Van Jones Martin

William R. Mitchell, Jr.

Landmark Homes of Georgia 1733-1983

ARCHITECTURE, INTERIORS, AND GARDENS

GOLDEN COAST PUBLISHING COMPANY • SAVANNAH

Landmark Homes
of Georgia 1733~1983

TWO HUNDRED AND FIFTY YEARS OF ARCHITECTURE, INTERIORS, AND GARDENS
BY VAN JONES MARTIN AND WILLIAM ROBERT MITCHELL, JR.

Co-editor's Notes

Augustus Baldwin Longstreet, author of *Georgia Scenes* (1835) described his book in this way: "There is scarcely a word of it from the beginning to the end . . . that is not strictly *Georgian.*"

Van Jones Martin and I, Georgians born-and-bred, first worked together for the old Georgia Historical Commission in 1972. We began this book on September 1, 1981, although we talked about it in 1980. Together we agreed on places to include, and collaborated on as many aspects as possible. Text was my major responsibility, but with few exceptions photographs were made while I was somewhere on the premises.

I do not believe that two people from anywhere else could, or would, have done this commemorative book. No other photographer *could* have done it. But perhaps, more important, Van and his wife, Barbara – an adopted Georgian – are Golden Coast Publishing Company. This is my acknowledgement to them. Acknowledgements to others – including my family – follow.

In 1975 E. J. Kahn wrote a two-part series about Georgia in *The New Yorker,* later published as *From Rabun Gap to Tybee Light,* and said: "Georgians on the subject of Georgia are something special." Something special for the 250th Anniversary has been our intention, and I know we traveled from Tybee Light to Rabun Gap – and back several times. . . .

William Robert Mitchell, Jr.

The History Business
P.O. Box 550113/Northside Station
Atlanta, Georgia 30305
September 18, 1982

Bill Mitchell and I began tilting at this idea a few years ago, and, spurred on by the impending 250th birthday of our home state, spent a frantic 1981-82 in production. For six months, in the fall of 1981 and the spring and early summer of '82, we were on the road, building this book house by house. As photographer, writer, and co-editors we had different yet overlapping roles, and this collaboration of visual and literary viewpoints had the most significant influence on the final form and appearance of *Landmark Homes of Georgia 1733-1983.*

Once back in Savannah, Bill dug in at his studio, a bunker lined with piles of accumulated notes, books, magazines, postcards, newspaper clippings, and maps, and wrote furiously for three more months. Periodically he would send out a stack of hand-written articles for my wife Barbara to transform into a neatly typed manuscript. Meanwhile, across town David Kaminsky was magically turning out wave after wave of beautiful color separations. With dedicated assistance from his wife Betsy Cain, he worked many a long night – with one eye scanning densitometer readings while the other kept track of the Braves' pennant chase. In Jacksonville at Miller Press, Bill Morton and Randy Taylor struggled valiantly to keep us moving in the right direction at the proper speed.

I salute this band of self-denying fanatics who have worked so hard to finish this book on time – to Bill, David and Betsy, Bill and Randy, and Barbara – thank you for your diligence and sacrifice. And to the lovely old 13th Colony – *Happy Birthday.*

Van Jones Martin

Savannah
September 18, 1982

Color film processed by Dataslide, Atlanta
Color separations made by Savannah Color Separations, Inc.
Printed at Miller Press, Jacksonville, Florida
Bound at Nicholstone Bindery, Nashville, Tennessee

•

1982 © by Golden Coast Publishing Company
Library of Congress Catalog Card Number 82-83560
ISBN 0-932958-01-X

•

GOLDEN COAST PUBLISHING COMPANY, 22 WAITE DRIVE, SAVANNAH, GEORGIA 912/352-2385

Dedicated to
The Georgia Historical Commission
1951-1973

Acknowledgements

Since the late summer of 1981 we have traveled thousands of miles and become indebted to many people for their help throughout the almost 59,000 square miles of this 250 year old state. Last fall we sent out a pre-publication notice to potential subscribers as we began to travel, photograph, interview, reseach, write and edit. The response to that announcement was encouraging, resulting in a list of over 250 subscribers (pages 6-7). We believe that a significant reason for such a positive response were the names we were able to list in that original announcement because of their interest in our idea. We want, therefore, to acknowledge their help first, for they were the first to put their names on the line:

Mrs. Ivan Allen, Jr.
Mrs. Jennie Tate Anderson
Mr. William N. Banks
Mrs. James J. W. Biggers, Jr.
Dr. Turner Bryson
Mr. David Richmond Byers III
Mrs. W.J. Dolvin
Mr. Alexander V.J. Gaudieri
Dr. Ben Grace
Mr. Henry D. Green
Mr. John C. Hagler III
Mr. John A. Hayes III
Professor John W. Linley
Mr. William Frank McCall
Dr. Hubert Bond Owens
Mr. and Mrs. Calder W. Payne
Mr. Philip Trammell Shutze
Mrs. Thomas Lyle Williams, Jr.

Then we would especially like to thank each subscriber listed on the following pages; many of those names represent more than one book; in one instance ten. Throughout the work, the doors of private homes and museum houses were generously opened, so we also especially want to acknowledge the help of each and every owner and each and every staff member of any historical organization that had to go out of his or her way to accommodate us. Their participation helped to make this book possible. Following is an alphabetical list of people who helped in various ways and, at the end, we acknowledge our families by name because, without their help, there would have been no finish to what seemed (sometimes) like a project with *no* end to it.

Dan Biggers, Martha Berry Museum; Walter Bowden and Mary Osborne, Savannah Bank and Trust; Mrs. Cecil K. Carmichael; Dr. George P. Cuttino, Emory University; Tony Dees, Georgia Historical Society; Mrs. James D. F. Evans II, Thomasville Landmarks, Inc., Jo Dollar, Days Inns; Faye Dill, Lori Fossum, and Nancy Jordan; President Jimmy Carter's Office; Professor James H. Grady; Mr. and Mrs. Hall, Chief Vann House; Mr. and Mrs. Bryan Haltermann; Henry L. Howell; Carolyn Humphries, Historic Augusta, Inc.; Kacey Jones, Historic Savannah Foundation; John Kerwood, Valli Hartrampf, and Nancy Lester, Atlanta Historical Society; Erica Kleine and *Colonial Homes* Magazine; and Ed Komerak, Greenwood Plantation.

F. Clason Kyle; Fran LaFarge, Johnston-Hay House Museum; Roy Lilly, Jr.; Mary Lane Morrison; Walter Mitchell, Jr. and Lisa B. Newsome, *Southern Accents;* Dean Owens; Dr. Hubert Bond Owens; Savannah College of Art and Design; Dr. William Seale; Ed and Esther Shaver; Denney Wells Spencer, Emory University; Kenneth H. Thomas, State Historic Preservation Section; Mary Jo Thompson, Old Capital Historical Society; Dolly Tyson, Owens-Thomas House Museum; Helena Zimmerman; Tom, Pam, Bill, Mark, Paul, Robert, and Robert at Worldwide Camera; John Petry, and all the folks at Miller Press.

To our families we give special acknowledgements:
Mrs. William Robert Mitchell, Sr.
Mr. and Mrs. John F. Robinson
Conrad and Donna, Gregory and Sandra,
John and Barbara, Patrick and Camille Scohier
Mr. and Mrs. Marion Fleming Martin, Jr.

The Semiquincentenary of Georgia

List of Subscribers for

Landmark Homes of Georgia, 1733-1983

Stephen W. Ackerman, Jr., FASID
Deborah D. Adams
Mr. and Mrs. Leopold Adler II
Mrs. William W. Alexander
Deborah S. Allen
Mr. and Mrs. Ivan Allen, Jr.
Judge Bond Almand
Mr. and Mrs. Bobby Joe Anderson
Mr. and Mrs. Halstead T. Anderson
Mr. and Mrs. Rodney Armstrong
The Atlanta Historical Society
Mrs. Louis Joseph Bahin
Harry J. Baldwin
William Nathaniel Banks
Leo T. Barber, Jr.
Mrs. Zeddie Barron, Jr.
Col. and Mrs. Claude A. Black
Mr. and Mrs. Dameron Black III
Mrs. P.L. Blackshear
Bates Block
James G. Bogle
Dr. and Mrs. James C. Bootle
Mr. and Mrs. Lloyd Bowers
Mrs. Lloyd G. Bowers
Mr. and Mrs. William R. Bridges, Jr.
Shirley A. Brother
Mrs. Joe L. Brown
Charles Berrien Browning
Mrs. John Frank Browning
Norris A. Broyles III
Frances Postell Burns
Mr. and Mrs. J. Derry Burns
Governor and Mrs. George Busbee
Mr. and Mrs. William G. Bush
Mrs. Clarence C. Butler
David Richmond Byers III
Mr. and Mrs. Maxwell M. Cain
Mr. and Mrs. Fuller E. Callaway, Jr.
Mark Clayton Callaway
William C. Callaway
Mrs. Asa W. Candler
Mr. and Mrs. Robert L.
    Carmichael, Jr.
Mr. and Mrs. Beauchamp C. Carr
Mr. and Mrs. Julian S. Carr
Rosalynn S. Carter
Alvin B. Cates, Jr.
Jane Alice Cauble

Anne Cox Chambers
Mrs. Alfred B. Chapple, Jr.
Mr. and Mrs. John H. Cheatham, Jr.
Cherokee Garden Library
Mrs. Reuben Clark
Mr. and Mrs. George S. Cobb, Jr.
Mrs. Linton M. Collins
Mr. and Mrs. John D. Comer
Virginia C. Courts
Charles R. Crisp
William Dixon Courtney
    Crusenberry, Jr.
William A. Cullens III
Joseph B. Cumming
Elizabeth Hay Curtis
Professor G.P. Cuttino
Mr. and Mrs. Hampton Lamar
    Daughtry
William H. Davidson
Mr. and Mrs. F.T. Davis, Jr.
Mrs. Cecil Day
Preston Waite DeMilly
Daniel Denny
Devours Funds (Deanne Devours
    Levision) The High Museum
    of Art, Atlanta
Mr. and Mrs. Arthur Forman
    Dismukes
Josephine Austin Dobbs
Doug H. Dorough
Cam D. Dorsey, Jr.
Mr. and Mrs. Hugh M. Dorsey, Jr.
Dr. A. Gatewood Dudley
Edward E. Elson
Mr. and Mrs. George Dwelle Elyea
Edward G. Engel
David E. Estes
Julian Tompkins Evans III
Mrs. Thomas M. Ezzard
Mr. and Mrs. Clayton H. Farnham
Mr. and Mrs. David Bryan Ferebee
Cathy Mitchell Fiebelkorn
Isabel and Cliff Fitzgerald
Dr. and Mrs. Robert Engram
    Fokes, Jr.
Mr. Alan Fort
Toby and Stan Friedman
Mr. and Mrs. William Michael Galardi

Mr. and Mrs. Gardiner W. Garrard
Franklin M. Garrett
Georgia Historical Society
The Georgia Trust
    for Historic Preservation
John L. Gignilliat
Mrs. Warren Gilbert
Alex and Jean Gilmore
Dr. Ben Grace
Mr. and Mrs. Henry D. Green
Sonia and Mickey Greenfield
Mr. and Mrs. Robert Irving
    Gresham, Jr.
Mr. and Mrs. William W. Griffin
Robert N. Griggs
Mrs. Fred C. Hack
John C. Hagler III
Mary Anne Tyler Hagler, M.D.
Mr. and Mrs. Jay Hall
John Screven Hand
Mrs. Lawrence M. Hand
Janice A. Hardy
Mrs. William B. Hartsfield
Guy M. Hays
John A. Hayes III
Mr. and Mrs. Zachary W. Henderson
Mr. and Mrs. Charles A. Hight
Historic Augusta, Incorporated
Historic Columbus Foundation
Historic Savannah Foundation
Mrs. Frank A. Hollowbush
Albert Howell (1904-1974)
Henry Lamar Howell
Mr. and Mrs. William Barrett Howell
Catherine M. Howett
Mrs. Charles D. Hudson
Charles D. Hudson, Jr.
Ellen Pinson Hudson
Ida Callaway Hudson
Mr. and Mrs. James P. Hudson
Jacqueline M. Ireland
Mr. and Mrs. Daniel B. Jeter
Mr. and Mrs. James M. Jeter
Mrs. Edward Vason Jones
Mrs. Joseph W. Jones
T. Ruben Jones
Mr. and Mrs. Albert H. Kaminsky
David J. Kaminsky and Elizabeth Cain

Mr. and Mrs. Stiles A. Kellett, Jr.
Mr. and Mrs. Thornton Kennedy
Mabry H. King
Amanda Kingery
Susan Kingery
Mr. and Mrs. Kevin Lee Knox
F. Clason Kyle
Sue and Alfred Langben
Mrs. Bernard A. Lazard
Dr. and Mrs. James E. Lee
Mr. and Mrs. Roy M. Lilly, Jr.
Ben H. Lovejoy
Mrs. Arthur Lucas
Rosalie Manan
Mr. and Mrs. Roy Mann, Jr.
Mrs. Harold H. Martin
Harry Edward Martin III
Mr. and Mrs. Jerry Martin and Della
Margaret and Donald Martin
Mr. and Mrs. Marion Fleming
    Martin, Jr.
Mr. and Mrs. Marion Fleming
    Martin III
Harriet Martin Cochran,
    Butch Dodd, and Gregory
Dr. and Mrs. Peter Winn Martin
    and James
McDowell Anderson Martin
    and Jessica
Mr. and Mrs. Thomas E. Martin, Jr.
Mr. and Mrs. Sherrod Garland
    McCall, Sr.
William Frank McCall, Jr.
Mr. and Mrs. Harold Franklin
    McCart, Jr.
Dr. and Mrs. James N. McCord, Jr.
Caro du Bignon McDowell
Ann McMillan
W.R. McNabb
Mr. and Mrs. Harmon B. Miller III
Miller Press
Thelma McCoy Miller
Walter H. Miller
Mr. and Mrs. Edward C. Mitchell, Jr.
Freeman and Margaret Mitchell
Mrs. R.L. Mitchell
Mrs. William Robert Mitchell, Sr.
Joseph H. Moore

Victor A. Moore III
Mrs. W.S. Morris III
W.T. Morton
Walter W. Morton
Alvin W. Neely, Jr.
Mrs. Howell Newton
Mr. and Mrs. Milton Henry
    Newton, Jr.
Henry Dole Norris
Joseph A. Odom
Mrs. Benjamin Osborne
Dean Owens
Dr. Hubert Bond Owens
Hubert Bond Owens, Jr.
Mr. and Mrs. Robert Glasgow
    Owens, Sr.
Sarah H. Owens
Mr. and Mrs. Robert D. Pannell
Diane Williams Parker
Mr. and Mrs. George Enslen
    Patterson, Jr.
Mr. and Mrs. Calder W. Payne
Donald C. Pierce
Mr. and Mrs. Rhodes L. Perdue
Parker Poe
James Zachary Rabun
Mr. and Mrs. Hansell W. Ramsey
Royal Forbes Rankin
Mr. and Mrs. George W. Ray
Mr. and Mrs. Brooke Reeve, Jr.
Mr. and Mrs. John R. Reiter
Mary Winn Rentz
Mr. and Mrs. J. Todd Robinson
Mr. and Mrs. John Fain Robinson
John Scott Robinson
Mr. and Mrs. R.L. Robinson
Bernard B. Rothschild
Minnie Lee Rountree
Albert D. Sams, Sr.
David G. Sands
Hazel and Paul Sanger
Mr. and Mrs. Emory Schwall
Mr. and Mrs. C.A. Scott
Mr. and Mrs. Charles Shaw
David M. Sherman
Dr. Olin Shivers
Mr. and Mrs. Edward S. Shorter
Philip Trammell Shutze

Charles O. Smith
Mr. and Mrs. D. Sidney Smith
Rev. and Mrs. Delbert Alan Smith
Mr. and Mrs. Linton H. Smith, Jr.
Dr. S. Dion Smith
Mr. and Mrs. William DuBerry Smith
Mrs. Robert R. Snodgrass
Hughes Spalding, Jr.
Mrs. Eugene A. Stanley
Jeanne G. Starnes
Albert H. Stoddard
Mary Ashworth Switzer
Mrs. John Cleves Symmes
Betty S. Talmadge
Mr. and Mrs. Ernest Shaw Tharpe, Sr.
Thomasville Public Library
Mary Jo Thompson
Edna W. Tucker
Mr. and Mrs. Robert A. Tucker
Mr. and Mrs. Cornelius Jasper
    Turner IV
Wesley Rhodes Vawter III
Leonoea Huguenin Victor
Christopher and Charlotte Vogelsang
Mrs. Bruce Wallis
Mr. and Mrs. William G. Welch
Dr. and Mrs. J. Herbert West
Jack E. Whitaker, Jr.
Mrs. Edward White
Norm and Mary White
Thomas Eugene White
James F. Whitnel
Mr. and Mrs. John Julian Wilkins
Thomas Hart Wilkins
Blanche Brooks Williams
James A. Williams
Mrs. Thomas L. Williams, Jr.
Barbara M. Wills
Mr. and Mrs. E. Ralph Wilson
Mr. and Mrs. Stephen A. Wilson
Mrs. Bernard Preston Wolff
Mr. and Mrs. Barry Wright, Jr.
Tate Wright, Jr.

Special Subscriber
Days Inns of America, Inc.

8

Contents

PROLOGUE 10

SECTION I: Domestic Architecture
in Georgia 14

SECTION II: Landmark Homes 34

    INTRODUCTION 36

THE HOUSES

LATE-COLONIAL TO MID-VICTORIAN

Harris-"Mackay" House 38
Hampton Lillibridge House 41
Chief Vann House 42
Gilbert-Alexander House 46
Richardson-Owens-Thomas House 50
Telfair Academy 58
Scarbrough House 60
Gordon-Banks House 62
Old Governor's Mansion 74
Mimosa Hall 80
Bulloch Hall 82
Barrington Hall 83
Tullie Smith House 84
Valley View 92
Andrew Low House 96
Charles Green House 100
Boxwood............................102
Hilsabeck-Symmes House 104
President's Home, University of Georgia 112
Founders Memorial Gardens 115
Owens House 116
Johnston-Hay House 120

VICTORIAN TO EARLY TWENTIETH
CENTURY 130

Liberty Hall 132
Sidney Lanier Cottage 134
Wren's Nest 134
Lapham-Patterson House 136
Baldwin-Neely 140
Beath-Griggs........................144
Plum Orchard 150
Greyfield 153

EARLY TWENTIETH CENTURY TO 1932 154
Mill Pond Plantation 156
Crane Cottage 160
Hills and Dales 162
Candler House 170
Callandwolde 173
Oak Hill 174
Swan House 178
Villa Albicini 189
Villa Apartments 189
Howell House 190

MID-TWENTIETH CENTURY, 1932-1966 198
Little White House 198
Augusta National Golf Club 200
Pebble Hill Plantation 204
Patterson-Carr House 208
Hightower House 212
Martin House 218

TWENTIETH CENTURY, 1967-1982 224
Snodgrass Apartment 225
Governor's Mansion 232
Carter House 236
Green House 237
Wright House 240
McCall House 244
Butler House 250
White House 258

SECTION III: Historic Preservation
in Georgia 262

Appendix A: National Historic Landmarks
in Georgia, Houses
and Districts 274

Appendix B: National Register of
Historic Places in Georgia,
Houses and Districts 275

Appendix C: Map of Georgia 276

Notes on Sources 277

Index 278

Prologue

Georgia is the southernmost, largest, and most geographically varied of the original thirteen states. Founded February 12, 1733, the colony was the youngest, most sparsely settled, and one of the most idealistically conceived in British America. One of the first colonists wrote in 1735, "I take it to be the promised land."

For her 250th birthday, February 12, 1983, we have produced this commemorative book which celebrates two and one-half centuries of domestic architecture and life. *Landmark Homes* illustrates how Georgians in each generation have lived and how present generations have become increasingly interested in understanding and enjoying their state's architectural heritage. Our overriding purpose is to show that Georgia has become a land of promise, fulfilling the high expectations of its founders.

Named for George II, and established at the beginning of the golden age of colonial culture, Georgia was envisioned by James Edward Oglethorpe, the soldier-philanthropist and member of Parliament who believed the colony would be a "land of liberty and plenty." Leader of the "Trustees for establishing the colony of Georgia in America," he sailed on the ship *Anne* in November 1732, less than six months after George II granted the trustees a twenty-one year charter. Aboard were a diverse but carefully chosen group of settlers, some 115, most of whom were needy, but only a few of whom were actually "debtors." On February 12, 1733, after brief landings in South Carolina, Oglethorpe and the colonists arrived at Yamacraw Bluff, fifteen miles up the Savannah River from the Atlantic Ocean. A few days before, with Colonel William Bull of South Carolina, he had visited the site, made friends with Tomochichi, chief of the Yamacraw Indians, and planned the first four of the expandable series of streets, building lots, and squares which came to be recognized as one of the world's most brilliant city plans. By June of that first year, Oglethorpe's imaginative plan (laid out, some believe, along the lines of military encampment) was taking form on the sandy landscape, and he was able to send to the other trustees in London – none of whom would ever see the colony – this description of the homes in which Georgians first lived: "Your new town of Savannah has nine framed houses finished, the sides covered with feather-edged board and the tops with shingles. These are 24 foot in length upon 16 foot in breadth. They have one story eight foot high with garrets over them. They are raised upon logs two foot above the ground and are floored with inch and half plank."

From that early eighteenth-century genesis on the southern frontier of the colonies, domestic architecture in Georgia has developed. None of those simple prototype cottages survives, but they influenced the form of Georgia houses for several generations. For many years their spartan colonial character was a standard way of building, especially in the eighteenth-century villages of eastern Georgia. Often, cottages such as these were the best that Georgians could afford. (Typical dwellings of the nineteenth-century upcountry frontier, prior to the Greek Revival, would be log cabins and two-story frame houses called Plantation Plain.)

People have had a special interest in Georgia's landmark homes, at least since the 1930's when Franklin Roosevelt's white-columned Southern retreat at Warm Springs became the Little White House after his election in 1932, and when Margaret Mitchell's *Gone With the Wind,* the novel of 1936 and the film of 1939, made household words of Tara, Twelve Oaks, and the March to the Sea. During that Depression decade, another work of fiction which dramatized Georgia in the popular imagination – although unromantically – was *Tobacco Road* by native Georgian, Erskine Caldwell; the plain pine tenant houses which he described had much in common with Oglethorpe's cottages. Popular interest, akin to that of the 1930's, was revived during President Eisenhower's administration when two second homes: Mamie's white clapboard cottage at the Augusta National Golf Club, and Milestone plantation, the hunting preserve at Thomasville of his Secretary of the Treasury, were constantly in the news. Then in the 1970's President Carter's one-story brick house at Plains added another chapter of interest.

Special status has usually arisen because of the people and events associated with a house.

Georgia's historic homes, from Martha Berry's Oak Hill near Rome to Joel Chandler Harris's Wren's Nest in Atlanta to the birthplaces of Sidney Lanier in Macon and Juliette Gordon Low in Savannah have had a special place in national affection. But more recently many houses have become famous on their architectural merits alone. For example the early to mid-twentieth century dwellings designed by Atlanta's Neel Reid and Philip Shutze were considered in their day to be exceptional examples of the traditional domestic styles, but now they are thought to be among the finest ever conceived in this country. The houses and gardens, interior decorating schemes and, in effect, whole neighborhoods Reid and Shutze designed prior to 1950 are recognized nationally for their truly remarkable beauty. In 1982, during Philip Shutze's 92nd year, he received the Arthur Ross Award of the Classical American Society for his greatness in classical architecture. (Georgians had loved his houses and respected his talents all along.)

This appreciation of Georgia's domestic architecture, regardless of who lived in the houses, is clearly related to the growing phenomenon of historic preservation. The public's interest in Georgia's landmark homes in the 1970's and into the 1980's is being expressed by the restoration and preservation of architecturally valuable houses and neighborhoods of varying degrees of historical value: whether the designs of William Jay in Savannah, Daniel Pratt in middle Georgia, John Wind in Thomas County, or Reid, Shutze, and their colleagues throughout the state. This interest has been expressed in the touring of restored houses and neighborhoods; the formation of historic preservation groups with large memberships, which have sometimes lavish – though needy – house museums and handsome publications.

Every generation rethinks and rewrites history from new perspectives. Over the years scholars and journalists have almost exclusively featured the domestic architecture of Georgia's antebellum period (c. 1785-1860), especially the romantic aspects, to the exclusion of the Victorian and later eras. The late Medora Field Perkerson's well-known *White Columns in Georgia* of 1952, for example, is an easily read journalistic story about famous Georgia houses, which frankly proclaims its nature in the title of the first chapter, "Gone With the Wind Country." The standard work for the houses of the colonial, federal, and Greek Revival periods is *The Early Architecture of Georgia* by Frederick Doveton Nichols, with black-and-white photographs by Francis Benjamin Johnston, published in 1957, and revised in 1976 with new photographs by Van Jones Martin. University of Georgia professor John Linley published *The Architecture of Middle Georgia* in 1972, a comprehensive architectural survey of buildings from all periods in seven counties around the antebellum capital of Milledgeville. For the whole state the volume closest to *Landmark Homes* appeared fifty years ago, the bicentennial *Garden History of Georgia* (reprinted in 1976). As much an architectural history, though informal, as a history of gardens, the *Garden History* documented the intimate relationship between Georgia's houses and gardens, with black-and-white photographs and landscape plans. Almost as many early-twentieth century houses and gardens were included as those from the pre-Civil

War era. Many of the same places were chosen for *Landmark Homes*. We have combined the earlier approaches to the subject to appeal to as many people as possible: to the general reader, who may be primarily interested in the manner in which Georgians have lived, as well as to the more serious student of domestic architecture – each of whom may also be interested in efforts to preserve, restore, and renovate. Each may find something of value from every period, 1733 to 1983.

Section One is a non-technical illustrated history of the state's urban and rural domestic architecture, starting with the first frame cottages at Savannah and ending with a house which was completed as the book went to press. Section Two is 228-pages of color photographs and text featuring the interiors, exteriors, and landscape settings of the most beautiful houses built in Georgia. The final section deals with historic preservation, illustrating the extraordinary value that present day Georgians place on their historic architecture and neighborhoods.

Landmark Homes is dedicated to the old Georgia Historical Commission (1951-1973). While working for that much-honored agency, we got to know our native state well as we recorded buildings for the National Register of Historic Places. As co-editors producing *Landmark Homes* we have traveled thousands of miles to study and photograph each house selected for its architectural, historical, or cultural significance. Many of the houses are on the National Register and several were restored by the Historical Commission, among them the Harris "Mackay" House at Augusta and the Vann House near Chatsworth. Our collaboration documents

Georgia's landmark houses for the first time in color, from coast to mountainous north Georgia, Old South and New. Not a catalogue or guide, it is a tour through public and private houses as they looked during the state's 250th year; some of them are being published for the first time.

Although the text is based on research, it expresses the spirit of the preservationist more than the antiquarian. Documentation is an important purpose, but even more crucial is encouraging people to admire and use houses within original contexts and neighborhoods.

The houses we have chosen demonstrate that many generations of conservation-minded Georgians have cared for these landmarks. The houses also show a long tradition of architectural conservatism. The late Georgia journalist-historian, Loretta Chappell of Columbus, summed it up when she wrote in 1928 at the time of the Columbus Centennial, "Anachronisms flourish with charming effect." Quoting Miss Chappell further: "A man's house is built to serve generations and no one thinks of discarding it when fashions change. So that city street is pleasantest which is lined with homes representing various periods. In Columbus the typical neighborhood is an assortment of new homes, old homes, and homes that are positively venerable."

These venerable homes of Georgia have set the pace for the design of newer houses. Georgia-based architects have recognized distinctly Georgia themes and used them creatively in their architectural designs. The landmarks of the twentieth-century domestic architecture they created, such as Hills and Dales (1916) at LaGrange, are now valued as much as those from the antebellum nineteenth century.

Veneration of the genuinely old continues as houses are built today in earlier styles, or in combinations of styles. The eclecticism of today is often less informed – and sometimes motivated by different aesthetic canons – than that of the early-twentieth century. But eclectic nonetheless. As historian James H. Grady wrote about Atlanta in 1975: "Eclecticism is still favored, although architects and craftsmen are no longer trained in historic design."

"Anachronisms" still flourish and the reader will find handsome examples illustrated here; some of them built within the past twenty-five years.

Landmark Homes, itself an eclectic selection of domestic architecture from every period and style found in Georgia, can serve as a primer for what some are calling the Post-Modern era; post-modernism means that the architecture of the past – even that of the Machine-Age – becomes the source of inspiration for romanticized present-day designs. Leading architect Philip Johnson (b.1906) has said, "We cannot *not* know history." Perhaps Georgia's anachronisms are, in fact, predictions of things to come.

We offer this heritage of domestic architecture to celebrate the Semiquincentenary of the founding of Oglethorpe's colony, as evidence that his dream is being realized and that Georgia's golden age of culture is now.

William R. Mitchell, Jr.
1982

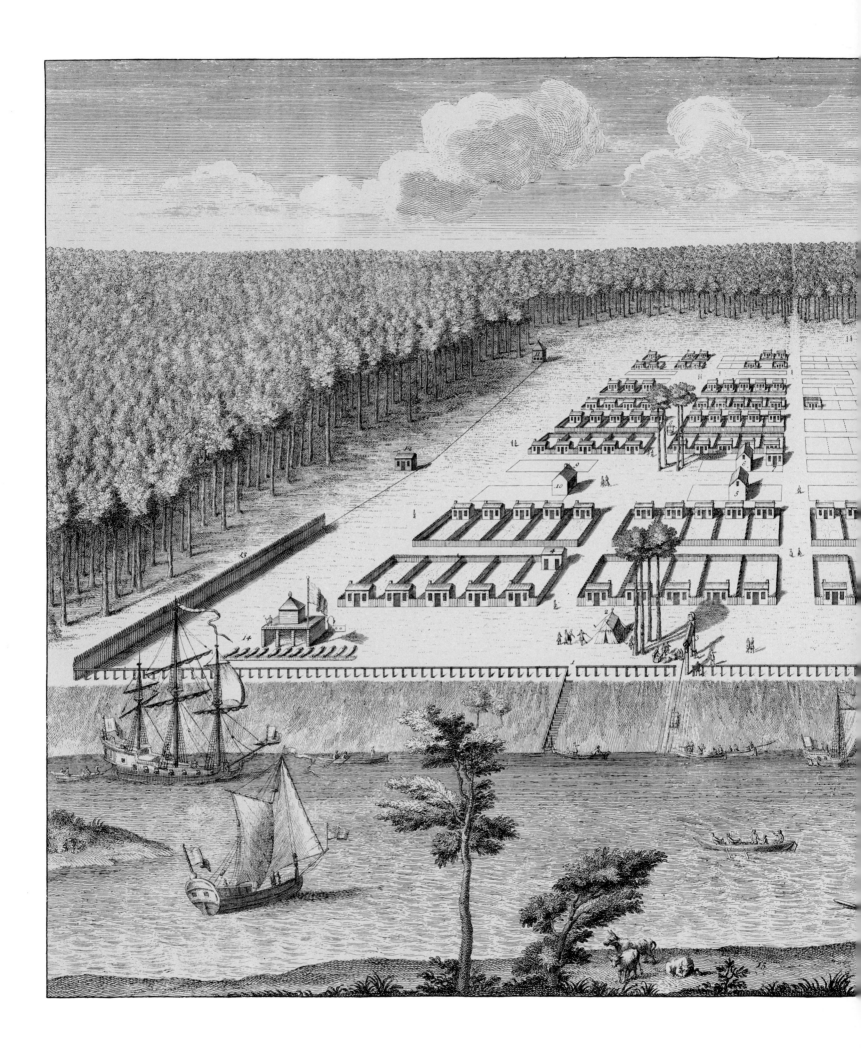

Section I
Domestic
Architecture
In Georgia

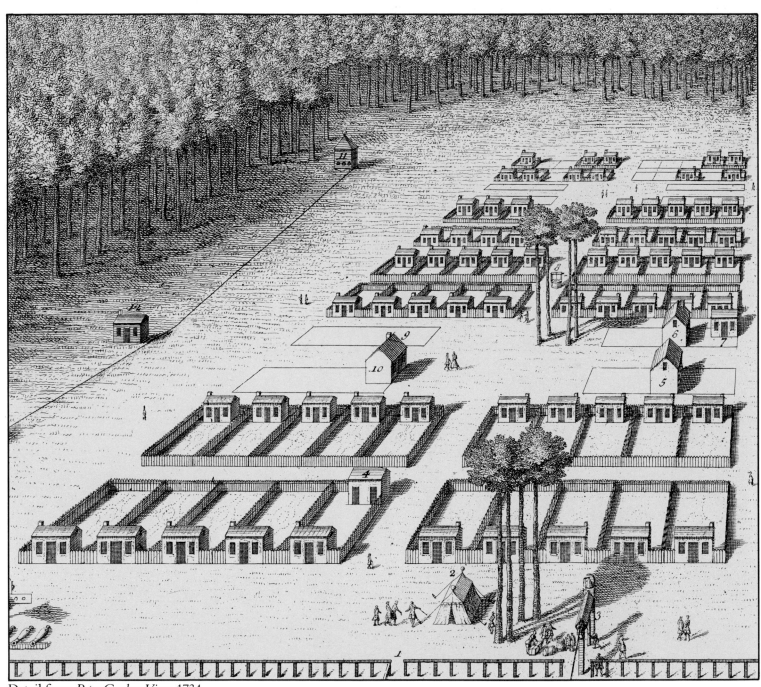

Detail from *Peter Gordon View*, 1734

SECTION I : Introduction

James Oglethorpe, Esq. – two books from subscription list, *Villas of the Ancients Illustrated*. London, 1728.

THE FIRST MAJOR WORK of architecture of any kind in Georgia occurred in 1733 almost as soon as Oglethorpe and the colonists reached the site of Savannah. It was not an individual building but the town plan of four wards arranged around four central squares, with a standard house, 24′ × 16′, to fit the overall design. Oglethorpe wrote to the Trustees in London soon after he arrived, "Upon the riverside in the center of this plain, I have laid out the town."

Many complex theories have been put forth as to the exact origins of this brilliant layout, but the simple fact is that the founder of Georgia had a rational plan which he executed on a perfect site, a plan which Savannah continued to follow until the last wards and squares were built in 1856, and which continues to be honored for its beauty and liveability. (In 1976, leading members of the American Institute of Architects chose Oglethorpe's Savannah plan as one of the most outstanding works of architecture in American history.)

That a soldier, a member of parliament, and of the landed gentry was interested in architecture would be normal, but that this interest was one of the catalysts for the founding of Georgia may seem surprising; yet it can be documented, and it may help to explain the unique plan Oglethorpe devised for the capital of George II's new colony.

In 1728, five years before he began the settlement of Georgia, James Oglethorpe, Esq., subscribed to two copies of *Villas of the Ancients Illustrated,* written and privately printed by Robert Castell, a gentleman-architect. Castell dedicated this folio to Lord Burlington, leader of the English Palladian school of Renaissance architecture, and it is considered to be an influential treatise in the history of English design. (The Georgia Historical Society in Savannah has an original copy.) Some scholars have considered Castell's folio to be the direct source for the design of Savannah. Indirect is perhaps a better word. Castell's text and engravings are characteristic of the way English architectural humanists thought about locating an appropriate site for a large estate and then distributing the elements in a regular fashion; in short, it was as much about landscape architecture as about the design of buildings. Thus, Castell addressed problems not unlike Oglethorpe faced when he founded Georgia.

Oglethorpe's subscription to Robert Castell's treatise is evidence of an interest in architecture, as well as to his acquaintance with the architectural theorist; this acquaintance – sometimes described as a friendship – matters in the history of Georgia, because Castell can be said to be the catalyst for the formation in 1729 of Oglethorpe's parliamentary committee to investigate the debtors' prisons. It was Castell's needless death that year in a London prison, where he had been placed because of the debt he incurred in publishing *Villas of the Ancients,* that sent Oglethorpe into action. It was this committee which in 1732 became almost in toto the "Trustees for establishing the colony of Georgia in America."

Thus, as with other aspects of the early history of the colony and state, it is to James Oglethorpe that one turns when beginning the story of domestic architecture in Georgia. Although he was not able to bring the debtor-scholar Robert Castell to America, he did bring Renaissance architectural ideas of symmetry and order, and he brought at least one well-trained "carpenter and joiner" to help carry them out, Thomas Milledge.

Thomas Milledge, whom Oglethorpe called his "best carpenter," helped lay out the town of Savannah and build the first clapboard cottages. (The cottages and the plan can be seen in the Peter Gordon view of 1734.) Although Milledge promptly died, he left an eleven-year-old son, John, who had accompanied him aboard the *Anne.* This son would live to be one of the colony's "principal inhabitants," as they were called in early Georgia, and his son – Thomas's grandson – also called John (1757-1818), would be a Georgia governor and U.S. Senator and have the antebellum capital of the state named Milledgeville in his honor.

It is to the colonists such as Thomas and John Milledge, which Oglethorpe brought with him to settle Georgia, that one must first look in piecing together an account of the development of domestic architecture in Georgia. What follows is arranged chronologically beginning with the generation of young John Milledge, eleven years old in 1733. The kind of house in which Milledge lived, designed by Oglethorpe with the help of Colonel William Bull of South Carolina and built by John's father, can be seen in the 1734 Peter Gordon View at left; and then, within 25-year spans, examples will be given of the sort of dwellings that generations of Georgians, following Oglethorpe and the Milledges, have built, with and without the help of architects, from 1733 to 1983.

Georgia, during these 25 years, consisted of low-country parishes along the Savannah River and the coast. Settlement in the up-country would not come until the next generation. Wild Heron, 1756, was the typical good house which settlers built throughout the area outside of the new towns; it is the only early example of the "raised cottage" (called in the Augusta area the Sand Hills Cottage) surviving in Georgia. Wild Heron was built by Francis Harris, Esq., a cotton and rice planter. Located fifteen miles outside of Savannah, near the Little Ogeechee River, it faces south and is on high ground. Note especially the cat-slide dormers which are one of the identifying characteristics of the early houses of Georgia.

Not all houses of this era were built of wood; both the Noble Jones and the Horton houses, now ruins, were of tabby, a local form of concrete made with oyster shells. Archaeology at these sites reveals some information; what is known may be found in *Captain Jones's Wormsloe,* William M. Kelso, the University of Georgia Press, 1979. At Frederica there were brick houses, sometimes with tabby foundations; these too are now in ruins.

The original freeholders' cottages built in Savannah and illustrated in the Peter Gordon View of 1734 have all disappeared, but similar houses survive on side streets in Savannah and are the Savannah equivalent of the shotgun houses of New Orleans. A fine restored example of one of these one-and-a-half story cottages built later is shown, the cottage of Henry Willink at 426 East St. Julian Street; note the sloping cat-slide dormers. Oglethorpe described these houses in a letter to the Trustees in 1733 soon after he, Thomas Milledge, and Colonel William Bull of South Carolina had completed nine of them: "The sides [are] covered with feather-edged board and the tops with shingles. They are 24 foot in length upon 16 foot in breadth. They have one storey eight foot high with garrets over them. They are raised upon logs two feet above the ground and are floored with inch and half plank."

Oglethorpe's own cottage at Frederica – founded in 1736 – is believed to have been similar to this, built on a tabby foundation, and possibly entirely of that material. After Oglethorpe permanently returned to

Wild Heron, near Savannah, 1756

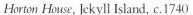

Frederica, St. Simons Island, 1736

Horton House, Jekyll Island, c.1740

England in 1743, this house was owned by John Spalding, whose son Thomas described the place as a "humble homestead" consisting of a "garden, an orchard of oranges, figs, and grapes, and a cottage" overshadowed by oaks. It was known as "The Farm."

Willink Cottage, Savannah, 1845

1758-1783
The Royal Colony and the Revolution

Georgia prospered as a royal colony as it had not as a Trusteeship. Although in theory a huge territory, it was colonized mainly along the Savannah River and the coast until the 1770's, when the area west of Augusta, the unofficial capital of the Piedmont upcountry, began to be settled. In 1780, during the Revolution, Washington in Wilkes County was named and laid out as a town near Fort Heard, around which settlers had already moved, building the sort of log cabins shown here. Those log houses were the upcountry version of the Oglethorpe cottages of Savannah. At the same time, Augusta was officially designated the capital, and the process of settlement of the entire state began, as well as the continuous process of removal of the Cherokee and Creek Indians, which would not be finally accomplished until the 1830's. For this 25-year span, from 1758 until the official end of the Revolution with the Treaty of Paris

in 1783, there is only the Wilkes County log house to show. The utter simplicity of this rare example tells much about the conditions of life in Colonial and Revolutionary Georgia. At the end of the Revolution, Georgia's boundaries extended from the Atlantic Ocean to the Mississippi River; it was an enormous Southern frontier and log houses were predominate. Of Savannah during this period, a visitor in April, 1762, wrote, "In the past two or three years much building has been going on in the city. At present there are about 200 houses. Of these I have seen but three of brick. The rest are of wood and are painted in shades of blue and red."

Log House, Wilkes County, c.1773

19

1783-1808
The New State/Post-Colonial Styles

After the Revolution Savannah and Augusta, which were both founded by Oglethorpe, vied for importance. Augusta became the leading town in the Piedmont upcountry, as settlers moved into the area, largely from the Carolinas and Virginia – instead of from the coastal low country. At that point tobacco rather than cotton was the chief money crop. Of the three houses illustrating this section, two are from the area west of Augusta: the Rock House of 1785 and the Thomas Carr House of 1805; the Savannah example from the 1790's is frame. Not until Savannah became a cotton port – after the invention of the cotton gin (1793) – would it begin to outdistance Augusta, and then Augusta would become a cotton market of national importance. During these years Milledgeville, named for the family that came with Oglethorpe on the *Anne,* would be founded as the new capital in 1803, as the settlement of Georgia began to expand westward towards the Chattahoochee River. In 1802 the western boundary of the state officially became the Chattahoochee as Georgia gave up her claims to western territory in exchange for the Federal government's promise to remove the Indians from within her new borders. During this period the new lands of Georgia's frontier (land lots were either 202½ or 490 acres) were the basis of wealth; however, a national survey in 1798 showed only 51 houses in Georgia in the $3000 to $6000 bracket; and only four from $6000 to $10,000. Not until after the War of 1812 would Georgia enter the national economy and begin to express her position

The Rock House, near Thomson, 1785

architecturally as a nationally important state. Architecture from 1783 to 1808 was Post-Colonial in character and only slowly becoming Federal in style. The Thomas Carr House, "Alexandria," at that time was possibly the finest house built in the Georgia upcountry and may have been one of the houses in the $6000 to $10,000 range. Carr owned 32,500 acres of land in Georgia and his fine brick house – with its rubbed and gauged brickwork – reflects his status; he was one of the Virginians and his house reflects his cultural background. (It is said to be the earliest surviving brick house in Georgia which can be documented as to the exact date of construction: 1804-1806).

LEFT: *Carr House,* near Thomson, 1805;
BELOW: *Oddingsells House,* Savannah, c.1798

1808-1833

Plantation Plain;
Post-Colonial, Federal, and Regency styles

During these years all of Georgia was settled and Indian territory disappeared. Macon (1823), Thomasville (1826), and Columbus (1828), among others, were established. Cultural and social patterns which Georgia, by and large, has to this day began to be developed. Much of Georgia was still frontier in character when compared with some of the original thirteen states, and fine architecture was still unusual enough that one of the examples in this section was called a "folly," it so outshown its neighbors in ornamentation, cost, and style – Ware's Folly (1819) in Augusta. At this time, "most houses were small and utilitarian" wrote Dr. Kenneth Coleman in the *History of Georgia* (1977). Some of the best houses were of wood in the Plantation Plain style but were still described by many travelers through the Georgia upcountry in somewhat appalled tones; James Silk Buckingham (1786-1855), an Englishman, described Traveler's Rest (Jarrett Manor) in this way: "We arrived before sunset at a large farm-house and inn united, kept by a Mr. Jarrett: the directions by which we were enabled to distinguish it from the other houses in the

Ware's Folly, Augusta, 1818

neighborhood was this – that it was the only house with glass windows in it on the road."

James Buckingham described the houses in Savannah, by comparison, with almost glowing pleasure; two of those he no doubt saw are included here: the William Scarbrough House (1819) by William Jay, and the Isaiah Davenport House (1820). Buckingham wrote in *The Slave States of America* (London, 1842): "There are many handsome and commodious brick buildings, occupied as

Traveler's Rest, or *Jarrett Manor,* near Toccoa, c.1815

Scarbrough House, Savannah, c.1819

Davenport House, Savannah, c.1820

private residences, and a few mansions, built by an English architect, Mr. Jay . . . which are of beautiful architecture, of sumptious interior, and combine as much of elegance and luxury as are to be found in any private dwellings in the country."

Although the Isaiah Davenport House was not by Jay, it was in that class – though in a more conservative, Post-Colonial, manner. Davenport was his own architect, as he was a builder-designer of the old school and the style of the house continued the Georgian Colonial

tradition, with only a few ornamental modifications in the Federal style. However, all four of these houses – three in Savannah and one in Augusta – could be described as combining "elegance and luxury." This tells a great deal about the direction life in Georgia took after the War of 1812 when the Port of Savannah was beginning to be well-supplied from the upriver cotton warehouses of Augusta; and when comfortable, if not always "folly"-class houses were beginning to be built here and there around the new state.

1833-1858
The Greek and other Revivals

Frederick Doveton Nichols, in *The Early Architecture of Georgia* (1957), described Greek Revival architecture as an unsurpassed "heritage of monumental beauty" and "the great cultural achievement of the Georgia Pied-

mont." In an article Nichols wrote: "The isolated towns of the Piedmont, where new villages, new settlers and new wealth had created an enormous demand for new buildings, saw the Greek Revival style achieve its most

Governor's Mansion, Milledgeville, 1838

Greenwood Plantation, Thomasville, 1839

pure and most uninhibited expression: the colossal temple form, the purity of which was never diluted in Georgia by the addition of the second-story gallery." ("Wooden Temples in Georgia," *The Walpole Society Notebook,* 1976)

In the main, nothing could be truer than Dr. Nichols' considered judgment, but there is a notable exception to what he says: Greenwood Plantation, in deep southwest Thomas County, Georgia, a monumental Greek Revival temple, far from the Piedmont upcountry – and displaying a fine second-story gallery. Begun in 1839 and completed in 1844, it was designed by John Wind, another one of those talented Britons who came to Georgia to help Georgians house themselves with style as they gave expression to their new agricultural prosperity and cultural nationalism.

Greenwood shows that during the period 1833-1855 all of Georgia was finally settled and unified, as similar cultural patterns were adopted throughout its ample borders. Symbolic of this cultural unification, as expressed in classic revival architecture, was the state's Executive Mansion at Milledgeville, designed by Charles B. Cluskey, an Irishman then working mainly in Savannah. (One beautiful example of the Gothic Revival, a Carpenter Gothic cottage from the Piedmont, is included to show an exception to the Greek Revival norm.)

Two of the houses built during this span did not start out as Greek temples, the Crawford-Talmadge House near Lovejoy and the Tupper-Barnett House at Washington-Wilkes. Both had columns added in the late 1850's, as the style became practically a statement of the Southern way of life, and as Georgia began to be called The Empire State of the South. In the next 25 years there would be many changes in Georgia, and these changes would continue to be expressed architecturally by the continued revival of historical styles. Although classicism would go out of fashion for awhile, eclecticism, or the selective use of past styles to create symbolic associations in the mind of users and observers, would continue in Georgia as it had since about 1800, and as it continues today.

(The frontier area's single-pen log cabins would continue to be the first houses built; often a second cabin would be added to create a dog-trot breezeway between the two "pens." Then a Plantation Plain frame house would come next. To this classical columns could be added, or it might become the wing of a formal Greek Revival house.)

Olney Ethridge House, Sparta, 1853

Crawford-Talmadge House, Lovejoy, 1855

Tupper-Barnett House, Washington-Wilkes, c.1840
(columns added 1860)

Rankin House, Columbus, begun 1859, completed c.1867

May's Folly, Columbus, 1862

1858-1883
Historical Revivalism and Eclecticism Continued

In 1859 in Columbus two fine houses, without Greek Revival columns, were conceived; one of them, the Rankin House, would not be finished until after the Civil War, and the other, Dinglewood, would rival Macon's W.B. Johnston-Hay House as an exemplar of the Italian Renaissance villa style. Temple-form houses were going out of fashion, and in 1862, in that same west Georgia Chattahoochee River town, a unique double Octagon house was built, May's Folly. Each of these houses reflects an increasing diversity of architectural thinking, and an increasing eclecticism which sought more picturesque, irregular silhouettes than the pure Greek temple had afforded. During these years Atlanta began to be the most important town in the state, and in 1868 it became the new capital as railroads became more important than river and sea-going transportation. This was the period after the Civil War when Atlanta proponents of the New South, especially Henry Grady, editor of the *Constitution,* sought to bring Georgia into the mainstream of nineteenth-century life. A new generation of Georgians built houses which were as "Victorian" in appearance as any to be found in the country and, as a result, as eclectic. Edgehill, near Rome, very well typifies a Georgia Victorian's flirtation with the Gothic for the latest in domestic architecture.

BELOW LEFT: *Edgehill,* near Rome, c.1880;
BELOW: *Dinglewood,* Columbus, 1859

Peters House, Atlanta, c.1885

The Edward C. Peters House, Atlanta, designed by the talented Atlanta architect, G. L. Norrman, is one of Georgia's finest examples of the High Victorian Queen Anne style; it is fine enough that it approximates what art historian Vincent Scully calls the Shingle Style, an American version of the English Arts and Crafts or Aesthetic movement. By the 1880's, Atlanta had surpassed Savannah in population and was the state's financial center. Edward Peters was one of the leaders of this small New South metropolis, and his house on three-and-a-half acres near Peachtree Street was one of its showplaces. The McGarvey House, Brunswick, was also one of the high points of Victorian eclecticism in Georgia; it is in the Stick Style, another particularly American version of Victorian architectural taste. Designed by New York architect J. A. Wood, it is a well-preserved example of Wood's manner which he per-

fected in the design of large resort hotels, among them the Piney Woods at Thomasville and the Oglethorpe at Brunswick, both now destroyed. The William Rockefeller Cottage at Jekyll Island was a Queen Anne, more-or-less Shingle Style resort cottage built at the height of that style's favor as a seaside mode, and at the height of the Jekyll Island Club's importance as a private resort. In 1907 columns were added to it as the fashion changed from picturesque architectural informality to neoclassical formality. The "Crescent" (1898) at Valdosta typifies this same turn-of-the-century combination of informal, open plan with the formality of a columned façade. This growing neoclassicism of the 1890's and early 1900's has been called part of an "American Renaissance," which was especially well-expressed at the World's Columbian Exposition at Chicago in 1893. Symmetrical, columned houses became fashionable

Rockefeller Cottage, Jekyll Island, 1892 (columns added 1907)

The Crescent, Valdosta, 1898

again. The Victorian picturesque taste for the assymetrical and exotic did not entirely disappear, however, but was continued in the informality and quaintness of bungalows; this one at Sparta is an especially fine example. A feature of this period, towards its close, were academically-trained architects who began to replace those who had started out in the building trades or who had been apprenticed to established architects; these more learned eclectics would go to France and Italy for a period of first-hand architectural history after they had finished a course of architectural schooling in America, especially at the Columbia University School of Architecture. One of the most influential of these academic eclectics in Georgia was born in 1885, as this quarter of the century began. Neel Reid (d. 1926) began the practice of architecture in Atlanta and Macon in 1909, and will figure greatly in the next 25 years.

ABOVE: *McGarvey House,* Brunswick, 1891
LEFT: *Walker-Moore House,* Sparta, c.1905;

1908-1933
The Creative Eclecticism of Academic Architects

In 1909 an architectural firm of much importance in the history of Georgia's domestic architecture was formed: Hentz and Reid. Hal Hentz and Neel Reid became partners in Atlanta after a time at Columbia University in New York and at the Ecole des Beaux Arts in Paris; that same year they joined the Atlanta Chapter of the American Institute of Architects, which would be incorporated as the Georgia Chapter in 1913 with their names as incorporators. They would be leaders of their profession for many years, and their firm would produce some of the finest houses ever built in Georgia. Reid was the principal designer, a fine example of his work is the Bach-Duncan House of 1915 in Macon. (Reid had moved to Macon in 1903 as an eighteen year old and much of his earliest work is to be found there.) Upon Reid's death in 1926, Philip Trammell Shutze, born in 1890 in Columbus, succeeded to the position Reid had held in the firm, and it became Hentz, Adler, and Shutze in 1927. Philip Shutze had been associated with the firm for several years, but his exceptional talent had been recognized as early as 1915, when he was awarded the Rome Prize while a student at the Columbia University School of Architecture. In taking this prize Shutze won the world's championship of architectural fellowships; it entitled him to three years of post-graduate study in Italy at the American Academy, sponsor of the Prize, and when he returned to Atlanta in 1919 he went to work for Hentz, Adler, and Reid. (In 1977 Henry Hope Reed of the Classical America Society described Philip Trammell Shutze, FAIA, as "America's Greatest Living Classical Architect"; in 1983 Shutze will be 93.) The beautiful English-Chambers House of 1930 is an example of his work in the Regency idiom; he knew of William Jay's Savannah work in that style but this is not a copy of any one of Jay's houses. Other outstanding academic architects who worked in Georgia were David Adler of Chicago who did the Crane House at Jekyll Island in 1916; and Henry Hornbostel of New York whose Charles Howard Candler House, Callanwolde, in Atlanta, 1917, is shown. It is in that Tudor-Gothic eclectic manner which some preferred to one of the more classical idioms. Atlanta architect P. Thornton Marye was another talented designer; his Lucas House of the mid-1920's is an outstanding American Georgian house and is one of the last major private homes on Atlanta's formerly residential Peachtree Street.

Perhaps the change in taste that occurred during these years, and the place that the Neel Reid firm had in that change, can best be symbolized by the Barnes-Cheatham House, at Griffin in middle Georgia; Reid transformed a Victorian period house into this grace-

Bach-Duncan House, Macon, 1915

ABOVE: *Chambers House,* Atlanta, 1929

BELOW. *Lucas House,* Atlanta, c.1925

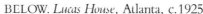

Barnes-Cheatham House, Griffin, c.1920

Callanwolde, Atlanta, 1917

fully landscaped American Georgian mansion, which seems eighteenth century but was formed out of the earlier house in 1920.

These academically-trained architects were consummate artists who could make any historical style of architecture into their own, so that their designs seemed always to have been in place, transforming suburban neighborhoods into historic districts; indeed the neighborhoods where Reid and Shutze worked are now being

so-designated only fifty years after they were developed. These were Renaissance men, not because they knew and admired classical architecture, but because they designed houses, gardens, and interiors, and helped select furnishings, to create period settings which are valued as though they were actually of the period chosen. For that reason these architects are often called "creative eclectics."

1933–1958
Academic Eclecticism Continued

With only one major exception, Academic Eclecticism continued in Georgia in the 1930's, 40's and 50's. The exception was this International Style house built in 1937 at Sea Island, the exclusive resort on the Georgia

coast. Few examples of this style, which tried to create a totally new precedent in domestic architecture, can be found anywhere in the state; it is a style which is itself being revived in the 1970's and 80's, as post-modernists

King House, Sea Island, 1937

chose to include early examples of modernism such as this in their repertoire; making the precedentless house itself a precedent.

Illustrating what the generation between 1933 and 1958 usually preferred are four houses which have a fundamental quality in common: they are each based on early American, rather than European, precedents. Edward Shorter of Columbus calls his house (1940), which he designed with the help of Georgia architect Henry Toombs, "Gulf Coast Creole." The Raymond Demere House (1941) near Savannah by Philip Shutze is based on Louisiana plantation houses, and the Goddard-Jones House by the Atlanta firm of Abreu and Robeson is a creative eclectic interpretation of a famous Lexington, Kentucky, Federal style house, Rose Hill, of 1812.

In point of time, the last of these houses is the Angus Alberson House at Albany, completed in 1953. A handsome version of several eighteenth-century Maryland houses, its designer James Means (1904-1979) was never a registered architect. He learned by doing; he was fourteen years old when he was first apprenticed to Neel Reid, and after Reid's death he continued to work with Philip Shutze, until Shutze's retirement in 1950. At that time Means went to Albany in southwest Georgia to work in partnership with Edward Vason Jones and designed this house. Means continued the tradition of design of the academic eclectics, ironically, since he was not himself academically trained. Means' houses were hand-crafted from old materials and were practically impossible to tell from the various originals from which his inspiration came. However, they were decidely not copies, even though prototypes and reminiscences of specific places come to mind. This is early American revivalism at its best; few architects anywhere in America have achieved, at any time, such masterpieces of quality as this native Georgian who began to build in the 1950's. As Means worked alone, without apprentices, he was possibly the last of his kind in Georgia or elsewhere. What he built perfectly expressed the continuing conservatism of taste in Georgia's domestic architecture and life.

Demere House, 1941;

ABOVE: *Goddard-Jones House,* Atlanta, 1949;
BELOW: *Alberson House,* Albany, 1953

Shorter House, Columbus, 1940

Watt House, Thomasville, 1961

Montgomery-Robinson House, Ansley Park, Atlanta, 1965

1958-1983
Academic Eclecticism Revived

A major theme in the architecture of this last 25 years is a renewed respect for tradition, especially the classical, and for traditional ways of designing buildings with references to historical styles of architecture. Philip Johnson who helped to coin the term, International Style, and who had been one of the leaders of "modernism" around 1961 began to change his basic tune when he said, "We cannot *not* know history." One of those who had always known his history well was Edward Vason Jones, a native of Albany; he was part of an "undercurrent of classicism" (as it was called in relation to James Means' houses) in twentieth-century architecture. The Vance Watt House at Thomasville, which Jones designed in 1961, is a perfect representative of his manner of design. It is a subtle variation on the theme of the James Semple House at Williamsburg, Virginia – one of the first classical revival houses in America, probably designed by the father of American classicism, Thomas Jefferson. Jones possibly knew the architectural vocabulary of early American architecture better than anyone who has practiced architecture in the last half of the twentieth century; he had made American architectural traditions his own as truly as only an academic can; the beautiful styles of the past served as a starting point, as a stimulus to creation. Jones was especially fond of the Regency, Federal, and early classical revival in Georgia. Its beauty, he said, was distinguished by great "restraint." There was an almost scientific precision in Jones' manner of working and taste, and the perfection of his art was thereby enhanced. He did work for, among others, the Metropolitan Museum of Art; the Telfair Academy and the Andrew Low House, Savannah; the U.S. Department of State; and the White House.

Architect Henry Jova, FAIA, of Atlanta has said, "More is More," as opposed to Mies Van de Rohe's, "Less is More." Jova is particularly adept at transforming something old into something new and attractive. He would agree with Philip Johnson that one cannot not know and use history. In the mid-1960's he transformed an early twentieth-century Georgian Revival house in Atlanta's Ansley Park into a contemporary house, saving some of the essentials of its original architectural character; this was a landmark in the revitalization of Ansley Park, a turn-of-the-century, garden suburb, now surrounded by metropolitan Atlanta. Jova showed what could be done with an old house – not how to restore it, but how to make "more" of it;

Williams House, Thomasville, 1970

expressing something of the diverse architectural character of our own era and creating a comfortable home.

The Thomas L. Williams, Jr., house in Thomasville is a similar example; it was an old, undistinguished house that Mrs. Williams remodeled in 1969 in such a way as to express the character of modern Thomasville, which reveres traditions and history above all else. The front porch she designed is based on the Thomas County classical revival vernacular, which places slender wooden columns on piers set out from the porch floor. (Marguerite Williams is the prime mover in Thomasville's architectural preservation, and her own home pays homage to local traditions in design.)

Girard Place, a new apartment building in an old section of Savannah, was designed by an Historic Savannah Foundation staff member to harmonize with its East Hall Street neighborhood – largely frame late-Victorian houses. This 1981 version of the sort of buildings which are typical of the Savannah Victorian Historic District carries on the tradition of academic eclecticism in the context of historic preservation. It is a new building which some might think was old and newly painted; it filled a void in the East Hall streetscape without duplicating any specific, now-destroyed Savannah building; it is contemporary but traditional in scale and character, and could be a model for what to do when adding a new structure to an old setting within an historic neighborhood. Lastly is the Post-modern Norman White house at Sea Island designed by the St.

Girard Place, Savannah, 1979

Simons architect Ed Cheshire; it is a meeting of the revived Shingle Style and the revived International Style. A resort house, it fits its site beautifully, and in all of these regards it confirms Leland Roth's definition of Post-modern architecture: "It is rooted in its context and makes allusions to the past."

This seems to be the trend in domestic architecture in Georgia – a renewed appreciation of the past architectural achievements of a 250-year-old state.

White House, Sea Island, 1982

Chronology, 1733–1983

1733	Founding; Savannah plan; first cottages; Trustee's Garden	**1808**	
1734	Peter Gordon View of Savannah	c.1815	Traveler's Rest, Jarrett Manor, Toccoa
c.1740	Noble Jones House, Isle of Hope, Chatham County	1817	William Jay, architect, arrived in Savannah from England
c.1742	Horton House, St. Simons Island	c.1818	Ware's Folly, Augusta
1743	Oglethorpe returns to England for last time	c.1819	Scarbrough House, Savannah
1752	Midway, St. John's Parish colonized	c.1820	Davenport House, Savannah
1754	Royal Charter of Georgia	1820	Savannah Fire
1756	Wild Heron, Chatham County	**1833**	Nutwood, near LaGrange
1758		1835	Cherokee Indian removal; there are 87 counties in state
c.1773	Log House, Washington-Wilkes	1838	Governor's Mansion, Milledgeville
1779	Siege of Savannah	1839	Georgia Historical Society chartered Greenwood Plantation, Thomasville
1783	End of Revolution (Treaty of Paris); Augusta is capital	1844	Aaron Champion House, Savannah
c.1785	Rock House, near Thomson	1845	Willink Cottage, Savannah
1793	Cotton Gin invented	c.1845	Taylor-Grady House, Athens
1796	Savannah Fire	1847	Atlanta incorporated
c.1798	Oddingsells House, St. Julian Street, Savannah	1853	Olney Ethridge House, Sparta
1802	Chattahoochee River becomes Georgia's western boundary	1855	Crawford-Talmadge House, near Lovejoy; Marshall Row
1803	Milledgeville authorized as state capital	1860	Tupper-Barnett House, Washington-Wilkes
c.1805	Carr House, near Thomson		

1858

1859–1867	Rankin House, Columbus
1859	Dinglewood, Columbus
c.1862	May's Folly, Columbus
1864	Fall of Atlanta and Savannah
1868	Atlanta becomes capital of Georgia
c.1880	Hatcher-Schwartz House, Macon
c.1880	Edgehill, Rome

1883

c.1885	Peters House, Atlanta
1891	McGarvey House, Brunswick
1892	(+1907) Rockefeller Cottage, Jekyll Island
1898	The Crescent, Valdosta
c.1905	Walker-Moore House, Sparta
1906	Atlanta Chapter AIA formed

1908

1909	Hentz and Reid architectural partnership formed
1915	Bach-Duncan House, Macon
1916	Crane House, Jekyll Island
1917	Callanwolde, Atlanta
c.1920	Barnes-Cheatham House, Griffin
c.1925	Lucas House, Atlanta
1927	Philip Trammell Shutze becomes partner of Hentz, Adler, and Shutze
1929	Chambers House, Atlanta

1933

1937	King House, International Style, Sea Island
1940	Shorter House, Columbus
1941	Demere House, Savannah
1949	Goddard-Jones House, Atlanta
1953	Alberson House, Albany

1958

1961	Watt House, Thomasville
1965	Montgomery-Robinson House, Atlanta
1970	Williams Porch, Thomasville
1979	Girard Place, Savannah
1982	White House, Sea Island

1983

SECTION II – LANDMARK HOMES

SECTION II. Introduction:

When first we came to this now beautiful home, it was a rough and uncultivated field.

From the journal of Mrs. Charles Colcock Jones (1808-1869),
Montevideo Plantation, Liberty County, Georgia, March 1865.

IN 1851, some fourteen years before Mrs. Mary Jones made that entry in her journal, the Right Reverend Stephen Elliott made a similar comment during his address to the state's leading plantation owners at a meeting in Macon. Elliott, the first bishop of the Episcopal Diocese of Georgia, said: "The recent settlement of much of our state has laid upon our people the necessity of hewing out for themselves homes in the forest and the wilderness." The Bishop added: "The very spot on which I now stand . . . was but yesterday the home of the Indian." Called *Georgia's Planting Prelate,* Elliott summarized in this address the true condition of life in much of antebellum Georgia, especially that in the recently settled areas west of Milledgeville. He went on to remark: "Our homes, with some exceptions, exhibit the most wretched specimens of architecture, our outbuildings are arranged in the most conspicuously awkward positions, our orchards are where our ornamental gardens should be, and our vegetable gardens . . . where the rose and the jasmine ought to be taught to twine."

The Bishop's candid words about architecture and ornamental gardening, addressed to the gentlemen-planters who were assembled as the members of the Georgia Agricultural Society, put antebellum culture into realistic perspective, and issued a challenge, especially when he said: "Instead of bare red hills crowned with great white houses glaring at you through the broiling sun with cotton and corn growing up to the very doors; we should have a variety of pretty country seats, or neat farm houses, peeping out of parks and groves, with lawns sweeping down to the entrance gate, and with pleasant associations all around."

Elliott described the way things actually were in much of Georgia, and how he hoped they might become. He said: "We should find a winding road running through native forest trees until it came out upon the ornamental gardens of the estates, and opening, as it wound towards the mansion, picturesque objects at every turn."

With few exceptions the Bishop's hopes were unfulfilled during the five generations from the founding of the colony in 1733 until the outbreak of war in 1861. Only later would the aspirations of men like Elliott be realized (as we shall see in this section).

A major exception in Bishop Elliott's own day was Montevideo, now utterly vanished, the winter plantation residence of the Rev. Dr. and Mrs. Charles Colcock Jones. Situated south of Savannah in Liberty County five and one-half miles from Midway Church, it was a place quite unlike the farms Bishop Elliott usually saw on his rounds through the state. Montevideo was a rice and sea island cotton plantation of 950 acres, at least twenty-five of which were landscaped park. The first house there was built in 1833 and in 1856 was remodeled into a spacious two-story mansion. In March 1865, when Mrs. Jones described Montevideo in her journal as "this now beautiful home," she was a widow recovering from a series of raids during occupation of the area by Federal General Hugh Kilpatrick.

During happier days, in an earlier journal entry, Mary Jones had described in detail the groves and lanes of hardwood trees, the gardens and orchards in the plantation's ornamental park on the south bank of the North Newport River; her account of Montevideo at its height is an exceptional description of an exceptional place. She wrote: "Attached to the house lot was a brick kitchen, brick dairy, smokehouse, washing and weaving rooms, two servants houses, a commodious new stable and a carriage house and wagon shed, various poultry houses and yards attached, a well of excellent water and a never failing spring."

In addition she said: "On the plantation settlement are a two-story cotton house, gin and gin house, barn, cornhouse, rice house, winnowing house, mill houses and fifteen frame houses, a brick shed and a yard of excellent clay and a chapel twenty by thirty feet."

Mrs. Jones' accounts of Montevideo come from *The Children of Pride* (1972), the epic historical re-creation based on the C. C. Jones family papers. These papers show that by the end of the nineteenth century the "now beautiful home" had once again become a rough and uncultivated field as it had been in the early 1830's. Its life as a plantation from wilderness to cultivation lasted essentially one and one-half generations.

Montevideo was never revived after Appomattox; in that sense it was typical of plantation culture in much of the state, which lasted about two generations, circa 1800-circa 1860, some 50 or 60 years. It must be said, however, that they were 60 formative years. Many aspects of life in Georgia – rural, urban and suburban – to this day continue the cultural traditions begun then, as the beautiful houses and gardens in this section will show. Indeed, the fruition of Bishop Elliott's thinking about architecture and gardening, expressed in 1851, has largely come in our own era. Scarlett O'Hara's dream in *Gone*

With the Wind that she would restore Tara after the War has largely been realized in the twentieth century; and many a non-fiction Tara has been fitted out and landscaped as it seldom could or would have been prior to 1860.

Here in fine twentieth-century color photographs are houses from the eighteenth century to the present, which express the domestic ideals to which Georgians have aspired. Arranged chronologically, beginning with the Late-Colonial to Mid-Victorian, they represent every major period and style of house found in Georgia. They are landmarks from Georgia's wilderness beginnings until her urbanized Semiquincentenary. From them we may discern much of the culture and heritage, the traditions, character, and personality of a state celebrating 250 years of history, 1733-1983.

Harris-"Mackay" House

c. 1795

Augusta, Richmond County

When fully restored and properly furnished it will be one of the finest examples of 18th Century frame residential architecture in the South.

Thomas G. Little, Architect, 1958.

THIS RED, WHITE, AND BLUE HOUSE – the original paint colors as restored in 1964 – is the most carefully documented landmark of eighteenth-century architecture in Georgia and a memorial to the early heritage of Augusta.

Augusta was established as a trading post on the fall line of the Savannah River by Oglethorpe during the decade that he founded Savannah. It became Savannah's rival as the colony's most important town and, after the Revolution, was the capital of the newly created state.

This is the finest American Georgian style doorway in Georgia; original to the house, it was based on an English design book, Salmon's *Palladio Londinensis,* 1743.

From that era of the state's history, few houses survived into the twentieth century. This one in Augusta was saved by its exceptional architecture and the belief that it had been the scene of a famous Revolutionary engagement. Its colonial appearance and its location in west Augusta caused it, as early as 1900, to be credited with an historic event that had actually happened before it was built on the tract where it stands. This confusion was fortunate, for it helped to preserve the house and has only enriched its value as a landmark.

Located at 1822 Broad Street on a portion of the historic "White House Tract," this house was built by a tobacco merchant, Ezekiel Harris (1757-1828). Harris bought 320 acres of the 500-acre tract in 1794 and built this three-story mansion on Lot 3. The entire tract had been owned from 1770 to 1775 by Robert Mackay, an Indian trader. During Mackay's time the Indians called the trading post the "White House," giving the land the name it bore when Harris bought his acreage. (By 1800 the area was called Harrisburg, the name it still carries.) Robert Mackay had sited his trading post on the tract closer to the river than Ezekiel Harris placed his house, and Mackay's White House was one of the centers of action in September 1780, when General Elijah Clarke attempted to retake Augusta from the British. But it was Harris' imposing house which would begin to be identified as the place where the patriots had lost their lives. By the turn of the century, it had become a symbolic landmark of the Revolutionary War.

In 1934 the architectural merits of the house were recognized and photographed by the Historic American Buildings Survey (HABS), and in 1947 the Richmond County Historical Society purchased the house with the conviction that it was Robert Mackay's historic White House. Occasionally the name Ezekiel Harris would be mentioned as having once owned the house; a newspaper story in the *Atlanta Journal* in 1935 described the place as "The White House at Augusta, the home of Ezekiel Harris," but added, "according to tradition built in 1750." Then in 1956 the Georgia Historical Commission, a state agency, became the owner of the property and retained a restoration architect who praised the house in these words: "When fully restored and properly furnished it will be one of the finest examples of 18th century frame residential architecture in the South."

Drawing Room. During restoration the original shade of blue was discovered on this fine mantlepiece, part of some of the best surviving eighteenth-century woodwork in Georgia. The furnishings were selected by the state to compliment the architecture.

ABOVE: Rear Elevation. The front and rear porches, exterior stair, and many windows are Southern and give excellent ventilation. The fine chimney laid in English bond and gambrell roof are notable features. RIGHT: Detail of rear stairs. BELOW RIGHT: Hampton Lillibridge House, Savannah, 1798.

About the same time a similar opinion appeared in *The Early Architecture of Georgia* (1957). Frederick D. Nichols wrote: "The interiors at the White House, Augusta, seem to be the earliest in the piedmont. The large room on the west is enriched with dog-ear motifs used on the mantel and doorways. The architectural evidence dates the room 1770-80."

In 1970 the house was listed in the National Register of Historic Places as the Mackay or White House. However, five years later new research proved that Ezekiel Harris, the tobacco merchant, and not Robert Mackay, the Indian trader, had built the house and, thus, the state decided to close the site. But citizens protested, and the old red, white, and blue landmark prevailed. Currently it is administered by Historic Augusta, Inc., under a lease arrangement with the state, and is open to the public as it has been since it was dedicated July 4, 1964.

By whatever name it is called, this fine frame house is the best preserved, restored, and researched example of eighteenth-century domestic architecture in Georgia. It exemplifies Augusta's place in the culture and economy of the era when it was built, and has no rival elsewhere in the state; its closest counterpart would be Savannah's Hampton Lillibridge House, 1798. (A mid-eighteenth century visitor to Savannah described houses such as these as "being of wood painted in shades of blue and red.")

The Chief Vann House

1805

Spring Place, Murray County

WHEN THE GEORGIA Historical Commission restored this extraordinary house in the mid-1950's, the archaeologist Clemens de Baillou wrote, "It was, in comparison with its surroundings, more than a Palais de Versailles in France." Long recognized as an unparalleled landmark of the Cherokee Nation, it is all that remains of the extensive plantation of Chief James Vann (1768-1809). Vann's mother was a Cherokee and his father a Scot who traded with the Indians. In 1801 Vann sponsored a mission of North Carolina Moravians at Spring Place to educate his children and tribesmen, and the missionary craftsmen helped him to build this late-Georgian, Federal style mansion. Archaeology showed that the bricks were fired on the place, and the north or front elevation is laid up in Flemish bond. On March 24, 1805, the Brethren, as they were called, recorded in their diary, "Vann moved into this newly built house today."

Several years after James's death, his son Joseph acquired the plantation and, in May 1819, entertained President Monroe, John C. Calhoun, and other governmental dignitaries as they traveled the Federal Road which the house faced. The mission diary recorded it this way: "Very late in the evening the President of the United States and his party arrived at Joseph Vann's."

In 1834, during the Cherokee Removal, a troop of Georgia guardsmen turned Vann and his family out of his home; in time he made his way to Oklahoma and became a leading citizen there. Later the Federal government paid Vann $19,605 for his property in Georgia; the inventory of that property lists, among other things: "One fine brick house, 800 acres of cultivated land, 42 cabins, six barns, five smokehouses, a grist mill, blacksmith shops, eight corn cribs, a shop and foundary, a trading post, a peach kiln, a still, and 1,133 peach trees." No wonder Vann's Georgia neighbors called him "Rich Joe."

The showplace of the Cherokee Tribe of Indians, when all of north Georgia was its republic, the Vann house had rapidly deteriorated until it was saved by public-spirited citizens and restored by the Georgia Historical Commission in 1952, as that agency's first preservation effort. In July 1958, the house was dedicated with the participation of a large contingent of leading Cherokee descendents, including 42 members of the Vann family. At that time relics such as Joseph Vann's gold signet ring were given to the house for display. The por-

ABOVE: Rear elevation. OPPOSITE: The Cohutta Mountains are the background for the "showplace of the Cherokee Nation."

trait of Vann over the dining room mantle shows this ring and gives an idea of how a well-to-do Indian dressed when north Georgia was the land of the Cherokee. Wild Indians they were not.

Today, visitors to the Chief Vann House see essentially what President Monroe saw in 1819 and no doubt experience something of his shock to find this small Versailles in the north Georgia wilderness.

TOP: Dining Room. A portrait of Joseph Vann hangs above the dining room mantle. The walnut table is set with period feather-edge Wedgwood, c. 1820. ABOVE: The workmanship of Moravian craftsmen from the Spring Place Mission, this cantilevered staircase has been restored to its original colors. OPPOSITE PAGE: Drawing Room. The late-Georgian style carved mantlepiece is highlighted with authentic colors: blue of the sky, gold of corn and wheat, green of the fields, and red of the earth.

It was, in comparison with its surroundings, more than a Palais de Versailles in France.

Gilbert-Alexander House

1808

Washington, Wilkes County

The Virginians were a remarkable group, constituting an element in the population of the state whose importance would be hard to overestimate."

E. Merton Coulter, Ph.D.
1965

RARE IN GEORGIA is a two-story brick house built in 1808 – especially outside of Augusta or Savannah – and rarer still a dwelling that has been the continuous home of the generations of a family which built it. As rare, too, are original furnishings still being used in the house for which they were made.

But this is not a fly-in-amber preservation; it is the main house of a working plantation, still working as it has been since the first decade of the nineteenth century. It is the home of Mr. and Mrs. Alexander Wright, Alexander and Lotte Uthes, a native of Germany. Squire Wright, as the Laird of this fine brick manor should be called, is a direct descendant of the Virginians, William and Felix Gilbert, who first saw this land lot with its clear spring and beautiful trees in the 1780's.

Although this is a private home, an on-going preservation and not a house-museum, it tells much of the history and character of the proud old town in which it was built. Founded in 1780, it was the first place in America to be named for General Washington. It is ten years older than Washington, D.C., and prefers to distinguish itself from the nation's capital with the distinctively alliterative name: Washington-Wilkes.

This area was the first of the Georgia Piedmont plateau to be settled. Beginning in 1773, after the Indian land cession of that year, the Carolinians and Virginians began to arrive. In 1777 Wilkes County was formed and, from the first, it was a stronghold of patriotism, especially when the British and their Tory allies controlled much of the rest of the state. The Battle of Kettle Creek, an important Loyalist victory, was fought near here in 1779. For that reason, in 1780 a Wilkes County town could be safely named for the General. By 1790 original Wilkes County had become the largest county in Georgia (later it would be subdivided) and had almost half of the people in the entire state, most of whom came south via the Great Philadelphia Wagon Road. This road south, through the Valley of Virginia and the Carolinas, was the main route taken by settlers of the Georgia interior in the eighteenth century. Few people moved inland from the Georgia coast and, as a result, the Piedmont developed a different culture from the Savannah low country. "The Virginians," wrote Dr. E. Merton Coulter, Georgia's preeminent historian, "were a remarkable group . . . whose importance [for Georgia] would be hard to overestimate."

The Gilbert-Alexander House is a living document of that Virginia-bred Georgia upcountry culture and of the first period of Wilkes County's prosperity, when tobacco was only beginning to lose out to cotton as the economic staple. This house dates from that pre-War of 1812, pre-Greek Revival, Early-Republican world. Many pieces of its original furniture are of the pre-Empire Period of Georgia-made Piedmont furniture, which Mr. Henry D. Green of St. Simons Island has collected and documented. The candlestand and the worktable shown here are family pieces from the earliest period of the house. They are both of walnut, the most popular wood for Piedmont cabinetwork; and both were shown at Mr. Green's High Museum of Art show in 1976 entitled "Furniture of the Georgia Piedmont Before 1830," as was the fine Pembroke table of mahogany with secondary woods of poplar and southern yellow pine.

The Gilbert-Alexander House is one of only a handful of early brick houses in Georgia. The side hall, rather than a wide central hall, is unusual for a Georgia house but is reminiscent of Federal period rowhouses in Alexandria, Virginia, familiar to the original builders. The wooden wing and porch were added by Adam Leopold Alexander, Alexander Wright's great-grandfather. Before these additions, the house would have resembled its Virginia cousins even more than it does now. One of the most architecturally interesting features is the Palladian window in the gable. The Federal style interior woodwork and plasterwork is original, and the drawing room chimneypiece, with three carved sunbursts and King of Prussia marble, is especially notable.

The Gilbert-Alexander House sits, among some of its original outbuildings, just east of Alexander Avenue

OPPOSITE: The Gilbert-Alexander House was built in 1808, with wooden wing and porch added later by Adam Leopold Alexander, the owner's great-grandfather, a graduate of Yale University.

OPPOSITE: This sofa was commissioned for the spot in the hall during Adam Leopold Alexander's time, c.1840. Note fine woodwork and plasterwork, original to the house. ABOVE: Adam Leopold Alexander was painted by Jocelyn at New Haven, Connecticut, in 1828 when Adam was a student at Yale. The portrait has hung in this house since that time. All of the brass fireplace equipment is original to the house, as are numerous pieces of the furniture. (The rocker on the right was rescued from a barn and restored.)

on 54 acres in a beautiful grove of old trees near the Washington-Wilkes town square. The burial ground on the property has generations of family members, including Adam Leopold Alexander, whose portrait by the painter Jocelyn hangs in the house. Born here, though buried in Augusta, was General Porter Alexander, co-founder of the U.S. Army Signal Corps, who was also a Brigadier General of the Artillery in the Confederate Army.

If Washington-Wilkes was, as it has been called, the "heart and soul of antebellum society," then the Gilbert-Alexander House remains as one of the truest legacies of that era. In 1983 it will have prevailed 175 years, only 75 years less than the state itself.

REGENCY ARCHITECTURE IN SAVANNAH

Richardson-Owens-Thomas House

1816–1819   William Jay, *Architect*

Savannah, Chatham County

LEFT: Richardson–Owens-Thomas House. Said to be "the finest Regency house in America," this two-story villa on a high basement permanently set the standard for domestic architecture in Savannah. The stucco has weathered to a tone similar to the Italian Renaissance villas of Andrea Palladio and to the Regency buildings at Bath, England, known to William Jay. ABOVE: East President Street elevation. This balcony, on the south side of the house, is of iron, cast and painted to resemble stone. Designed by William Jay, there was to be a matching balcony on this elevation off of the front reception room. This is one of the most beautiful and unusual verandas in all of early-American architecture. The Marquis de Lafayette spoke from here in 1825.

You would be astonished to see the number of handsome Fire-proof dwelling houses that have been completed here since the last War, and those that are now erecting. There are several houses here that would be an ornament to any city.

Petit De Villiers, Savannah, to General Charles Cotesworthy Pinckney, Pinckney Island. December 29, 1818. Georgia Historical Society Collections; previously unpublished.

EXACTLY ONE YEAR after this letter was written, the young British architect, William Jay (c. 1792-1837), arrived in Savannah from England to supervise the completion of the Richard Richardson house. It would have been one of the "handsome Fire-proof dwelling houses" the writer, a well-known Savannah merchant, described as "now erecting." When this letter was written, the Richardson house had been underway for two years; begun in 1816, it was finished in 1819, and in December 1818 was fast becoming one of the houses which the correspondent believed could "ornament . . . any city."

The merchant's letter nicely summarized conditions in Savannah after the War of 1812. The Port of Savannah began to see a time of unparalleled prosperity based on the cotton trade, which created a class of merchant princes including Richard Richardson, who built in the latest taste and who looked more to England – in this case the English Regency period – and to the North, economically and culturally, than to their own region.

This house is the preeminent surviving architectural expression of that first major phase of Savannah's prominence. It was one of the first to be built in the Classical Revival style which reigned, along with cotton, for about 30 years, ending its dominance during the five years before the War Between the States. This house is still one of the ornaments of Savannah and is the only one of the houses William Jay did during his brief sojourn (1817-1821) which still may be experienced as a residence. It is so uniquely a part of Savannah that one cannot imagine it actually ornamenting another city; without a doubt, it reflects in stucco-covered bricks and tabby much of the historical character of the town in which it was built.

The reception room at the Richardson-Owens-Thomas House has many interesting features: ceiling as designed by William Jay; original mantlepiece, attributed to the English sculptor, Richard Westmacott, Jr.; polished steel fireplace equipment; portrait of Anne Jay Bolton (1793-1859) by William Etty, R.A., on Indefinite Loan from New York State Historical Society. The furnishings are largely American, pre-1830's. Sofa is by Duncan Phyfe.

Clearly the honor for this remarkable "ornament" is not entirely due to the architect William Jay. In some ways it is as much a landmark of eighteenth-century Savannah as it is of nineteenth. And, in other ways, of the twentieth century which chose to preserve, restore and furnish it as a house museum.

A list of acknowledgements for its architecture and preservation would be lengthy. In reverse chronological order one would start with Miss Margaret Gray Thomas, whose family had made it their home for 121 years until her death in 1951; her grandfather purchased it in 1830.

Miss Thomas gave it at her death to the Telfair Academy of Arts and Sciences to be a museum honoring her grandfather, Owens, and her father, Thomas. It was opened to the public in October 1954.

In normal sequence, however, the acknowledgements would begin, strange perhaps to say, with Colonial Trustee James Oglethorpe, whose brilliant city plan of 1733 provided the unusual building site: a Trust Lot on Oglethorpe Square in Anson Ward. When this house was begun in 1816, Savannah consisted of the original four wards laid out by Oglethorpe, plus eleven more.

LEFT: The dining room as designed by Jay has a black-marble mantel and a shallow niche with a built-in Regency console. The banquet table and twelve chairs are American, from Philadelphia, owned in Savannah for many generations. Pine floor boards spanning the length of the room, are painted in light and dark shades, as originally. ABOVE: Detail of dining room niche. The architect provided this indirect lighting instead of windows on the north wall. The marble top console table is part of the original furnishings of the house; it was in Richard Richardson's inventory. The carved pedestal is of mahogany and ebony.

Anson Ward, in which the house sits on the northeast Trust Lot, was also laid out by Oglethorpe; he did so in 1742, one year before returning permanently to England. Thus, the house sits in the oldest part of Savannah on one of the Trust Lots especially designed to accommodate and display important buildings. A Trust Lot is like a corner lot, doubled, so that the architect has a setting for a particularly three-dimensional composition; thus, in this case, the East President Street side gives the chance for the profile of a fine balcony; and then there is a walled garden and the chance for a garden elevation partly on view to the passing parade.

Library-sitting room, second floor. This room was refurnished in 1980 when the walls were restored to their original color. Portrait of Robert Bolton, husband of Anne Jay Bolton, William Jay's sister, on indefinite Loan by the New York State Historical Society. Furnishings are American, nineteenth century. The sofa is from a Savannah house; the straight chairs are from Hofwyl Plantation, in Glynn County.

After the recognition of Oglethorpe's eighteenth-century plan, which provides a Trust Lot building site, must come Richard Richardson's early nineteenth-century prosperity and taste. Richardson was president of the Savannah branch of the Bank of the United States, a cotton merchant and prominent citizen. In 1811, he married Frances Bolton whose older brother, Robert Bolton, had married Anne Jay, William Jay's sister, in Bath, England, in 1810. Through the Savannah Boltons, Richardson became acquainted with Jay.

At what point Jay, in fact, became associated with the project to build the house is not known; it was underway at least by 1816. An inscription incised on the masonry foundation under the portico gives the name of the builder and the dates: "Began house A.D. 1816 – Finished June A.D. 1819 – J. Retan." John Retan was a Savannah contractor and is known to have built the Jay-

designed Branch Bank of the United States (1820), of which Richardson was president. Since Jay arrived in Savannah in late December 1817, Retan would have been underway. Traditionally it is said that the 21-year-old designed the house in England and sent over the plans to Richardson and his contractor. Conclusive documentation for that may never be found. But client, builder, and architect produced a masterwork on this Trust Lot site which permanently affected architecture in Savannah and Georgia.

Based on the work of early nineteenth-century English architects such as Sir John Soane, the Richardson House introduced curves and movement, and varied room sizes and shapes, up to then little seen in Savannah. At the same time, Jay brought a more archaeological use of the classical orders, characteristic of the developing classical revival. Jay, like Soane, molded space

56

Garden. As planned and planted in parterres (for the 1954 house museum opening) by Clermont Lee, Savannah landscape architect. Lee described it as a "Georgia-style Regency Garden." Plants as used in Georgia in 1820 were put in the beds at that time. All of it was based on careful research into gardens, in Savannah and related places.

three-dimensionally and used precise but personalized classical ornamentation on the exterior and interior. The entry portico demonstrates Jay's use of a spatially exciting series of curves, and then, inside the door, screening the foyer from the stairway, are two Corinthian columns with gilded capitals derived from the Choragic Monument of Lysicrates (from the book by Stuart and Revett, *Antiquities of Athens,* 1762, which inspired the classical revival).

William Jay left Georgia in 1821 for Charleston, South Carolina, after designing four or five important houses (see pages 58-61) and several other buildings, and in 1824 returned to England. Richardson sold his house in 1822 after his wife's untimely death, and it was during its brief use as a boarding house that the Marquis de Lafayette and his son stayed here in 1825 as guests of the City of Savannah. Five years later, George Welch-

man Owens purchased it and thus began the sequence in which this "handsome Fire-proof dwelling house" was preserved as a continuing ornament on Savannah's Oglethorpe Square.

(Pages 58-61 show two other houses designed by William Jay: the Alexander Telfair and the William Scarbrough; both are used by organizations and neither is a house museum, but each has a room restored with great care to the way it looked when new.)

Telfair Academy of Arts and Sciences
The Octagon Room

1819   William Jay, *Architect*

Savannah, Chatham County

"In Savannah there are a few mansions built by an English architect, Mr. Jay – son of the celebrated divine of that name at Bath – which are of beautiful architecture, of sumptious interior, and combine as much of elegance and luxury as are to be found in any private dwelling in the country."

James Silk Buckingham, 1842

Telfair Academy of Arts and Sciences, 1886. Alexander Telfair residence, 1818-1819, William Jay, Architect; with additions in 1883 by Detlief Lienau (1818-1887) of New York City. This is another one of the "handsome Fire-proof dwelling houses" Jay designed for Savannah; it was also on a Trust Lot. Now an art museum. OPPOSITE: The Octagon Room, Telfair Academy. Alexander Telfair's octagonal reception room, which he called the Oak Room, as restored and furnished 1981-82. Some of the *faux bois* surfaces of this room had survived behind bookcases in the niches, and, with that as evidence, the oak-grained plaster walls have been re-created as designed by William Jay in 1818. The furnishings are largely nineteenth-century American; the c.1800 globes are Telfair family items.
The gilt-bronze oil chandelier is original to the house.

Scarbrough House

1819   William Jay, *Architect*

Savannah, Chatham County

The Scarbrough House hall is a kind of atrium. It is one of the grandest special compositions in American domestic architecture.

Frederick Doveton Nichols
The Early Architecture of Georgia, 1957

Scarbrough House, home of William Scarbrough, merchant; William Jay, Architect, 1818–1819; since 1972 the headquarters of Historic Savannah Foundation, Inc. William Scarbrough entertained President James Monroe here in May 1819, soon after the house was completed. At that time Scarbrough described his architect's taste as "pure and genuine." OPPOSITE: Atrium entrance hall. *Faux marbre* restoration, 1982. This resembles an atrium design of Regency tastemaker Thomas Hope in his *Household Furniture and Interior Decoration* (1807).

Gordon-Bowen-Blount-Lamar-Lindsley-James-Banks House

1828   Daniel Pratt, *Architect*

Bankshaven, Coweta County

ABOVE: Drawing room mantlepiece and niche; with original *faux marbre,* gilded carving, and plasterwork. BELOW: Gordon-Banks House garden elevation, as designed by Daniel Pratt, c. 1828, with balancing wings by Robert L. Raley, 1970. (William N. Banks moved the house from Jones County to this site in 1969.)

Sister Mary's fine home – built by Daniel Pratt with exquisite use of gold on fluted woodwork, artful paint to transform Georgia pine to exotically patterned wood grains, and Greek motifs in small designs on mantels, windows, and mouldings – was undamaged by the detachment from Sherman's army which took over the lower floor in 1865.

Dolly Blount Lamar
(Mrs. Walter D. Lamar)
When All Is Said and Done, 1952

SISTER MARY was Mrs. Thomas O. Bowen, Dolly Blount's aunt. The Bowens owned this house when it was in Jones County, near Haddock, living in it through the Civil War. They were the second owners, having bought it in 1848 from John W. Gordon who built it with the help of the architect Daniel Pratt in the late 1820's. Gordon was a cotton planter, state senator, and brigadier general in the Georgia militia. Pratt (1799-1873) was an architect-builder from Temple, New Hampshire, who moved to Georgia when he was twenty and built a remarkable group of early classical revival houses in and around Milledgeville, then the capital of Georgia. The third owner was James H. Blount of Macon who bought it in 1881 and left it to his daughter, Mrs. Walter D. Lamar, Dolly Blount. She used it as a weekend retreat, calling it "Hale Nui," supposedly meaning "Big House" in the language of the Sandwich Islands. Mrs. Lamar gave picnics at "Hale Nui" where the treat of the occasion, according to her account in *When All Is Said and Done,* was the "singing of spirituals by the two Negro women who lived in separate cabins just below the Big House and acted as caretakers." The spirits of these two women are supposed to be one of the things which helped to save the house after they and Mrs. Lamar had passed on. When the present owner, William Nathaniel Banks, first saw the place it was said to be haunted by these old care-

OPPOSITE: The Gordon-Banks House, 1828. (The three-tiered Carrara marble fountain in the background came from the fabled Barnsley Gardens, Bartow County, c. 1850; the fountain was damaged during the Civil War but repaired, restored and erected here by William Banks.)

ABOVE: Bankshaven: Panorama from portico showing lake and established boxwood gardens, originally planted in the 1920's. This is an English-style landscape of the "Landscape Gardening School" as advocated by Humphrey Repton about 1820. William C. Pauley of Atlanta designed it in 1929. There are 300 acres and five major gardens within the "park." LEFT: "Spring"; Italian marble, garden figure, c. 1845.

takers. But before Banks there was Dr. L. C. Lindsley of Milledgeville, a historian and teacher who admired Daniel Pratt's architecture and helped the "caretakers" until his death when he left it to his daughter, Mrs. John James, from whom Banks bought it in 1968. At that time it had seldom been occupied except for weekends for more than fifty years. But "Sister Mary's fine home" was still as described by her niece, Dolly Lamar, as she remembered it in the 1870's. William Banks says that it was like a "fly-in-amber."

This house has had everything. It was designed and built by one of the best antebellum architects to work in Georgia outside of Savannah; it survived Sherman; was haunted by protective ghosts; and when it was languishing in Jones County (on what was by that time called "Rattlesnake Hill"). A teacher who loved architecture bought it to protect it; and then along came someone (Banks) who not only cared for beautiful old buildings but could afford to rescue one, completely and permanently, by moving it 100 miles to a beautifully established site in Coweta County; this new owner was actually looking for such a place to house an exceptional early nineteenth-century American table found in Charleston, South Carolina (see p. 69).

RIGHT: Looking from "Gothick" style gazebo designed by Robert L. Raley. FOLLOWING PAGES: Formal rose garden, Spring 1982.

Handsomely built and preserved, this fortunate antique house was moved with surprising ease; it was given the most careful sort of renovation/restoration clean-up and a pair of balancing wings, and then it was furnished as if it were a museum of early-American decorative arts, with antiques – some of them masterpieces comparable to the house – from the Federal and Empire periods.

By 1972 it was perfect enough to be featured in *The Magazine Antiques* in the "Living with Antiques" section as "The Gordon-Banks House in the Georgia Piedmont." In that same issue Robert L. Raley, the distinguished architect who helped Mr. Banks with the renovation, also had an article, "Daniel Pratt, Architect and Builder in Georgia." Although additional *objects d'art* have been added since 1972, it remains much as it was then: a landmark of historic preservation in Georgia. The owner says that it will be "a house museum in the future." In effect it is this already, as these photographs show. (William Nathaniel Banks, a native of Coweta County, also has a beautiful old house in New England; it is in Temple, New Hampshire, the birthplace of Daniel Pratt.)

LEFT: Drawing room as furnished c. 1970 with early nineteenth-century Americana of exceptional quality. ABOVE: Card table, with winged support, attributed to cabinetmaker, Charles-Honoré Lannuier, c. 1815. This piece, which needed to be housed in a comparable setting, caused Mr. Banks to begin the restoration project. Note similarity of table top to woodwork design.

LEFT: Dining room with fine French needlework rug, c. 1830. Portrait of William Nathaniel Banks by Aaron Shikler. The dado and door paneling is painted to imitate flame-mahogany veneers with tiger-maple borders, and the baseboards are marbleized. The dining table is English, c. 1825. ABOVE: Study with New York state bookcase; worktable is from Boston, Massachusetts. Next to bookcase are lithographs from the McKenny and Hall portfolio of Indians, c. 1836.

TOP LEFT: Hall looking towards staircase. Note marble-topped pier table, New York City, c. 1815; pine painted and gilded; attributed to New York cabinetmaker, Lannuier. Sofa: New York City, c. 1815, with gilded winged-paw feet. TOP RIGHT AND LOWER LEFT: This spacious upstairs hall, larger than the downstairs hall, would have been used as a sitting room; it is fitted-out with Empire furniture, c. 1835, all of it attributed to Philadelphia cabinetmaker, Anthony Querville. The center pedestal table is especially fine. LOWER RIGHT: Hall looking through original fan light towards the garden and pond. Shows original woodwork and gilded plasterwork.

TOP: From master bedroom through hall into guestroom. "Gathering Wood for Winter," (1855) by George Henry Durrie (1820–1863) over the mantlepiece, is one of a number of fine American paintings at Bankshaven. ABOVE: Bedroom with mahogany bedstead in the French Empire style with ormolu decoration. The original bill of sale for this bed, dated "1813 March 13," documents it as by Duncan Phyfe, New York City.

"The old Governor's Mansion is an acknowledged masterpiece."

John W. Linley, AIA
The Architecture of Middle Georgia, 1972

Old Governor's Mansion

1838   Charles B. Cluskey, *Architect*

Milledgeville, Baldwin County

Charles B. Cluskey, a native of Ireland, is, after William Jay, the most significant architect of Georgia. He and his work deserve to be better known. Among his superb houses is the monumental, Palladian-inspired Governor's Mansion at Milledgeville.

Frederick Doveton Nichols
The Early Architecture of Georgia, 1957

CARVED IN GRANITE above the massive front door is the inscription, "Executive Mansion 1838." Nine governors, beginning with George R. Gilmer and ending with Charles J. Jenkins, lived here. Its most unwelcome overnight guest was General William T. Sherman who occupied the house as his headquarters in November 1864. The governor most responsible for its design and construction was William Schley who spent $50,000 and turned the masterful results over to his successor.

Milledgeville was founded and laid out as the capital of Georgia during the four-year term of John Milledge (1802-1806), for whom the carefully planned town was named. Milledgeville served as the capital from 1804 until the seat of government was moved to Atlanta in 1868. This Executive Mansion was the fifth place in Milledgeville to house governors, but it was the first that the Georgia legislature built for that purpose; the second, which is officially named the Executive Center (pages 232-235) is a 1968 Atlanta version of classical revival.

In Milledgeville the old Governor's Mansion is simply called The Mansion, which it clearly was when no other dwelling in the area was of masonry, nor of this architectural quality and scale. Then, as now, a landmark of neoclassical architecture, it has hardly been rivaled in the state. Of 60 feet square and three stories, it was one of Charles B. Cluskey's most important public commissions and, if not the finest house that he built, it was certainly the most handsomely preserved and presented.

Inspired by Thomas Jefferson's neoclassicism and Andrea Palladio's sixteenth-century Renaissance villas, The Mansion is planned around an impressive central rotunda, 25 feet in diameter, which rises 50 feet to a sky-lighted dome. The entrance elevation is similar to Palladio's Villa Foscari and Villa Rotonda; it shared with them a monumental portico in the Ionic Order. Similarly, it is of stucco in a stone color and has two stories set on a high basement floor, where the cooking and many other necessary household chores were accomplished.

ABOVE: Portrait of John Milledge II (1757-1818) by John Field. Milledge was a second-generation Georgian. His father, also John, came over with Oglethorpe on the *Anne*. He was a Congressman from Georgia; and Governor from 1802-1806, when Milledgeville was founded; later he was a U.S. Senator. He donated the land on the Oconee River for the campus of the University of Georgia. Overton was his home in the Summerville/Sand Hills district of Augusta.

The colossal, pedimented porch is said by F. D. Nichols to be the "earliest documented Greek Revival portico in Georgia." Certainly it set the fashion and was an important model for the fine houses built in the 1840's and 50's throughout the state. (As with this house, the finest houses in Georgia were usually built within villages and towns, and not out in the countryside. The neoclassical houses on pages 80-83, for example, were

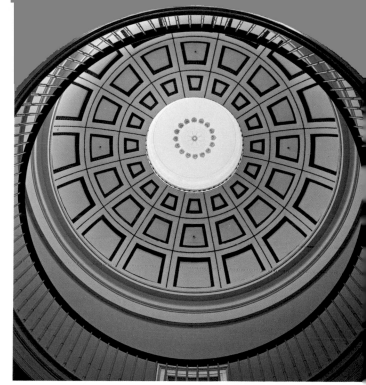

LEFT: Entrance Hall. The classical symmetry of the house is emphasized here with architecture and furnishings. Looking through the rotunda, on axis to the octagonal library. TOP: Dome. This is 50 feet from the floor of the rotunda. ABOVE: Rotunda. The main staircase is in a side hall to the right of this central circular room. A concealed spiral staircase winds from the basement floor up through the north rotunda wall to the third floor.

town houses on large acreages within a New England-like village.)

Cluskey was paid $100 on April 19, 1837, for his plans. An Irishman by birth, he practiced architecture and constructed buildings in Georgia from 1829 or '30 until 1847; he returned later to St. Simons Island where he died June 14, 1871, during construction of the lighthouse and keeper's dwelling. His building for the Medical College of Georgia (1835) at Augusta is another of his important public commissions. Cluskey's work in Savannah in the 1840's was outstanding. Using the columned Greek Revival idiom William Jay introduced there, he contributed several notable houses to the otherwise conservative, late-Georgian "townscape"; among his best was the Aaron Champion House (1844).

Also important in the construction of the Executive Mansion was a Connecticut Yankee with family members living in Georgia: Timothy Porter (1802-1876). Porter arrived in Milledgeville in 1837 with carpenters,

bricklayers, and other skilled workers, and the house was ready by the fall of 1838. It is considered a masterpiece of construction but, by 1855, was evidently shopworn; that year a state referendum voted to keep Milledgeville as the capital and, with that encouragement, the legislature appropriated monies to refurbish The Mansion. In 1856 it was given a new coat of stucco, scored to simulate stone and stained a red-pink color (said to resemble Georgia clay). Also at that time, the grounds were re-landscaped and $2,200 spent for furnishings. (Presumably these facts about the c. 1855 renovation were in mind when the house was restored in the mid-1960's.)

In 1889 The Mansion became the home of the presidents of the state college at Milledgeville, for a long time known as The Women's College of Georgia and now called Georgia College. The Mansion has continued in that capacity, but in 1967 the first two floors were opened to the public for tours after the two-year

ABOVE: Dining Room. This bowfront sideboard was made in Athens, Georgia, about 1815; it is of walnut with southern yellow pine secondary wood. This room is as refurnished in the mid-1960's. BELOW: Dining Room detail. American silver of the Federal period on tray; the earliest piece is a teapot with duck finial made in Philadelphia in 1815 by Joseph Lownes. Worktable – Athens, Georgia, area, c. 1800; walnut; southern yellow pine; maple inlay. LEFT: Drawing Room. Running the 60-foot extent of the north side of the house is this grand salon, refurnished in the mid-1960's with antiques of the 1820's, 30's, and 40's. The matching black marble mantles have been in this room since 1838, as have the ceiling medallions. The crystal and gilt-bronze chandeliers in the French Empire style were made for the room when the house was refurnished.

renovation and restoration of most of the building. The ground floor and the *piano nobile* were furnished by a Georgia College Foundation committee. This committee enhanced the architectural style and character of The Mansion with appropriate furnishings; therefore, the Regency, Federal and Empire periods (1800–1850) predominate with several early nineteenth-century Georgia-made pieces for local flavor.

In 1974 The Mansion was designated a National Historic Landmark, specifically because of its architecture. Georgians would agree that such recognition is deserved but, from whatever point of view, they feel their old Governor's Mansion is a landmark. The first photographs made for this book were of this house because it is the most symbolic of Georgia houses: it is for Georgians, as Georgians, the landmark home of their hearts.

THREE HALLS AT ROSWELL
Bulloch, Barrington and Mimosa
1840's   Willis Ball, *Architect*

Roswell, Fulton County

The Bulloch and Hansell houses at Roswell, Georgia, are almost purely Jeffersonian. The full temple form – as it had been employed in Jefferson's pavilions at the University of Virginia – was imitated widely.

Fiske Kimball
Thomas Jefferson, Architect, 1916

Mimosa Hall, 1840's. Originally Dunwody Hall, then Phenix Hall, now Mimosa.

IN THE LATE 1830's, a group of families from the coastal counties of Georgia, led by Roswell King, began colonizing the former Indian lands just north of the Chattahoochee River in what was then Cobb County. The colonists envisioned classical temples (symbols of their civilization) crowning the hills and brought in a builder/architect, Willis Ball from Windsor, Connecticut – Roswell King's birthplace. In several years Roswell resembled a New England town, built around a church and village green. Down on the creek, as it flowed into the Chattahoochee, textile mills were built. Incorporated as the Roswell Manufacturing Company in December 1839, its incorporators were the founders of the town, among them Roswell King (town name); Barrington King, son of Roswell King (Barrington Hall);

James S. Bulloch of Savannah (Bulloch Hall); and John Dunwody, brother-in-law of James S. Bulloch (Mimosa Hall).

This was an extraordinary antebellum Georgia town: a textile manufacturing village – one of the first in the state – and each founder was a prominent man. Roswell was one of General Sherman's targets: he sent General Kenner Garrard to occupy the town in 1864; Garrard used the houses as officers' quarters and burned the mills to the ground. However, by 1865, the mills were back in operation and for many generations were the main source of the town's wealth.

Mimosa Hall was the home of General Andrew Jackson Hansell who, in 1869, became the president of the reactivated manufacturing company. The present owner, C. Edward Hansell, a great-great-grandson of General Hansell, inherited the house from his father, Granger Hansell, who re-acquired the property in 1947 after it was out of the family for a generation. During that break in Hansell ownership, one of the owners was Neel Reid, Georgia's preeminent architect of houses. Reid bought the place in 1916, renovated the house and grounds, and died there ten years later.

These three halls have long been praised for their architecture, at least as much as for their history. The year that Neel Reid bought Mimosa Hall as his own home, the great art historian Fiske Kimball cited the Roswell houses as an important derivation of Thomas Jefferson's Neoclassicism. Neel Reid must have agreed with Kimball's opinions and, presumably, even thought of it as more suitable for a modern classicist than anything he could design for himself. (That year of 1916, Reid completed one of his masterpieces: a Palladian-inspired Renaissance villa, pages 162-169.)

But prior to 1916, architectural historians and architects discovered the neoclassical houses in Roswell, giving them national recognition. In 1902 Mrs. Thaddeus E. Horton, an Atlanta journalist whose writings deserve to be better known, published these houses – for the first time nationally – in *The American Architect*

*The great portal, opening with hospitable welcome, Closes as a fortress gate
Upon a world hostile to ancient leisure.*

"Mimosa Hall"
Dr. Thomas H. English, 1953.

and Building News. C.R.S. Horton, as she signed herself professionally, was an astute amateur architectural historian, and hers was the first serious work on the domestic architecture of Georgia to appear in the twentieth century. She was the first to rediscover the work of William Jay in Savannah. Her insightful article was entitled "Savannah and Parts of the Far South." In it Mrs. Horton featured *two* Bulloch houses in Georgia: the house in Roswell and the now-demolished Bulloch house in Savannah (often called the Bulloch-Habersham house, Orleans Square, 1820, by William Jay). Oddly, however, she was seemingly unaware that the houses were built by relatives, a nephew and uncle: Major James Stephens Bulloch (1793-1849) of Bulloch Hall was the nephew of Archibald Stobo Bulloch who commissioned Jay to build the house on Orleans Square, later owned by Robert Habershan, Esq. This obscure piece of "architectural genealogy" is important as it is one of the links between the first classic revival houses in coastal Georgia, by Jay, with those of the Georgia upcountry by builder/architects such as Willis Ball. (Roswell is on the northern edge of the Piedmont and was an exception to the rule that the Piedmont was settled by Virginians and Carolinians.)

It would not be stretching the imagination to think that the design of houses and other buildings in Savannah influenced Major Bulloch's taste when he came to build a house in Roswell; or that of his sister Jane when her husband John Dunwody built what is now called Mimosa Hall. Bulloch had been president of the United States Branch Bank of Savannah (now demolished), an important Jay essay in Regency neoclassicism; therefore, he was used to classical revival buildings of the first quality.

The sort of people who founded Roswell were truly low-country aristocrats, as literature usually calls them. Normally, James Stephen Bulloch is described first as a grandson of the Revolutionary patriot Archibald Bulloch who was elected President and Commander-in-Chief of Georgia in 1776; and then, second, as the father of Martha (Mittie) who married Theodore Roosevelt, Sr., on December 22, 1853, at Bulloch Hall. Thus, he was a grandfather of Theodore Roosevelt, Jr. (26th President of the United States) who visited Bulloch Hall in 1905, and a great-grandfather of Eleanor Roosevelt, daughter of Elliot Roosevelt and wife of her fifth cousin, President Franklin D. Roosevelt. It is no wonder that Bulloch Hall was nominated to the National Reg-

ABOVE: Barrington Hall. OPPOSITE: Bulloch Hall.

ister of Historic Places with these words: "Architecturally, historically and culturally, one of the most significant houses in Georgia."

Barrington Hall was also nominated to the National Register and described in this way: "In many ways the most significant landmark in Roswell, and Roswell is one of Georgia's most historic towns." Mimosa Hall was not nominated because the owners declined. But in 1974 all three halls were included in the nationally registered Roswell Historic District, and Mimosa was singled out as an important element.

The three halls – Bulloch, Barrington and Mimosa – are the major landmarks of Roswell. With many satellite buildings throughout the historic town, they constitute a major reflection of Thomas Jefferson's American classic revival, a cultural nationalism which had no exact English or European counterpart; these were Jeffersonian pavilions on the North Georgia frontier. As Talbot Hamlin wrote in his *Greek Revival Architecture in America* (1944): "Nowhere did the Greek Revival produce a more perfect blending of the dignified and the gracious, the impressive and the domestic, than in the lovely houses of the thirties and forties in upstate Georgia . . . . ."

Tullie Smith House

c. 1845

Atlanta Historical Society, Fulton County

This is the most serious and purposeful house museum in Georgia.

The Architecture of Georgia
1976

THE LAST RESIDENT of this house, before it was relocated and restored, was Miss Tullie Smith; she lived in it in the eastern outskirts of Atlanta as expressways and office parks grew up around her. After Miss Tullie's death, the house and its outside kitchen were moved to the grounds of the Swan House, the Atlanta Historical Society's museum in northwest Atlanta (page 178). There, with the help of the Georgia Historical Commission, the Atlanta Junior League, and others, the Historical Society carefully restored the frame buildings in 1971 and '72 to their original appearance.

At that time the house and kitchen were placed in the National Register of Historic Places because of their significance as examples of the Plantation Plain style of building. They were chosen because they represented the way a yeoman farmer in the Georgia upcountry built during the time of the Greek Revival. Research shows that in 1842 and '43, Robert Hiram Smith of Rutherford County, North Carolina, and his father Robert had acquired the property in Dekalb County on which the buildings stood before they were moved to their present location. Because Miss Tullie was the last member of the Smith family to live in the house, and because she loved the way of life her home had symbolized, the Historical Society named the museum in her honor.

During the generations of ownership, changes had been made in the house and kitchen. For educational purposes, the Society's Restoration Committee decided

OPPOSITE: The swept front yard with flowerbeds is typically rural Georgia, and the paling fence is based on a prototype from the Georgia Piedmont. Note Parson's Room on end of shed front porch. ABOVE: This view shows the Plantation Plain profile, with gable and end chimneys. The house colors are authentic as restored in 1971. Frame dependencies can be seen at the side and rear within the picketed yard. FOLLOWING PAGE: The living hall is arranged for dining. The hunt board against the far wall and the other plain-style Southern antiques are part of a fine collection of early Piedmont furnishings in the house and kitchen.

on restoration inside and out to return the buildings to their original appearance. Carefully researched and thoughtfully interpreted, with authentic furnishings and landscaping and with additional Georgia outbuildings, this complex of buildings illustrates a seemingly obvious, but often ignored, historical truth – that not all Georgians of the antebellum period lived in white-columned plantation houses.

There was a plain-style plantation built from the eighteenth century until the 1870's, in which the upstairs of the main house was only one room deep and a one-story porch extended across the front; one end of this porch was usually enclosed for a guest room or office, often called the "Parson's Room," which opened onto the front porch and not into the house. The back always had shed rooms instead of a porch. These simple houses

were of wood covered with weatherboard and with chimneys on the gable ends. The interiors were completely sheathed with matching boarding and with the simplest of trim. This was what the small planter built after log cabins — a two-story dwelling with a steep staircase. It was the upcountry equivalent of the low-country raised cottage. Sometimes these houses were outwardly converted to Greek Revival with the addition of tall columns and, sometimes, wooden gingerbread. They were a basic "root stock" of domestic architecture in Georgia and throughout the upcountry South.

No better example of this type of small planter's farm in Georgia may be found than these restored buildings and gardens, which show the way people lived in the 1830's and 40's as the Atlanta area was first settled. By contrast the Historical Society's Swan House of 1928 is as much a Versailles as the Chief Vann House (page 42) seemed to be at Spring Place. Each mirrors the people and generation which produced it, and each is a house museum open to the public because of the landmark qualities each clearly possesses.

OPPOSITE: At the rear of the house is a shed room with a quilt-frame and quilting in process. ABOVE: The bedroom is simply furnished with Georgia-made pieces. Plain-style houses had only two main rooms; usually there was no hallway. The profile of the stairs shows here.

OPPOSITE ABOVE: Rear view with kitchen building on right. OPPOSITE BELOW: The log farm buildings relocated from other parts of Georgia can be seen beyond the front yard fence. The crepe myrtle tree was moved here with the house; it and other plants have been carefully selected for their period authenticity. ABOVE: The restored kitchen is furnished with Georgia-made items. LEFT: In the kitchen is this combination hunt-board and pie-safe, with stoneware "Face Jug" made by the Meaders family of White County, folk potters.

Valley View

c. 1849

Etowah Valley, Bartow County

*Valley View was built in the late 1840's by James Caldwell
Sproull, a well-to-do planter from Abbeville County, South
Carolina. Since that time, the place has been owned by his
direct descendants, the present owner
being the fourth generation.*

"Notes on Valley View"
Helen and Robert Fouché Norton
June 1976

THIS IS a magnificently sited, imaginatively designed
and handsomely preserved plantation – always owned
by the same family. Because of site, authenticity, preservation, and beauty, it is the crown jewel of old brick
houses in the Etowah River Valley. It is the choice example
of the classic revival as imaginatively interpreted to suit
the situation. The Ionic capitals are what might be called
Carpenter's Classic; the fluted wooden columns (ten in
all) are unusually slender and set out from the porch
floor on tapering brick piers, forming a pedestal for the
tall shafts. The overall form of the house is itself unusual
– unique in Georgia. The massive two-story façade,
which seems to reach out to embrace the magnificent
view, masks a main block which is only one room deep.
The central stairhall, which ascends to the bedrooms,
is therefore comparatively shallow in depth, even though
it is handsome in conception and detail. The staircase,
wood-grained paneling and door trim were all made
by a German cabinetmaker who lived on the place, Mr.
Vitenger (called Witey). He evidently finished the cab-

inetwork and other details after the local builders, Glazner and Clayton of Euharlee, completed the main body of the house. (Witey also made some of the walnut bedsteads, tables and cabinets which are still on the place.)

The gardens of English boxwood and the brick walks, bordered with boxwood and Carolina cherry, are all as old as the house and characteristic of mid-nineteenth-century Georgia. This "front-yard," as it would be called, is as vernacular as the house itself, and the two elements of house and yard together make a

OPPOSITE: Ten tall Ionic columns create a monumental porch for a one-room deep, brick house with flanking one-story rear service wings. French doors open out onto the first-floor porch, which is mirrored by a gallery above; the balustrade of this second-floor gallery was not completed until 1963 – the original was of iron melted down for use during the Civil War. ABOVE: Looking east from the second-floor gallery towards the Etowah River Valley, over the English boxwood and Carolina cherry bordered brick walk. This and the boxwood parterre garden are as old as the house. On an elevation 250 yards from the river, which flows southwest in the meadow below, the house is a quarter of a mile from the main road.

This central hallway, unusual in design and impressive in detail, is short because the house is one-room deep, possibly for ventilation. The house takes grand advantage of the elevated site from all standpoints, aesthetic and functional.

picture of a Georgia plantation home which is rare in its authenticity.

Classic revival houses in Georgia almost always had just such formal gardens made up of beds and sandy walks, sometimes bordered with boxwood or some other green plant, and sometimes with terra cotta tiles; but rarely, if ever, a lawn – at most (as at Valley View) perhaps a meadow. The fundamental concept of this formal treatment is early nineteenth-century English landscape gardening of the Humphrey Repton school, wherein the transition from neoclassical architecture to lawns and park is made by a garden divided into beds or parterres.

And, just as it should be, beyond the Valley View parterres is a cattle-dotted meadow sweeping down to the river valley, with a sublime view of low-peaked mountains in the far distance. All in all, it is a rural and picturesque setting of which Repton would have approved. The site is not unlike Thomas Jefferson's Monticello. Certainly the house is the sort of American villa that Jefferson encouraged: classically inspired and romantically beautiful, even if vernacular in character.

The Garden History of Georgia (1933; reprinted 1976) includes a drawing of the Valley View landscaping and of similar gardens that existed or were known in 1933. Those at Valley View are still as they were diagrammed, and as they have been growing since the late 1840's. There are only a handful of comparable gardens surviving anywhere in the state. The front yard at the University of Georgia's president's home is one of this quality; see page 162 following.

One of the most delightful of the Valley View family possessions is an extraordinary journal and scrapbook kept by Mrs. Rebecca Sproull Fouché (daughter of Colonel James Sproull) dated 1912, with the title *Our Mother's Memories,* "Of That Other Beautiful World We Used to Live in Before the War." According to Mrs. Fouché's account, the plantation was used as headquarters by General Schofield for several months in 1864. The house survived, she said, because of the intervention of Mr. Vitenger, the German cabinetmaker. Although Witey convinced the "Yankees" not to damage his workmanship, one of his built-in cupboard/closets in an upstairs bedroom has an invader's scrawled autograph and the date: September 7, 1864.

An interesting account of Valley View and of the other antebellum houses in the Etowah Valley is that in *White Columns in Georgia* (1952) by the historian/journalist Medora Field Perkerson of Atlanta. She reported that Mrs. Sproull Fouché, who lived at Valley View in the 1940's, had "spent many years with her late husband in Roumania where he was American charge d'affaires." Mrs. Perkerson said that Edith Fouché had become a "friend of the late Queen Marie of Roumania."

A regal friendship seems entirely conceivable for a resident of this white-columned, red-brick villa overlooking the Etowah Valley; the place evokes romantic visions, for it is an ancestral family seat of great presence, a gracious Georgia country house existing from antebellum days and not gone with the winds of change, of war, nor of any of the other incivilities wrought by the passage of time.

ABOVE: Detail of Porch. The slender columns in a vernacular version of the Ionic Order rest on brick piers which taper to form a naive and charming but functional pedestal. This Greek Revival temple seems to reach out to embrace the view. BELOW: The one-story rear service wings open onto this U-shaped veranda and courtyard. In the background are some of the original outbuildings.

MID-NINETEENTH-CENTURY SAVANNAH

The Andrew Low House
c. 1848   John S. Norris, *Architect*

The Charles Green House
c. 1853   John S. Norris, *Architect*

Savannah, Chatham County

They are tremendous men, those cotton merchants.

William Makepeace Thackeray
Savannah, 1856

THESE ARE TWO of the finest houses ever built in Georgia; they were designed by the same architect for two business associates who were British subjects, cotton factors, and exporters residing in the Georgia cotton port. Andrew Low and Charles Green had made what one of their fellow countrymen called "a speedy fortune in trade." Low was one of the richest men in the English-speaking world; he helped his partner, Charles Green, become one of Savannah's wealthiest businessmen. When the English writer, William Makepeace Thackeray, came to Savannah to lecture in 1853 he stayed with Andrew Low, and when he returned in 1856 he was Low's house guest again, and that of the second Mrs. Low, Mary Couper Stiles. While their guest on this second visit, Thackeray wrote home to say that he had "the most comfortable quarters I have ever had in the United States" and described the cotton merchants of Savannah as "tremendous men."

The late Walter Charlton Hartridge, a Savannah historian, commented on these British-born cotton capitalists and the aura of England that pervaded the port: "Savannah, indeed, was ruled by the cotton merchants whose activities had called forth Thackeray's admiring tribute. The Cotton Exchange at Liverpool was the magnet which held the aspirations of the town; as a result, the British Consul in Savannah enjoyed more prestige than any Royal Governor of Colonial days."

As Mr. Low and Mr. Green were two of the leaders in this Anglo-Southern cotton empire, naturally their residences were exceptional. Their elegant houses were in the second generation of such places built by the cotton barons. The first generation, dating from around 1820, had been designed by William Jay, the English-bred architect; but by the mid-century Jay's classical revival houses were somewhat out of fashion. One British traveler described them as "decayed" and "melancholy." (An exception was the William Scarbrough House

OPPOSITE: The Andrew Low House is the headquarters of the National Society of Colonial Dames of America in the State of Georgia. In foreground, original tile-edged parterre garden and in background, across East Charlton Street, is the Battersby-Hartridge House, c. 1852. ABOVE: Low House, Central Hall, as refurnished in the late 1970's, guided by Edward Vason Jones, the Georgia and Americana specialist; a fine nineteenth-century American sofa, c. 1820, selected by Jones.

owned by Scarbrough's son-in-law, Godfrey Barnsley, a cotton factor originally from Derbyshire, England. Barnsley made it his residence when he was not in Liverpool or at his Italianate villa in the northwest Georgia mountains.)

LEFT: Low House Front Parlor. The room overlooking Lafayette Square as refurnished under Edward Vason Jones's direction; the *méridienne* is American mid-nineteenth century; the piano is English, c.1810, John Broadwood & Sons of London. The Bristol crystal chandelier is from another fine Savannah house. The carpet, selected by specialist Jones, is Wilton. ABOVE: Back Parlor. A *méridienne* and a crystal chandelier match those in the front drawing room. The mahogany sofa table with hairy paw feet is attributed to Michael Allison of New York. Note the recently restored marbleized baseboard.

By 1845 Savannah was becoming a particularly important port because the Central of Georgia Railroad linked Savannah with the cotton fields and growing towns of upcountry Georgia: Augusta, Macon, and even brand-new Atlanta. Savannah itself began to expand and add new wards and squares according to the original plan conceived by James Oglethorpe. Lafayette Square, on which the Low House was built, dates from 1837, and Madison Square, the site of the Green House, was 1839. These new wards provided choice trust-lot building sites which gave the architect, John S. Norris (1804–1876), the opportunity for architectural display as William Jay had done to such an advantage with the Richardson House on Oglethorpe Square, pages 50–57. Both the Low House and the Green House sit majestically on double-trust lots, taking up 60′ × 180′ spaces rather than

ABOVE: The Charles Green House, c.1853. Parish house and rectory of St. John's Church. The Gothic Revival ironwork is exceptional; the tile-edged parterre garden on the Madison Square side is original. This was the finest Gothic Revival style house built in antebellum Georgia. (In the right background across Harris Street is the Sorrel-Weed House, c.1840, designed by Charles B. Cluskey.) RIGHT: The Green House Double Parlor. The windows in these drawing rooms slide into the walls to create doors onto the Gothic Revival piazza. A grandson of Charles Green described the ornamentation in these rooms as "semi-Gothic, semi-Louis XV." Another writer said that the house, designed by New York and Savannah architect, John S. Norris, had "New York Fifth Avenue character."

the less-deep, normal-sized lots of 60′ × 90′. Norris, of New York City and Savannah, expressed the exuberance and prosperity of the era with an architectural eclecticism that today seems particularly mid-nineteenth century. The early-Victorian Renaissance villa Norris designed for Low is a bit more subdued than the elaborate Gothic Revival mansion he did for Charles Green, which cost $93,000 to complete and was possibly the most expensive house built in antebellum Savannah. It had just about everything, including indoor plumbing. (See *John S. Norris, Architect in Savannah, 1846-1860,* by Mary Lane Morrison, 1980.)

A grandson of Charles Green, a writer and French Academy member, Julien Green came from Paris to Savannah in 1934 and recorded in his diary some impressions of his grandfather's house (published in 1964). When Julien Green saw the house it was still stuccoed as it had been originally. He described it as a "vast Tudor house, painted a tawny yellow." He said that to him it was "both hideous and magnificent" and he characterized the eclecticism of the drawing rooms as "semi-Gothic, semi-Louis XV," but summed up his opinions on a positive note. He thought, "The whole

thing remains splendid in a manner that seems peculiar to the Southern states."

Julien Green's private and personal views about his grandfather's house are interesting. But, as each of these houses has long been an acknowledged landmark, there is a large fund of such information. They have become historic sites and, in a sense, public buildings; since 1943, the Charles Green House has been the parish house and rectory of Saint John's Episcopal Church and, since 1928, the Andrew Low House has been the Headquarters of the National Society of the Colonial Dames of America in the State of Georgia. Each is partly a house museum and as such is open for tours on a regular basis. Each has been owned or visited by unusually interesting people.

Andrew Low's son William (Willie) inherited his

father's house and was married in 1886 to Juliette (Daisy) Magil Gordon. Daisy Low founded the first Girl Scout troop in America there in 1912 and continued to make it one of her residences until her death in 1927. Daisy Low's mother, Mrs. William Washington Gordon, founded the Georgia Society of Colonial Dames so it was particularly appropriate that the Dames bought the house as its headquarters.

"The Man Who Came to Dinner" at Charles Green's was a figure quite unlike Thackeray – General William T. Sherman. He arrived in December 1864 after a protracted and unpleasant journey through Georgia (usually called his March) and stayed until January 21, 1865. (That may have stretched Southern hospitality a bit far.) In 1892 Judge Peter Meldrim purchased the property from Edward Green, Julien's father, and it

remained in the Meldrim family until purchased by St. John's Church. It is usually called the Green-Meldrim House; the state historical marker in the churchyard refers to it as "Sherman's Headquarters," and points out that in 1976 the house was declared a National Historic Landmark.

A description of Savannah written by an English journalist in 1863 perfectly summarizes these two Norris–designed mansions, built for the business associates Andrew Low and Charles Green: "The wealthier classes have houses of the New York Fifth Avenue character. One of the best of these, a handsome mansion of rich red sandstone [actually stucco] belonged to my host Charles Green who, coming out of England many years ago, raised himself by industry and intelligence to the position of one of the first merchants of Savannah."

ABOVE: The Kolb-Newton House, Boxwood: Built by the gentleman-farmer, Wilds Kolb (1804–1861), it is based on "A Suburban Cottage in the Italian Style" in *The Architecture of Country Houses* by Andrew Jackson Downing, 1850. The trellis-work veranda almost duplicates the Downing design as does the overall form of the house. This was a very up-to-date house; it even had a first-floor bathroom with hot running water. It is preserved today, inside and outside, much as it was when it was new. OPPOSITE ABOVE: The old Post Road side of the Kolb-Newton House has a classical portico, showing the transitional character of the architecture. The boxwood parterre garden, one of Georgia's finest, is as old as the house.

MADISON, THE PRETTIEST VILLAGE

The Kolb-Newton House
c. 1852

The Hilsabeck-Symmes House
c. 1840

Madison, Morgan County

Madison is the prettiest village I've seen in the state. One garden and yard I never saw excelled, even in Connecticut.

Sgt. Rufus Mead, Jr.
November 19, 1864

SERGEANT MEAD, a Connecticut Yankee with the Federal Army, passed through Morgan County and Madison on his way to Savannah with General H. W. Slocum. Perhaps because of its beauty, Madison was largely spared; it is still one of Georgia's prettiest villages and a model for those interested in historic preservation, which many Georgians are. These two houses are textbook examples of two aspects of historic preservation: The Kolb-Newton House is almost "as is," inside and outside – a preservation in purest terms – and the Hilsabeck-Symmes House is one of the most perfect examples of restoration and conservation to be found.

ABOVE: Madison, founded in 1809, the county seat of Morgan County, was one of the most prosperous and civilized Piedmont towns. Today it leads in historic preservation, and many of its residents commute to Atlanta. The W.H. Broughton House, c.1852, in middleground and the Stokes-McHenry House on far right.

ABOVE: Cedar Lane Farm, the Hilsabeck-Symmes House, Morgan County c.1840; restored late 1960's. This farm house was almost in ruins and the farmlands were eroded when the John Symmeses bought this property for a wholesale nursery in 1966. It is now a prize-winning example of historic preservation – a model for others to follow. RIGHT: Central Hallway and Dining Room. The mantlepieces throughout the house are simple Greek Revival and the walls are unpainted except in the parlor. The door on the right leads to a closet under the stairs.

These, with many other places in Madison and around the county, present "antebellum" Georgia at its best. Sgt. Mead saw it during wartime. He should see it now; he would have no trouble recognizing landmarks such as the Kolb House, which easily could have been the garden and yard that he commented on in his diary.

Madison, the county seat of Morgan County, is north of Milledgeville and almost in the middle of the fertile Piedmont Plateau. These lands were ceded to the state by the Creek Indians in the cession of 1802-1805; Morgan was created in 1807 and Madison in 1809, as Louisville was being replaced by Milledgeville as the state capital. Madison was one of the most prosperous of the Piedmont towns; by the 1850's it was the center of a civilized way of life similar in many ways to that in the rest of the Union with the exception that the labor force was in servitude. The Reverend George White wrote in 1849: "Madison is the wealthiest and most aristocratic village along the stagecoach route between Charleston and New Orleans."

The Georgia Railroad came to Madison from Augusta in 1841 and reached the new town of Atlanta

in 1845. By 1861 Georgia had an extensive railroad system, the best in the Deep South. This system was one of General Sherman's targets. On the 19th of November, 1864, the day that Sgt. Mead recorded his visit, General Ward's division destroyed the Madison depot, water tank, warehouses, switching tracks, side-tracked cars, and other railroad facilities and quantities of cotton and Army supplies. That was the worst of it, and then the Army moved east towards the sea.

Boxwood, the Italianate villa of Miss Kittie Newton, is practically as it was that day 180 years ago. At that time it would have been 11 years old. (Antebellum culture in much of Georgia was only one or two generations old when the War came.) The grounds take up half a block and the house has two façades. The one towards the old stagecoach/post road has a classical one-

story Doric portico, and that towards the steepled brick church, a trellis-work veranda – lacy and cool. Boxwood is a mid-Victorian, transitional house in combining these two porches, looking backward to the classical revival and forward to the picturesque eclecticism of the rest of the century. As with other fine antebellum houses in Georgia there are formal parterres of boxwood in the place of a lawn, except that here both the front and rear yards are landscaped in this manner.

The entire historic neighborhood surrounding Boxwood *is* pretty. Among the comparable places are the W. H. Broughton and the Stokes-McHenry houses; and about half a mile out on the old stagecoach road is Bonar Hall, home of Miss Therese Newton, which also could have been the exceptional place the Connecticut Yankee saw as he made his way to Savannah.

OPPOSITE: Dining Room. The corner cupboard was repainted this blue-green color to match the original paint. Otherwise, this room is a symphony of wood tones set off by the blue-and-white china. ABOVE: Parlor. The mantlepiece is black as was the custom, and the walls are painted as they were originally. The Sheraton sofa and other antique furnishings dress up this plain-style Greek Revival parlor and emphasize its early character.

An old house in Georgia without some sort of porch is a great rarity, especially a farm house. Out in the county is such a place, which predates these town houses by a decade. The Hilsabeck-Symmes House, which was named Cedar Lane Farm as it was being restored in the late 1960's, has caught up with the authenticity of its in-town neighbors by means of the twentieth-century art of restoration. Unlike the town houses, it is not mid-Victorian in character but is an unusual example of the Greek Revival vernacular with Plantation Plain style characteristics. The profile of the house is Plantation Plain but the plan and detailing is Greek Revival: the doorway (with transom and sidelights) leading into a wide central hallway with a spacious staircase, and the mantlepieces, are what identify it as Greek Revival, though a vernacular interpretation. The Plantation Plain style is practically defined by the Tullie Smith House, pages 84–91, and one of the things missing at Cedar Lane Farm is a shed porch. However, with Tullie Smith, it shares an utter simplicity, Shaker in feeling, in which plainness is the aesthetic. The interior walls are completely sheathed with horizontal boards and there is a

minimum of trim. Mantlepieces are the main cabinet-work unless one counts wide, unpainted "pine panelling."

Facing north, its need for a porch was minimized and one was never built, but the doorway, though severe, could easily rest under a classical porch as on the stage-coach road side of Boxwood. Like Boxwood, this is a transitional house, looking in more than one stylistic direction. The way that Cedar Lane Farm is furnished emphasizes the pre-1840 aspects of its architecture: a c.1800 Sheraton sofa in the parlor (the only room in the house ever to be painted) and other furnishings are country Federal. Little or nothing of the post-1840 Empire Period directs one's thoughts to the mid-Victorian – so typical of Madison.

This house appeared in the Spring 1981 issue of *Southern Accents* magazine, which details the restoration procedure Jane and the late John Symmes followed to bring this house to its present condition. John Symmes was a graduate nurseryman; the conservation of the entire property is as much a part of the story as the restoration of the main house and grounds. The beautiful boxwood

OPPOSITE: Bedroom: Throughout the house Mrs. Symmes has placed flower bouquets from her garden. Ornamental horticulture is one of her specialties, as is the decorative art of early America. ABOVE: Porch. Shaded by a Cedar Lane Farm's cedar is this screened-in porch, a concession to modern comfort.

garden in parterres is done in homage to that form of garden so characteristic of mid-nineteenth-century Georgia.

If Sgt. Mead's great-grandson marched through Georgia in his Yankee ancestor's footsteps, he would see a town possibly even prettier than it was in the 1860's. Certainly out in the county, Cedar Lane Farm shows how the South has transcended its dirt-poor, worn-out, cotton-field period. This plain-style Greek Revival house with no columns is now as beautiful as any in the state; and Sgt. Mead's descendant, we daresay, would find no place which excells it, even back home in Connecticut.

ABOVE: The view from the central hallway into the backyard, where the old spring has been made into a small lake. RIGHT: A historically accurate formal boxwood garden designed and created in the late-1960's as part of the restoration. Flowers and plants of the period of the house are used exclusively, such as this old rose.

ATHENS AND A CONTINUING TRADITION

The President's Home, 1857; restored 1949, 1967

Founders Memorial Garden, 1939-1950

State Headquarters, the Garden Club of Georgia, 1857; restored 1964

Dr. Hubert B. Owens House, 1940-1941
Athens, Clarke County

ABOVE: The President's Home, 570 Prince Avenue, c.1857. The architecture and front landscaping are very much as they were when John T. Grant, a University of Georgia alumnus, built this on the five-acre tract as his town house. There were a series of distinguished owners including Benjamin H. Hill, and in 1949 it was purchased by the University of Georgia Foundation. It has long been considered one of the most outstanding Greek Revival houses in the United States. Dr. Fiske Kimball wrote in 1922, "The most superb of all the fine Athens houses is the Hill house, with its peristyle of tall Corinthian columns."
RIGHT: Double Drawing Room, 20' × 40'. One of the most sumptious houses built in the King Cotton era, it was the last of the great classical revival houses of antebellum Georgia. The interior architecture, especially the splendid plasterwork and carved marble mantlepieces, are mid-Victorian in character. (The furnishings in this room date from the 1949 and 1967 redecorations.)

But where are our lawns? There are literally none. A green sward is almost as rare in Georgia as a pavement of jasper. In the art of landscape gardening we are more deficient than in anything else.

Bishop Stephen Elliott, Jr., 1851
From *Georgia's Planting Prelate,*
Hubert B. Owens, 1945

"BUT WHERE ARE OUR LAWNS?" asked the Bishop as he addressed a large gathering of Georgia planters in 1851. In matters of gardening and architecture the Right Reverend Stephen Elliott, Jr., followed Andrew Jackson Downing, author of *Cottage Residences, Rural Architecture and Landscape Gardening* (1842). Elliott was one of the first to concern himself with improving the architecture and landscaping of Georgia communities. He was part of a continuing tradition in which Athens has been the center of activity. The person most identified with it in the mid-twentieth century was the founder of the Landscape Architecture program at the University of Georgia, Dr. Hubert Bond Owens. Owens's house and garden in Athens, both of which he designed, are on pages 116-119. Among his outstanding Athens projects are the grounds of the President's Home (restoration and design) and the Founders Memorial Garden, page 115. Dr. Owens first came to Athens as a student in 1922 and in 1973 he was made Dean Emeritus. His life's work, centered in Athens, traces back to Downing and to Bishop Elliott's question, "Where are our lawns?"

Andrew Jackson Downing was America's first nationally important landscape gardener, as they were first called; he advocated spacious lawns and consciously naturalistic landscapes as settings for picturesque, asymmetrical houses. His books spread his influence widely, helped to end the classical revival and created the fashion for exotic and eclectic architectural

styles. He encouraged domestic ornamental gardening by knowledgeable amateurs, which led to the formation of ladies' garden clubs (the Athens Garden Club of 1891 was the first in America) and to landscape architecture on a professional level. Frederick Law Olmsted (1822-1903), Downing's pupil and friend, was the first of those. By the turn of the century an American Society of Landscape Architects was formed, and academic departments of landscape architecture similar to the program Dean Owens began at the University of Georgia in 1928.

With good reason Bishop Elliott asked about Georgia's antebellum lawns, as we have seen at Valley View; the Andrew Low and Green-Meldrim houses; at Boxwood; and the two restorations – Tullie Smith House and Cedar Lane Farms. At these places, instead of lawns there were formal parterre gardens enclosed by fences. The same is true with the Colonel John T. Grant House (since 1949, the University of Georgia President's Home).

The fine garden here works especially well today because the house is so often used for formal entertaining, and the rear yard has been made into a garden-party lawn following Professor Owens's design. For the social life of antebellum Georgia, the house and garden Col. Grant created in 1857 was perfect, and it continues to serve equally well for President and Mrs. Fred C. Davison. These formal gardens were no doubt admired more from verandahs, balconies and windows than from the sandy walks separating the beds. Repeating the sort of formal ornamental patterns found inside, they were outdoor parlors – more to be admired than actually used. Divided by a central walk, they were symmetrically lined up with the central hallways which antebellum Georgia houses often had, whatever their size and style.

The Grant House was the last of the great Georgia houses built in the Greek Revival style, and one of the greatest of that style ever built anywhere. (It is the frontispiece illustration for *Southern Architecture,* a new his-

President's Home Dining Room. Looking into front sitting room. Both rooms have items from the 1949 and 1967 refurnishing. In the sitting room is a Gilbert Stuart portrait on loan from the University of Georgia Museum.

tory by Professor Kenneth Severens.) It was a culmination of the American classical revival begun by Thomas Jefferson in the late eighteenth century. This house was built when that style had already run its course nationally, as it was beginning to do in Georgia: the Johnston-Hay House of 1859 at Macon, for example, is one of America's really magnificent Italian Renaissance revival villas (page 120).

That the last great house in the old South's favorite style was in Athens is understandable, for those built in Athens were some of the finest. Athens was named and designed as a center of classical learning and culture. It came at the start of the classical revival. Faithful to that revival longer than the rest of the country, Athens actually pre-dated the Greek aspect of the revival by more than two decades: it was named Athens in 1801, long before

the War for Greek Independence. It was founded as an educational center by, among others, John Milledge, the Oglethorpe colonist's son who represented the best of early Georgia. Milledge was on the state-appointed committee that selected the Oconee River site even before the creation of Clarke County. The committee named the town, and Milledge personally gave 633 acres to start the college and settlement. The state charter of 1785 authorized this work, so that if 1785 is the official birth year, the University of Georgia is the earliest state-char-

RIGHT: The Garden Club of Georgia, Inc., State Headquarters House, 325 South Lumpkin Street. Built as a residence for professors, it has been a house museum since 1964. It is surrounded by the 2½-acre Founders Memorial Garden on the North Campus of the University of Georgia. Both the house and garden are cooperative projects of the University of Georgia (especially the Landscape Architecture Department) and the Garden Club of Georgia, Inc. BELOW: The Founders Memorial Gardens, the Boxwood Parterre. The 2½-acre Memorial Garden was developed beginning in 1939 to honor the twelve matrons who established America's first garden club, the Ladies Garden Club of Athens, in 1891. It was designed by Dr. Hubert B. Owens and planted under his supervision.

tered college in the United States.

The Georgia legislature incorporated Athens in 1806, that same year the first major building in the town was completed: a three-story, all-purpose brick structure called Franklin College. It still stands on part of the 37 acres the committee set aside for the original college yard. The remaining acreage was either used for college purposes or sold to develop the town. Colonel John Grant bought some of that land along Prince Avenue in the early 1850's to build his house. By that time Athens was a thriving community, connected by railroad with all of the major points in the state. William Bacon Stevens,

the first to write a Georgia history of any consequence, wrote in his *History of Georgia* in 1859: "The legislature placed the college on the very borders of civilization, on its western frontier, which now proves to be a most admirable selection." When that was published the Grant House stood on Prince Avenue, where it is still a symbol of the civilization and traditions of Georgia's Classic City.

The Dr. Hubert Bond Owens House, 215 Rutherford Street, 1940-1941. The doorway and sheaf-of-wheat railing are from the Moore-Reaves House (c.1825) which stood on Thomas Street in downtown Athens. Dean Owens, founder of the University of Georgia's Landscape Architecture Department, designed this house to be in keeping with the earliest architectural traditions of Athens. (Dr. Owens first came to Athens as a student in 1922.)

Parlor of Dean Emeritus Owens. The mantlepiece is from the Moore-Reaves House, Athens c.1825. On the center pedestal table are Lenten roses from Dean Owens's garden. The copy of Raphael's Sistine Madonna belonged to the late Mrs. Owens's grandfather, the Right Reverend Telfair Hodgson.

ABOVE: Owens Entrance Hall. This shows a native walnut handrail from Dr. Owens's family plantation at Canon, Georgia. Dr. Owens salvaged the Federal style doorway in 1937 to use as the frontispiece for his traditional house, built in 1940–1941. RIGHT: Rear Garden. As designed by Dr. Owens. This is a downtown garden with a rural atmosphere, a twentieth-century garden with a traditional flavor. Dr. Owens has written: "A garden, or any other landscape development, should provide the best use possible for the people who live with it."

The Johnston-Felton-Hay House

1855-1861

Macon, Bibb County

An opulent, Italianate palazzo which adds a startling note to the architecture of the region. The mansion was originally built for W.B. Johnston, a hugely successful merchant, who took his bride to Italy for their honeymoon.

G. E. Kidder Smith, FAIA
The Architecture of the United States,
1981

WILLIAM BUTLER JOHNSTON (1809-1887) and his wife, Anne Clarke Tracy, returned to Macon in 1854 after spending almost three years in Europe. Their trip began as a honeymoon and became a Grand Tour. They came back prepared to build the finest mansion in Georgia, which they did. It has not been surpassed to this day. Work took almost five years. Not completed until the spring of 1861, it can be said to be the last great house of antebellum Georgia.

Johnston's architect was a firm of Yankees of New York City, Thomas Thomas and Son, the leading practitioners of that day's newest styles. The Thomas firm consisted of several generations. It was said of Griffith Thomas (1820-1877) that he built in a "princely way." He and his father were both trained in England and have been described as "rather academically-minded eclec-

ABOVE: The Johnston-Felton-Hay House (1855–1861) sits on an elevation near downtown Macon. Macon is on the Ocmulgee River at the fall line in middle Georgia. This is the most opulent house of antebellum Georgia. Of the Italian Renaissance Revival style, it was designed by the New York City firm of T. Thomas and Son. There are 24 rooms not counting the halls and the two-story cupola. OPPOSITE: Looking from the cupola towards Coleman Hill, which is the beginning of the Georgia Piedmont. In 1823 the Georgia legislature founded Macon as a "trading town" near the geographical center of the state.

OPPOSITE: Carved lion's head on massive front door: a traditional symbol of nobility and strength. ABOVE: Portico with patterned marble floor and Corinthian columns of cast iron. In the center of the marble floor is a glass block which lets light into the wine cellar below.

tics and medievalists." The detailed drawings and specifications for the house, some of which survive, read: "W.B. Johnston, Esq., Country House in Macon, State of Georgia, Oct 1855, T. Thomas and Son, Architects, corner of Broadway and Grand Street, New York." The Thomas firm designed many of the most imposing buildings in New York City, including the old Astor Library, also in the Italianate manner. Thomas Thomas, the father, helped to form the first professional organization for American architects which became the AIA in 1857. Johnston's builder was James B. Ayres, originally from New Jersey, a prominent Macon contractor.

It is said that Johnston imported furnishings, art treasures, and Italian artisans who did the carving on the site and created the plaster embellishments for the interior. It is also said that the massive front doors with lions' heads and sand-etched glass panels weigh 500 pounds each, and were brought from Europe along with Carrara marble for the mantlepieces, front steps and intricately-designed portico floor.

A 24-room, 18,000 square foot house of this opulence, completed on the very eve of the Civil War, helps to explain why the South felt it was ready to challenge the North. This is especially the case when it is known that Macon, Bibb County, did not even exist in 1820. The county dates from 1822 and Macon from the next year. Is it any wonder that Georgia and its sister states believed their cotton-based affluence could support a successful war between the states? During the war, Johnston was named Premier of the Confederate States Treasury and his house was made a gold and silver Depository which held the largest monetary reserve south of Richmond. That is the stuff of romance and, appropriately, a stained-glass portrait of Lord Byron, the romantic poet and hero, is found in a window lighting the staircase.

The very fact that Johnston's sumptious mansion was in the height of national fashion (an aesthetic challenge to the Yankees on their own stylistic terms) truly makes this home a landmark; it was part of a turning point, not only in architecture and taste but in politics as well. It symbolized the South's determination to prevail nationally and to establish a nationality equal to, if not superior to, that of the North.

Thus, here is a place which contradicts what Maj. General William T. Sherman wrote about some Georgia houses in his *Memoirs* (1875): "The houses, though comfortable, would hardly make a display on Fifth Avenue." The General, of course, was writing about Savannah; he did not *see* Macon – for which Macon has been eternally grateful. In 1865, when William Thackeray came to Macon on a lecture tour which also took him to Savannah, he wrote: "Mr. Johnston keeps a shop here. Almost everybody keeps a shop. He is rich though and has left the shop to his brother. They all have pretty houses a little way from their businesses." Even though

the Johnston's house was not finished, Thackeray was their guest, for he always stayed with the most fashionable couple.

Johnston had, in fact, begun his fortune in the jewelry business which he started in 1831, hardly a decade after the founding of the town. That led to a bank, the presidency of the Central Railroad and Manufacturing Company and, in 1869, to founding a life insurance company. At his death in 1887 his wife, Anne, inherited all of his property and continued to live in the house until her death. The Johnstons' daughter, Mary Ellen, wife of Judge William Hamilton Felton II, inherited the house and lived there until her death in 1926. Her son sold it in December 1926 to Parks Lee Hay.

P. L. Hay had come to Macon in 1897 and, in 1904, founded the Bankers Health and Life Insurance Company. He was the Johnston sort of entrepreneur, in a new century. His skyscraper office was in downtown Macon, only a few blocks from the Johnston-Felton House. He and Mrs. Hay (Maude Saxon Murphy) furnished the house much as it is today. In 1964, after the deaths of Mr. and Mrs. Hay, the P.L. Hay Foundation, a family-directed charitable trust, opened the house to the public. (The tour guide and man-in-charge from that time until his retirement in December 1981 was Chester Davis, who had worked for the Hay family as butler and chauffer.)

In December 1977, the P. L. Hay Foundation gave the house, its contents, and a partial endowment to the Georgia Trust for Historic Preservation, Inc. The Georgia Trust continues to operate the house as a museum, and the Macon Junior League has offices on the basement level. During the recent exterior restoration (which cost about $350,000), the resident coordinator continued to open the house for tours and special events. The Georgia Trust welcomes the public's interest; the preservation of this monument of mid-nineteenth-century American and Southern taste is a public trust in which all of us share. (It is said that if this house could be reproduced, it would cost $25,000,000.)

PRECEDING PAGES: Double Drawing Room, 41' × 18'. Mr. and Mrs. Parks Lee Hay purchased the house in 1926; this room is furnished as it was during their lifetime. (Note the condition of the fabric wall-covering on the right; conservation is a never-ending process.) ABOVE: Reception or Morning Room, facing east of the front of the house. The portrait is of Parks Lee Hay, who came to Macon in 1897 and purchased the property in 1926. This is one of the 19 carved mantlepieces. All of the plasterwork is sculptural in quality, made in hand-carved molds according to the architect's designs in the Renaissance Revival style. RIGHT: The Picture Gallery-Ballroom, 54' × 24'. This was designed as a picture gallery, so clerestory windows were necessary for light; these windows were also part of the ventilation system which functioned from the basement to the cupola – seven levels. The marble statue of "Ruth Gleaning" by Randolph Rogers, at the far end of the room, is one of the Johnston's imported art objects that P.L. Hay purchased in 1926.

OPPOSITE: Looking from the Picture Gallery through the Central Hallway into the Dining Room. The plan of this house is classical, symmetrical, and formal, but rooms lead into one another through wide, arched openings with sliding "pocket-doors" which, when opened, create a gracious openness and a spacious informality which looks to the future. ABOVE: Dining Room, 42′ × 24′. The high, dark ceiling and the cabinetwork in the Renaissance Revival manner create a somber, baronial space which seems more "Victorian" in mood than any room in the house. The stained-glass, which is more characteristic of the styles of the 1880's and 90's than the 1850's, contributes to this mood.

Victorian to Early Twentieth Century

Never at any time did politics become the all-consuming passion of Georgians, white and black . . . Life and making a living were the chief passions, as they had always been.

Charles E. Wynes, from
History of Georgia, 1977;
Part Four, "1865-1890."

THE TIFFANY STUDIOS' lamps in the vignette on the facing page are from the original furnishings of the George Lauder Carnegie House on Cumberland Island, pages 150-152. Called Plum Orchard, it combined a new, turn–of–the–century neoclassicism with late-Victorian elements. The tall Tiffany lamp in the center of the group expresses this same eclecticism: a neoclassical column of bronze supports a naturalistic poinsettia shade made from a mosaic of opalescent glass.

Lamps such as these were patented in 1899; Louis C. Tiffany designed them to use light bulbs and electricity, but they were almost entirely handmade. They were partly of the opulent Victorian era, with its medievalistic mood of Arts and Crafts, and partly of the more rationalistic, early-twentieth century. They express the eclectic character of the transitional period sometimes called the "American Renaissance" (c.1875–c.1915) in which professional artists like Tiffany, and clients like Carnegie, expressed an extremely romanticized but expert knowledge of history and an equally romanticized but almost scientific love of nature.

Eclecticism was found before the Civil War, as we have seen with the Johnston-Hay, Green-Meldrim, and Andrew Low houses. These set the stage for an aesthetic point of view which continued despite postwar problems; Reconstruction probably seemed interminable, but officially ended in Georgia by 1872. Nevertheless, houses continued to be built and embellished, inside and out, with richly creative combinations of historical and naturalistic motifs. At the same time, there was an element of underlying change, represented by lamps designed for electricity, instead of for oil, gas, and kerosene. This was the period when professional architects came more and more into the picture, and when some of the finest houses built in Georgia were for part-time citizens. Those were the houses that set the standard which Georgians often followed. This was the period when the state capital was moved from Milledgeville to Atlanta (1868), and soon thereafter when the *Atlanta Constitution* promoted the idea of the New South. It was the time, too, when the Port of Savannah was possibly even more prosperous than it had been in the 1850's.

The history of Georgia is too often divided into antebellum and postwar, as though military affairs, politics, and the location of the state capital were the only concerns of most people. A tradition independent of front page news, although interrupted by it, continued in the arts of daily living; of domestic architecture and life; of such things as getting a new lamp for the parlor; and of landscaping the yard; of telling stories and reciting verses by the hearth fire. The following lines which express the Victorian's love of nature and of home, were written during this period by Sidney Lanier, "The Poet of the South," a Confederate veteran whose birthplace appears on page 134:

All down the hills of Habersham
All through the valleys of Hall,
The rushes cried Abide, abide
The willful waterweeds held me thrall,
The laving laurels turned my tide,

. . . .

And the little reeds sighed Abide, abide
Here in the hills of Habersham
Here in the valleys of Hall.

"Song of the Chattahoochee," 1877

THREE FAMOUS GEORGIANS, THEIR LANDMARKS AND MEMORIALS:

Alexander Stephens (1812-1883), *Crawfordville*
Sidney Lanier (1842-1881), *Macon*
Joel Chandler Harris (1848-1908), *Atlanta*

Alexander Stephens purchased an old house on this site in 1845; in 1858 he added a rear veranda and wing, and named the place Liberty Hall. In 1875 he tore down the oldest part of the house and built this larger replacement, which was his home until he died in 1883. Outbuildings remind the visitor that at one time this was a thousand-acre plantation.

THE VICE-PRESIDENT of the Confederacy, the "Poet of the South," and the creator of Uncle Remus each survived the Civil War and Reconstruction, living long enough to make contributions of such value that Georgians have preserved these landmarks as their memorials: the statesman's home, Liberty Hall; the poet's birthplace; the journalist-author's Wren's Nest. These modest and unpretentious places reflect the character of these exceptional men and of the trying times in which they lived.

Alexander Stephen's Liberty Hall is a fine memorial for an extraordinary "Little Aleck," a giant among the men of his day. He was a United States Congressman and the Vice-President of the Confederacy; and after the war, he was elected U.S. Senator but was prevented from taking his seat because of Reconstruction policy. Subsequently, he was again elected to Congress, and in 1882 to the Georgia governorship. He died in office. Liberty Hall was his home before, during, and after the Civil War. The name he gave it was a reflection of his political and constitutional philosophy, as well as of his hospitality; he entertained visitors from throughout the Union and held open house every day. An upstairs rear bedroom was known as "The Tramps' Room," as it was always open to anyone who needed it.

Liberty Hall dates largely from 1875. During that year Stephens replaced most of the original house, which stood on the place when he bought it. The architectural style could be called "Native-Son Victorian Classical." Stephens was a Reconstructed Rebel, unlike his friend and fellow Georgia Statesman, Robert Toombs, but the place does harken back to antebellum days, and it is said that during the postwar years he lived as though the South had won the war. He wrote his two-volume *Constitutional View of the Late War Between the States* (1868-1870) in his office at Liberty Hall, the office in which a Union officer arrested him in May 1865, because of his role in the Confederacy.

Alexander Stephens's bedroom. It is furnished as it has been since 1875. In 1882 Stephens was elected Governor, but less than a year later he died. A memorial association bought the place in 1885. The United Daughters of the Confederacy presented the property to the state in 1932, and in 1935 the house was opened as a memorial.

Stephens is buried in front of Liberty Hall. He was an uncommonly popular man who never married; never weighed as much as 100 pounds and was in pain, of one sort or another, most of his life. He openly opposed Secession but, even so, was chosen to be the Confederate Vice-President; part of the inscription on his grave reads: "Here sleep the remains of one who dared to tell the people they were wrong when he believed so . . ." (One of Stephens' congressional colleagues tried to bully him with the taunt, "I could swallow you whole in one gulp." Stephens replied, "And if you did, Sir, you would have more brains in your stomach than in your head.")

LEFT: This is the house in which Sidney Lanier was born in 1842 when his grandparents lived here. Later remodeled in the Victorian "gingerbread cottage" taste, it appears as it was when Lanier was writing his most famous poems. In 1973, because it was Lanier's birthplace, the cottage was purchased as the headquarters of the Middle Georgia Historical Society. BELOW: Joel Chandler Harris bought this house in 1881 and in 1884 remodeled it in the Queen Anne style; it has not been changed since. He named it the Wren's Nest and the property, Snap Bean Farm. In 1913 the Joel Chandler Harris Memorial Association bought it to preserve and to open as a museum.

Sidney Lanier lived to be only 39, was in bad health most of his life, and nearly died of tuberculosis in a Northern prison camp during the War. Of worldly goods he had few, but from his poetic genius he left a legacy of great works including his two famous poems: "The Marshes of Glynn" (1877) and "The Song of the Chattahoochee" (1879). Lanier spent the last years of his life in Baltimore, Maryland, playing first flute with the Peabody Symphony Orchestra and lecturing at the Johns Hopkins University. He and his wife, Mary Day of Macon, often stayed with her brother in Glynn County, on the edge of the marshes he immortalized with these lines: "I stand / On the firm-packed sand, / Free / By a world of marsh that borders a world of sea." He is buried in Greenmount Cemetery, Baltimore.

Joel Chandler Harris, newspaper editor, author, and humorist, was born in Putnam County; he joined Henry Grady on the staff of the *Atlanta Constitution* in 1876, where he remained for 24 years. In 1880 he published *Uncle Remus: His Songs and Sayings,* and in a short time it became an international classic and he a celebrity. But Harris was a shy, retiring, modest man; his refuge was the Wren's Nest on Snap Bean Farm in Atlanta's West End, which was at that time a suburban neighborhood – a charming village of Queen-Anne-style cottages. He died there on July 3, 1908, and in several months a ladies memorial association was formed which eventually bought the property and still preserves it. The most enduring event at Snap Bean Farm is the annual May Day (since 1909) when a grammar-school May Queen

reigns over a festival in which her "court" revives the Uncle Remus characters: Br'er Rabbit, Br'er Fox, Sis Cow, and all the rest of the "critters" for a day. The Wren's Nest is the "Brier Patch" in which Harris preferred to be, and it is kept very much as he knew it. (Harris' house is the best preserved of any of the neighborhood's Victorian period cottages. West End began to decline as a neighborhood during World War II, but restoration efforts around the Wren's Nest in the 1970's have been returning the area to the way it was when Harris and his family knew it.)

Stephens, Lanier, and Harris contributed to the true reconstruction of Georgia after the bitter defeat of 1865 and the equally bitter postwar decades. During the years of the New South's success, they are still remembered for their contributions. Their most tangible memorials are these three houses: a birthplace and two homes, all open to the public.

Joel Chandler Harris's bedroom. It has been kept exactly this way since the early part of this century. Harris moved here with his family in 1881 as he began to publish his world-famous Uncle Remus stories. This is the typewriter he used and the hat he habitually wore as he typed.

Lapham-Patterson House

1885

Thomasville, Thomas County

*Driving down Dawson Street we passed the most original specimen of architecture I ever laid eyes on.
It was built by a wealthy gentleman named Lapham.*

Atlanta Constitution
March 26, 1887

THOMASVILLE, the county seat of Thomas County, is fifteen miles from the Georgia-Florida border and less than 100 miles from the Gulf of Mexico, but is on a ridge 285 feet above sea level. This unusual elevation at that southern latitude was one of the fundamental reasons why Thomasville became a Victorian winter resort of international renown. Also, Thomasville was the southernmost railroad depot of the eastern seaboard states for a few years before and after the end of the Civil War. This fundamental combination of location and access brought an influx of visitors, among them Charles W. Lapham of Chicago. Lapham chose Thomasville as his winter home in 1883, and had this exceptional house built in 1884 and 1885.

Planters and yeoman farmers from the older settled parts of the state, especially from the Piedmont, were the original settlers of Thomas County. They came in the 1820's and 30's and brought with them an established way of life. In the 1840's they built some of the finest Greek Revival houses in Georgia, including Greenwood Plantation (page 22). During the Civil War, Thomasville's accessibility by rail and its healthy location attracted refugees from coastal Georgia. After the War many of these coastal people stayed, adding a low-country element to the county's developing sophistication.

After the war, moreover, a new kind of refugee began to arrive – the "winter visitor." The local people welcomed these new refugees as a source of income and diversion during a frankly bad time. At first, like C. W. Lapham, the visitors were escaping northern winters and seeking a healthful climate. But, in time, Thomasville became fashionable; some of the people who originally came because of their health returned because of the good society in town and the quail shooting out in the piney woods. They were joined by others who came for social reasons only, and a winter colony was formed. (Thomas County is still the best quail-shooting and field-trial territory in America.)

Among the first to come for his health was Baron Vicco von Stralendorff, a German nobleman who arrived in 1870. The Baron's doctors thought that a dry atmosphere laden with the resinous scent of Thomasville's longleaf pines would cure his tuberculosis. In 1875 a handsome small hostelry was opened and, in 1885, an enormous resort hotel of pine was built: the three-story, 400-foot long Piney Woods, designed by a resort/hotel architect, J.A. Wood of New York. He was also responsible for the design of another grand Victorian hotel in Thomasville – The Mitchell House. Completed in 1886, it was lighted by gas, heated with steam, and built of brick in various colors. Four dollars a day, American Plan, was the average charge for each hotel.

Both hotels closed in the first few years of the twentieth century for several reasons: by then people could get farther south by railway, and doctors had new theories about the treatment of tuberculosis. Thomas County had outlawed the sale of liquor, and private resort houses were the fashion. The Piney Woods burned in 1906 and The Mitchell House, stripped of its elaborate ornamentation, became offices and shops.

Charles Lapham's place was always considered one of the most singular of the resort houses. It is one of the few remaining, the best preserved, and the only one open to the public. Lapham built at the height of Thomasville's popularity, when Harper's *New Monthly Magazine* included it among "The Winter Resorts of Three Continents" (November 1887). Lapham was a successful shoe manufacturer from Chicago who owned retail shoe stores. His wife was related to the well-known Charles Goodyear family. Lapham said that he lost his health in the Chicago Fire (1871). He was one of the first winter visitors to build his own house, possibly because he was afraid of being trapped in a burning hotel. Many other winter visitors wanted houses and, in time, the antebellum places out in the county were purchased; many of these are still owned by descendants

OPPOSITE: 626 North Dawson Street, Thomasville. Charles W. Lapham said in a front page *Thomasville Times* account: "I lost my health during the great Chicago fire, but regained it in Thomasville, where I built my winter home and return to it every December to remain until May."

of the visitors who bought them in the 1880's and 90's.

Lapham stopped coming to Thomasville in 1894 and sold his house to James Larmon of Cincinnati, Ohio. In 1905 the property passed to James G. Patterson of North Carolina who bought the place as a year-round residence. It remained in that family until 1970 when it was sold to the City of Thomasville and then deeded to the State of Georgia's historical commission.

Now called the Lapham-Patterson House, it has been described as "innovative in form, detail, and construction; an architectural tour-de-force." Because of its outstanding architecture it was designated a National Historic Landmark in 1974. Recent information suggests that the architect may have been T.J.P. Rommerdall (1849-1887), a native of Denmark who advertised himself as an "Architect and Builder." Rommerdall came to Thomasville from Chicago at the time Lapham's house was constructed, and it is certain that he built structures

in the town, including a large water tower. The owner's and the probable architect's connection with Chicago suggests influences from the experimentation of such Chicago architects as Louis Sullivan. Few Victorian period houses in Georgia are as free in form, plan, and the use of interior space. The main staircase in the expansive central living-hall, for example, winds through the chimney stack, forms a balcony, and then passes on to the second floor!

The *Atlanta Constitution* writer who described the house in 1887 as "the most original specimen of architecture [he had] ever laid eyes on," also wrote: "There are corners and nooks, balconies and projecting windows, piazzas and porticoes, all thrown together in a pell mell fashion that is delightfully picturesque." Some specialists call this manner of building Queen Anne, a Victorian style the English originated; others say that it is strictly American and call it "Stick Style," a term

BELOW: Front Sitting Room. ABOVE: Upstairs Bedroom. LEFT: Central Living-Hall. Such halls were usual in Queen Anne style houses but this is unusually spacious; the staircase is unique, winding through the chimney and forming a balcony. Specialists call the ornamentation of this house "Stick Style," a variant of Queen Anne, in which wood is used in diagonal, vertical, and horizontal patterns. The wood is longleaf pine; note the curly pine on the stairs in alternating bands. The plan defies description, and rooms are of odd sizes and shapes.

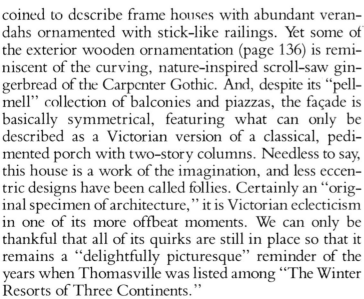

coined to describe frame houses with abundant verandahs ornamented with stick-like railings. Yet some of the exterior wooden ornamentation (page 136) is reminiscent of the curving, nature-inspired scroll-saw gingerbread of the Carpenter Gothic. And, despite its "pell-mell" collection of balconies and piazzas, the façade is basically symmetrical, featuring what can only be described as a Victorian version of a classical, pedimented porch with two-story columns. Needless to say, this house is a work of the imagination, and less eccentric designs have been called follies. Certainly an "original specimen of architecture," it is Victorian eclecticism in one of its more offbeat moments. We can only be thankful that all of its quirks are still in place so that it remains a "delightfully picturesque" reminder of the years when Thomasville was listed among "The Winter Resorts of Three Continents."

Baldwin-Neely House

1887   William Gibbons Preston, *Architect*

Savannah, Chatham County

Because there was so little building in the South at the time, High Victorian architecture never swept the region as it did the rest of the country. The South was largely spared the intrusion of Victorian irregularity and eccentricity.

Professor Kenneth Severens
*Southern Architecture, 350 Years
of Distinctive Buildings,* 1981

THE ARCHITECTURE OF THE SOUTH in the decades after the Civil War is little appreciated and little understood; this is doubly true since the same may be said generally about American architecture in this period. Dr. Severens's new book has very little more

about Victorian architecture in the South than the statement quoted above. His remarks, however, do not apply to Savannah and Georgia, at least not for the 1880's and 90's. This was a period of great building in the state, especially in Savannah, and much of it was done with the help of architects. A talented architect from Boston, Massachusetts, was responsible for many of the Savannah buildings: William G. Preston, FAIA (1842-1910), the designer of this house. Whether Preston's designs were "irregular" and "eccentric" is perhaps a matter of taste and historical perspective. Dwellings as distinctive as this handsomely restored Queen Anne villa, however, are not easily ignored, and they are part of Southern architecture despite theories to the contrary.

W. G. Preston helped to transform the face of Savannah with twenty-three commissions for buildings of various types. This transformation reflected Savannah's post-Reconstruction recovery, a prosperity based on cotton, especially the Sea Island variety, on naval stores, lumber and phosphates. Preston followed the pattern of other talented architects – Jay, Cluskey, and

Norris – who had come to Savannah during expansive periods and found much work to be done. (Preston was not the only significant national architect to work in Victorian Savannah; Detlief Lienau of New York was another.)

Among Preston's most important Savannah commissions were the Cotton Exchange (1886-1887), his first, which was awarded to him as the result of a national competition; the Desoto Hotel (1888-1890) now demolished; the Chatham County Courthouse (1889-1890); the Independent Presbyterian Church rebuilding (1891); and the Volunteer Guards Armory (1892-1893), now the Savannah College of Art and Design. His major residential design for Savannah was this house, built as the home of George Johnson Baldwin in 1887, and now restored.

Preston has been characterized as little more than

in the midst of the late-Gothic Revival. Consciously "Aesthetic," rather than moralistic in character, it was also nationalistic. Early eighteenth-century English ornamentation was revived, and in America it was sometimes combined with hints of Early American or Colonial. The English often called it the Aesthetic Movement, but here the popular name was Queen Anne, or sometimes Shingle Style, if the house were frame, covered with wooden shingles. Craftmanship, a cottage-like informality, and varied materials were emphasized. The chief building material was red brick with molded terra cotta details, although frame houses were also built. Chimneys were tall and highly ornamented. There were stepped gables in the Dutch manner and tall sash-windows, often subdivided by colored glass panels. A large central space with a decorative staircase was the primary feature of a rambling, open plan which was

a follower of a more famous Bostonian, Henry Hobson Richardson, who died the year that Preston received his first Savannah commission. Certainly these near contemporaries had things in common. Richardson was born in 1838 and Preston in 1842, and both were graduated from Harvard. Preston was a native of Boston, the son of a successful builder/architect. Richardson was from New Orleans of an equally established family, and he was the second American to study architecture at the École des Beaux-Arts in Paris. Preston, a few years younger, was at the École soon thereafter. But there the similarities stop. Richardson is famous for his personal brand of Victorian medievalism, featuring bold stone masonry and rounded arches, now called Richardsonian Romanesque. Preston did not design in that style. His Savannah buildings are not take-offs on any one aspect of Richardson's Victorian eclecticism, as others have written. Both men were well-trained eclectics, but Preston created in Savannah his own version of the equally popular High Victorian Romantic style (which originated in England) called Queen Anne.

Queen Anne originated as the domestic architecture of the Arts and Crafts movement which occurred

expressed on the outside by an assymetrical silhouette.

Preston's architecture, domestic and otherwise, was all of that exactly, with details such as the small steppedgable, ornamented chimney, and colored-glass window (shown here). A Richardsonian aspect of his designs were rounded arches. These became a hallmark of Savannah's Queen Anne buildings, and later the motif was used in Richard Aeck's design for the new Desoto Hotel (late 1960's).

The most Queen Anne of all Preston's designs was this house which he built for George Baldwin in 1887. Baldwin was an unusually successful businessman whose fortune was founded on phosphates and the other valuable commodities which passed through the busy Port of Savannah. Born in Savannah in 1856, he graduated from Boston's MIT in 1877, returning to Savannah to become one of its leading citizens. Baldwin's wife was Lucy Harvie Hull of Athens, Georgia. At his death he was Chairman of the Board of Directors of the Savannah Electric and Power Company. His lengthy obituary March 5, 1927, described this house as "the center of social and cultural life" in Savannah.

During World War II, it was broken up into apart-

ments, but in 1973 Alvin W. Neely of Waynesboro, Georgia, purchased it to restore as his residence. Alvin Neely was looking for a late-Georgian row house, but George Baldwin's Queen Anne villa at the corner of Lincoln and East Hall streets won out. Located near the southern boundary of the Savannah Historic District, about two blocks east of Forsyth Park, the house is a center of social and cultural life as it was during the tenure of George Baldwin; it is a landmark of Victorian Savannah, thriving again in the last quarter of the twentieth century.

LEFT: Living Hall: Large central stairhalls were major features of Queen Anne style houses. Other major rooms opened onto these impressive spaces. To the far right is the Reception Room which is just to the left of the main entrance. W.G. Preston's interior ornamentation is a romantic interpretation of early English Renaissance. Mr. Neely's furnishings complement the eclectic Victorian aura. This room might be in Boston, or in London's Kensington, Chelsea, or Bedford Park; but it is in Stephens Ward, Savannah. ABOVE: This stairway in form and detail has every characteristic of the Queen Anne style. The contrast between the rich, dark staircase and paneling, colored glass, and large, clear panes is typically Queen Anne, as is the window seat. The furnishings enhance the English Arts and Crafts mood of the space: if William Morris (1834–1896) and W.S. Gilbert (1836–1911) could descend these stairs today, they would feel right at home.

144

Beath-Griggs House

c.1890; restored 1970's

Inman Park, Atlanta

The architect of the Griggs House is unknown but it is a good example of the rich, picturesque, infinitely varied English Aesthetic Movement. Interiors are richly detailed and have been carefully restored.

James H. Grady "A Question of Style,
Houses in Atlanta, 1885-1900"
Yale *Perspecta,* 1975

THIS QUEEN ANNE VILLA is a landmark in the preservation of Georgia's Victorian architecture; a landmark in the restoration of Victorian houses in metropolitan Atlanta; a landmark in the rehabilitation of an entire Victorian-period neighborhood; and, finally, a landmark of private restoration in Atlanta of the kind that now occurs more frequently, largely because this restoration encouraged others to do the same – especially those born since World War II.

In many ways, this house is more significant as a restoration than it was as an Inman Park residence of the 1890's, although it was one of the best houses built in the neighborhood. As Inman Park's most important remaining house, it has *become* historic, rather than beginning that way. In July 1973, the entire Inman Park neighborhood – as originally planned and developed – was recognized as a historic district and added to the National Register of Historic Places; the Beath-Griggs house was singled out for its preeminent place in the community's renovation.

Inman Park was begun in 1888 as Atlanta's first planned suburb. The engineer and entrepreneur, Joel Hurt, bought a large acreage several miles east of the newly built State Capitol. Using an overall plan similar to that of the picturesque garden suburbs of Llewellyn Park in New Jersey (1860) and Riverside, near Chicago (1868), he developed the existing terrain, respecting native trees and plants, adding curving streets, fair-sized building lots, a park, a lake, and exotic plant materials such as live oak trees, which continue to thrive throughout Inman Park.

OPPOSITE: Beath-Griggs House, Inman Park. This landmark of house restoration in Atlanta led to the rehabilitation of the entire neighborhood. Of the American Queen Anne style, it features a decoratively rich display of materials: granite, brick, marble, slate, wood, wood-shingles, terra cotta, glass and paint. The architecture of the American Renaissance era freely combined the formal classicism of Palladian windows and Tuscan columns, with an informal medievalism in ornamentation and in forms such as cylindrical towers topped by a helmet-roofed belvedere. RIGHT: Rear verandah with view of swimming pool.

This planned suburban setting for the display of Victorian villas was based on the land-use and design ideas of Andrew Jackson Downing and Frederick Law Olmsted. Other comprehensively planned, visually appealing neighborhoods were built soon afterwards, notably Ansley Park, Druid Hills, and then northwest Atlanta, giving other choices of fine neighborhoods in which to build. The automobile soon made Hurt's streetcar line passé and, by 1920, Inman Park was not considered suburban enough, was no longer fashionable, and the architecture was out of date. Atlanta's most sought after and talented architect of suburban houses, Neel Reid, designed only one Inman Park house.

But by the early 1960's the trend had slowly begun to change as growing problems of commuting coincided with a change in architectural taste and an interest in inner city life. Inman Park was not the first to expe-

RIGHT AND ABOVE: Living Hall, showing American Renaissance-style woodwork.

rience this change; there were young couples at that time who moved into Ansley Park – definitely not a slum – and later were able to sell their improved property at an advantage. The person who led the trend in the more adventurous direction of Inman Park was Robert N. Griggs, a bachelor. Perhaps only a single man would have attempted what he did in 1969.

That year Robert Griggs paid $22,500 for his three-story dream house, which most people thought was a Charles Addams nightmare – in architecture and condition. The whole of Inman Park had become a flop-house which was producing considerable income for respectable people in more genteel parts of town, so Griggs had to pay a premium rate. The 15 original rooms had been subdivided into eight apartments for 40 wretched human beings. Griggs, a professional designer and artist, had first seen his landmark in the late 1950's and fallen for it as a romantic quest. By the time he was able to buy it in 1969, it was in even worse condition, of course, but the exceptional architecture and the challenge appealed to him. He knew that it would be difficult to match the unknown designer and builder of 866 Euclid Avenue. The house was filthy, but it was beautiful underneath the ugly paint and dirt. He spent over $50,000 in the early 1970's to turn it into a one-family dwelling again.

That was the beginning. Next came the entire neighborhood which had only a few old-timers who had hung onto their homes. It was Griggs's ground-breaking example to other adventurous young people

that would bring the neighborhood to a point it had never achieved when new.

Among those who followed his lead to Inman Park, one should be singled out: James Whitnel, still a resident in 1982. Whitnel helped to start both the Atlanta Chapter of the Victorian Society in America and Inman Park Restoration, Inc. The latter organization is one of the most successful neighborhood conservation associations in Georgia.

Griggs shares the three-story Queen Anne villa with a landscape architect, Robert B. Aiken, a native of Brunswick, Georgia, who became part of the household in the early 1970's. The grounds show his professional touch, and with two professional designers in residence, the house, inside and out, is a showplace that is the realization of a dream and probably exceeds even the original owner's expectations.

ABOVE: Drawing Room. Exceptional woodwork – a Victorian interpretation of classicism – which the furnishings complement. LEFT: Drawing Room Mantlepiece: the American Renaissance combination of classicism and naturalistic ornamentation beautifully interpreted. (Note handmade tiles with John M. Beath's monogram and Georgia flora and fauna.) OPPOSITE: Library. This beautiful woodwork survived all the years when the house was divided into apartments. The mantlepiece, especially its troubadour tiles, demonstrates the romantic historicism of the American Renaissance era.

The house was built around 1890 for John M. Beath, who had come to Atlanta, made a fortune, and lavished it on this house as a honeymoon gift to his bride. The mantlepiece in the drawing room has his monogram (page 146) and Georgia's most beautiful Victorian fireplace tiles, an unequaled Arts and Crafts display of local flora and fauna. Everything about the place shows the Victorian's exuberant love of history and nature. The interior and architecture has that oddly attractive combination which characterized the American Renaissance: formal and classical, and informal and naturalistic (almost-medieval motifs), imaginatively and eclectically combined. The English called this the Aesthetic Movement and the architecture Queen Anne, but Americans took it up and made it their own. The Shingle Style, for example, which this house reflects in some of its exterior ornamentation, was an American Queen Anne sub-style. Trained architects such as H.H. Richardson and the firm of McKim, Mead, and White designed houses with free-flowing plans and an intimate feeling of oneness with nature, symbolized by a taut skin of earth-toned shingles. Tuxedo Park, a garden suburb in New York state, had such houses. In 1890 the whole phenomenon in which this house and neighborhood were aspects was as American as baseball, but in only a few years it would be as old fashioned as gas lights and peacock feathers in the parlor.

This house and neighborhood were part of Atlanta's renaissance in the years after its wartime destruction when the Phoenix became the city's symbol and Atlanta became the individualistic, future-oriented capital of the New South. Inman Park's developer and the builder of this house were both typical of the entrepreneurs who came to Atlanta to join in the fray and create such successes as the series of cotton expositions held in the 1880's and 90's. Almost 100 years later, one of the real estate developments of that renaissance, Inman Park, became the setting of another rebirth, led by a new breed of individualist/entrepreneurs: the Victorians of our own era. This house was their model and their meeting place. In 1982-83 it is the landmark home of the neighborhood they saved and of a reborn interest in Georgia's Victorian architecture and culture.

Plum Orchard, the George Lauder Carnegie House, was built in 1891. It was designed by one of the oldest and best known Boston architectural firms, Peabody and Stearns, FAIA. The entrance portico is based on the north elevation of the White House; the wings were added in 1906. There are thirty main rooms, twelve bathrooms, and numerous service areas.

TWO CARNEGIE COTTAGES
Plum Orchard
1898

Greyfield
1903

Cumberland Island, Camden County

Where Georgia's oaks with moss-curled beards
Wave by the shining strand.

Sidney Lanier
1876

PLUM ORCHARD AND GREYFIELD are two of four Cumberland Island "cottages," Mrs. Thomas M. Carnegie built at the turn of the century for her children. Today both houses are accessible to the general public on a limited basis: Plum Orchard, as part of the National Seashore site established by Congress in 1972, and Greyfield as an inn belonging to Mrs. Lucy Ferguson (a Thomas and Lucy Coleman Carnegie granddaughter).

Cumberland Island is on the intracoastal waterway near the Georgia-Florida border. It is the southernmost and largest of Georgia's barrier sea islands, and may be reached only by boat or airplane. It is sixteen miles long and three miles wide at its widest point. In the eighteenth and early nineteenth centuries sea island cotton was grown here on several plantations, among them Dungeness, the home of the widow of Revolutionary hero, General Nathaniel Greene. Plum Orchard is near the center and Greyfield is toward the southern end. Cumberland is largely undeveloped and unspoiled because after the Civil War the wealthy Carnegies of Pittsburgh (and later the Candlers of Atlanta on the northern end) used most of the island as a retreat and hunting preserve.

When these American Renaissance era houses were built, Mrs. Lucy Coleman Carnegie, widow of Andrew Carnegie's younger brother and partner, owned 90% of the island. She managed the island plantation from Dungeness, her now-ruined plantation manor, which was the largest and finest house built in Georgia in the post Civil War period. Although some of the Carnegies and other private owners still have a foothold here, approximately 90% of the island now belongs to the United States Congress, including the northern tip which Atlanta's Coca-Cola rich Candler family sold to the federal government in 1982. Congress in theory will protect the island permanently as a natural and historical park. Plum Orchard is part of that 90% but Greyfield, Mrs. Ferguson's Inn, is part of the 10% in which longtime private owners have retained rights for themselves and their heirs.

These houses came at the height of the American Renaissance when the classical, formal, and rationalistic features of the Queen Anne style were winning out over the informal, picturesque, and "Victorian" aspects. Plum Orchard's neoclassical, pedimented portico, based on the north elevation of the White House, is part of this new formalism in which the eighteenth-century architecture of early America was revived to become a dominant theme in twentieth-century domestic architecture. Plum Orchard's interior was less formal and featured late Victorian, Queen Anne ideas like the large, central living and stair hall with fireplace alcove and inglenook, page 152. But in time, this sort of eclecticism would almost disappear as interior architecture began to match the historical styles of exteriors, and as both became more photographically and literally like the original sources of inspiration. Early American precedents would be added to the English and European sources already used and all would become part of the more academically correct eclecticism of the twentieth century (exemplified by the Julian Hightower House, pages 212-217).

Greyfield, the Margaret Carnegie Rickeston House of 1902 and '03 is a fine example of early-American revivalism, in this case of a Southern plantation persuasion. A Pittsburgh architectural firm, MacClure and Spahr, worked with Oliver Ricketson on the design and construction. According to Ricketson's great-granddaughter, Mrs. William R. Bullard, he was "a man of great taste." Mrs. Bullard has said that the design of Greyfield was her great-grandfather's inspiration; he wanted the place to seem like a large, late-eighteenth-century coastal plantation house raised on a high base-

This large, entrance foyer continues the traditions begun in the Queen Anne Style. The fireplace alcove, inglenook, and open stair-case recall a similar, though highly eccentric arrangement at the Lapham-Patterson House, page 138. The hall table is original and rests on an antique Isfahan. The Tiffany-like hanging fixture is a reproduction which replaced the original.

ment, as the local eighteenth-century cottages usually were. His romantic evocation of a Southern plantation house has made a particularly fine inn.

In 1970 Carnegie heirs donated Plum Orchard with twelve acres to the National Park Foundation. Some of the family's furnishings were also given, among them the items shown on page 130. The house is open by reservation from March through October as part of the National Seashore site.

These houses are glimpses of a time now equally as gone with the wind as the plantation life of antebellum Georgia, which they evoked. Gone is the Gilded Age of the American Renaissance when Georgia's sea islands became a Gold Coast far more gilded than when the Spanish first called them the Golden Isles: "Where Georgia's oaks with moss-curled beards / Wave by the shining strand."

RIGHT: Greyfield, the Margaret Carnegie Ricketson House, 1902–1903, was designed to seem like a late-eighteenth century, coastal plantation house. It is now an inn owned by a Thomas Carnegie granddaughter, Mrs. Lucy Ferguson. ABOVE: Mrs. Lucy Ferguson's bedroom suite, now used as part of the hostelry. The small Tiffany studio's bedside lamp has been there since 1905 when the house was furnished. "Miss Lucy" and her two sisters are shown in the oval frame above the headboard. This, as well as the rest of the house, shows the comfortable aristocratic mix of excellent and ordinary objects, old and new, which gives present-day Greyfield its special charm.

Early Twentieth Century until 1932

THESE YEARS from just before the first World War until the election of Franklin Roosevelt have been called the Country House era. On the next 35 pages we have brought together some of the first and most beautiful of the suburban country houses built in Georgia during that era. They were the first landmarks of a domestic ideal which has prevailed in Georgia throughout the rest of the century.

Each of these houses was designed and built with the help of architects. The first, completed in 1916, and the last two were variations of the style of the Italian Renaissance villa as interpreted in Georgian England and reinterpreted in the early twentieth century by academically trained architects: Hills and Dales, LaGrange, 1914-1916, Neel Reid, architect; Swan House, Atlanta, 1926-1928, Philip Shutze, architect (with glimpses of the Villa Apartments, Atlanta, 1920, and the Villa Albicini, Macon, 1926); and the Albert Howell House, Atlanta, 1930-1932, Albert Howell, architect. Although not Renaissance in style, the other houses in this series were essentially villas in the sense that Charles A. Platt had used the term: an important, well-sited suburban house with fairly extensive gardens and grounds; designed inside and outside as a harmonious unit in which all of the parts contribute to the owner's pleasure and that of his guests.

Four of these houses are in suburban Atlanta; one is in Macon; one in LaGrange, another in Rome. By 1920 Atlanta was not only the state capital but had become the dominant urban area in the state, and the four Atlanta houses reflect its new position. All of these houses illustrate the general growth of urban areas in Georgia; the well-to-do usually moved from town into suburban neighborhoods to small estates where they lived full time. (During this era in the East, the true country houses were part-time residences and much grander in scale.) These suburban estates also reflect new sources of wealth in Georgia. The Fuller Callaway house in LaGrange was built with a textile mill fortune, and the two Candler houses in Atlanta's Druid Hills were made possible because of Coca-Cola.

These houses were indeed landmarks; they were built when most people could have built only one room of any of them, so they were as much little Versailles as the Chief Vann house when it was the showplace of the Cherokee Nation (pages 42-45). Oak Hill, Miss Martha Berry's home on the 30,000-acre campus of the Berry Schools, was purposefully a showplace. Miss Berry remodeled the family plantation house into a monumental, classic revival house as part of her educational program for deserving young people. (She was the Thomas Jefferson of north Georgia because she used the architecture of campus buildings, including her own home, as part of the education of the young – as Jefferson had done at the University of Virginia.)

Except for the last, each of these houses was built before the Great Depression, during the prosperous years before, during and after World War I. The Albert Howell house was built as the Depression began when work on a fine house was welcome and the house could be built unusually well, for less money; some of the special embellishments were possible because of the economy.

All of these houses were built when the interior decorating field was getting underway and, over the years, decorators have helped furnish them. The original leaders of that business were women. It was the ladies – the theorist, Edith Wharton, and the professionals, Elsie de Wolfe and Georgia-born Ruby Ross Wood – who led the field, and their work was published in the women's magazines. Architects (Neel Reid, for example) often helped with the fundamentals of interior decoration, but decorators and decorating firms such as Atlanta's W.E. Browne, Inc., came from this period. It was also the era of residential landscape architecture and there, too, architects usually conceived the fundamental outlines; specialists helped to carry out the scheme established by the character of the architecture.

Perhaps the most interesting aspect of this period is that for the first time, a native-born Georgia architect began to design houses. Philip Trammell Shutze was born in Columbus, Muscogee County, Georgia, in 1890 less than 70 years after the area was settled. He was also trained in Georgia, at least for his collegiate education and that, too, is significant. Shutze graduated in 1912 in the first class of the Georgia Institute of Technology's School of Architecture (directed by Francis P. Smith, FAIA). He did postgraduate work at Columbia University and the American Academy of Rome, Italy; but he returned to Georgia to practice. Until that time, architects had come to Georgia from elsewhere: Jay from England, Pratt from New Hampshire, Norris from New York, William G. Preston from Boston, to name only a few. (Neel Reid, architect of Hills and Dales, the first house in this series, was born in Alabama. He moved to Macon in 1903 and to Atlanta in 1909 to practice architecture, so he almost qualified as Georgia-born. But he was a Southerner, and he and Philip Shutze were professional associates beginning in 1902.)

Founded in the reign of George II, Georgia produced its first native-born and native-trained architect during the reign of George V, 1910-1936. That was a propitious time for a Georgian to begin the practice of architecture. Settling in the suburbs of the growing towns and cities of Georgia were potential clients who had known a more rural South, where ladies and gentlemen were reared to respect the classical house as a symbol of a family's social position and cultural status. That was the classical Anglo-American tradition which had developed in the South during the reigns of the eighteenth-century Georges, and had not been entirely lost. In Georgia it was a taste quite naturally revived in the reign of George V. Philip Shutze's Anglo-Palladian Swan House (pages 178-188) was a landmark of that taste; as was Neel Reid's Hills and Dales (pages 162-169). These were houses that conditions would not permit to have been built in Georgia during the reigns of George II and George III; but in the days of their descendant, George V, Georgians were ready, and no monument of the neo-Georgian taste in America or in Britain surpassed these country houses in Atlanta and LaGrange.

In spirit, therefore, these suburban houses built in the New South were continuations of the ideals of the Old South, begun in the eighteenth-century Georgian period and realized in Georgia, to an extent, in the antebellum years. Where more appropriate than in Georgia? As a colony it had been reluctant to declare its independence from George III, and as a state in 1861 it had tried to make a King Cotton alliance with England. Where more appropriate an early twentieth-century Georgian Revival country house than in conservative Georgia?

TWO WINTER VILLAS
Mill Pond Plantation,
1905, *Thomasville*

Hubbell and Benes, *Architects*
Crane Cottage, 1916, *Jekyll Island*

David Adler, *Architect*

In Italy the term "villa" refers to the place as a whole – not to either house or grounds alone, but to the total complex as a unit: a combination of indoor and outdoor space, of architecture and landscape architecture fitted to its site.

Norman T. Newton,
Design on the Land, 1976

A T FIRST GLANCE these two houses might seem to have little of significance in common other than the fact that they were built as "winter homes" in the southern part of Georgia prior to the first World War. After closer examination one notices that each has a tile roof and an interior courtyard; the Crane Cottage courtyard is open to the sky and Mill Pond's is covered with an unusual skylight. Each is of stucco, but the walls of Mill Pond are almost completely covered with vines. Each is two story, large, long, and horizontal, and both have handsomely designed settings with formal gardens, terraces, and fountains. These elements add up to an early twentieth-century interpretation of the Italian Renaissance villa; but very different interpretations in the resulting visual effect. In this difference lay two approaches to domestic architecture in the early twentieth century: one academic and conventional – Crane Cottage; and the other experimental and unconventional – Mill Pond. The former approach became the norm in the first decades of the century, and the latter pointed towards attempts to break with the past and find new forms of expression.

Each of these is a villa in the sense of the type of country estate developed in the warm Mediterranean climate of Italy during the Renaissance. Houses, gardens, and grounds were conceived as a unit with ties between indoor and outdoor spaces; an integrated composition of architecture and landscape architecture. Whether the Renaissance villa was a working farm or a gentleman's retreat, the house and garden were designed to take advantage of the site – the solar orientation, the views and breezes – and to give the fullest opportunity for the enjoyment of country life. These two winter homes in Georgia conform to this historic domestic ideal; Crane Cottage more obviously than Mill Pond.

In 1928 the late architect Rexford Newcomb described houses of this kind as "Mediterranean . . .

disposed around an open courtyard or 'patio.'" This became an especially popular form of dwelling a few years after these Georgia resort houses were built, but some were built even earlier than these. An influential book on the subject was published in 1894, Charles A. Platt's *Italian Gardens*. Another less epochal book was Edith Wharton's *Italian Villas and Their Gardens* (1904). Platt and Wharton were enamored with Italian architecture as Americans had been since the 1850's: the Hay House (pages 120-129), in Macon, is an example of this. They did not recommend so much a revival as the use of design principles, a study of models, for the design

ABOVE: Mill Pond Plantation, front elevation. RIGHT: Garden facade.

of American country houses and suburban villas. The houses and gardens which Platt designed in his own interpretation of the Italian villa influenced a generation of designers and laymen. Georgia's Neel Reid was one of those, as was David Adler (1882–1949) of Chicago, designer of the Crane Cottage.

These two winter villas in Georgia differ in this matter of the interpretation of how a twentieth-century Italian villa in America ought to look. The Crane Cot-

LEFT: Courtyard, indoor patio, and greenhouse. All of the major rooms and the bedrooms open onto this exotic, plant-filled space. (This glass canopy was designed to be opened.) TOP: Detail from enclosed courtyard. ABOVE: Entrance Foyer.

This looks like a seventeenth-century Italian villa, but it was a winter home on Jekyll Island, the once private sea island off southeast Georgia. Designed by the accomplished residential architect from Chicago, David Adler, for Richard T. Crane, Jr., of the Crane Company, it was a grandly informal resort house in a colony of winter "cottages." The season started in January and ended at Easter; a studied informality prevailed. Georgia's "Golden Isles" preceded Florida's playgrounds for the very rich. Millionaires like Richard Crane came to Jekyll on yachts by way of the inland waterway or on private railway cars on the mainland. In 1942 the Jekyll Club closed for its final season and in 1947 the State of Georgia bought the island for a State Park. On the island's western shore, a clubhouse and several cottages still stand; the Richard Crane House is perhaps the most beautiful. (It is now an administrative office.) David Adler's architectural mastery unified plan, ornamentation, decoration, furnishings, and landscape making a harmonious composition for island-resort living. The Crane Cottage is what an early-twentieth-century architect from Chicago could do in Georgia with stucco, arches, pediments, tiles, urns, courtyards, loggias, terraces, and formal gardens.

tage is photographically realistic and academically authentic so that it seems convincingly like an Italian villa and, in the courtyard, it possibly even resembled a Spanish hacienda. On the other hand, Mill Pond is novel in its overall appearance and in detail, so that it is more difficult to classify. It does not resemble any other villa that one has seen. And that is the point, for it is part of the experimentation in domestic architecture which occurred in the midwest, largely in Chicago, and was called the Prairie School.

Prairie School architects, led by Frank Lloyd Wright (1867-1959), searched for a new architectural language not based on the well known and conventional historical precedents. They believed that they could invent a totally new architecture based on the nature of sites, materials, and functional requirements. Mill Pond, of course, is Prairie School only by influence, but the influence was strong enough to make this house different from anything else built in Georgia at the time.

In 1903 Jephtha H. Wade of Cleveland, Ohio, a financier, philanthropist, and art collector, commissioned Hubbell and Benes, Cleveland's most outstanding firm of architects, to design this hunting lodge/winter home for his 10,000-acre plantation in Thomasville. (A Wade descendant still owns the place and uses it seasonally.) Warren H. Manning, ASLA, of Boston, Massachusetts, a former student of Frederick Law Olmsted, laid out the extensive gardens and grounds. Manning designed these to suit the house and the terrain. Thus the architecture and landscape architecture reflect the Coastal Plain landscape as the Prairie School houses did the horizontal plains near Chicago. Its function as a southern vacation villa is perfectly stated with few references to ornamental precedents: the curvilinear gables may refer to either the Spanish Colonial Revival or the Mission Style, but they are exceptions. The vine-covered stucco walls emphasize even more the non-revivalist quality of the house. And the 100-foot square arcaded courtyard, covered by the boldly engineered steel-and-glass skylight, seems particularly Prairie School.

In 1900, however, most architects and clients wanted buildings to look as if they belonged – not so much to a specific place and time as to the great tradition of western civilization begun in Greece and Rome, revived in the Renaissance, refined in the seventeenth and eighteenth centuries, and codified by the royal academies, especially by the École des Beaux-Arts. David Adler, the designer of the Crane Cottage, was part of that tradition. He had studied for a time at the École, and although he was from Chicago, he was decidedly not of the Prairie School. His villa for the Crane Company millionaire, Richard T. Crane, Jr., was a very fine example of what an American trained in the French academic tradition could do. In the Beaux-Arts tradition the monuments of past architecture were analyzed,

Courtyard: The floor plan of the cottage reflects this "ritzy" causualness perfectly. There was no entrance hall; one stepped from the balmy Georgia outdoors into a large living room which in turn opened into this loggia and cloistered courtyard overlooking terraces and gardens. A small villa in northern Italy supplied inspiration but David Adler's design perfectly suited its place and time.

sketched and made the basis of a conventional and conservative design vocabulary which, in theory, did not lead to the revival of any particular style. This was true in Adler's career. The Crane Cottage was only one of fifty superb houses – no two of them alike – which Adler designed. For each one of them he planned the landscaping as an integral part of the architecture, and often did the decoration and furnishing so that the entire setting would be stylistically consistent and harmonious.

Both of these winter homes in Georgia – differ as they might in aspects of their appearance – were interpretations of the Italian villa ideal. Mill Pond is a landmark of the end of the era in which the interpretation was likely to be an individually-inspired creation of the sort which characterized the work of Louis Comfort Tiffany. The Crane Cottage is a landmark of the transition to the era which follows, in which academic classicism and academic eclecticism, fine craftsmanship, and good taste will be the watchwords.

Hills and Dales
The Fuller Callaway House

1914-1916   Neel Reid, *Architect*

LaGrange, Troup County

Hills and Dales is a villa in the true Italian tradition. Now the home of Mr. and Mrs. Fuller Callaway, Jr. it is a work of excellence in design and execution. Landscape, architecture, and details form a satisfying total expression. Neel Reid was thirty-one when he started work on this design but it must be considered a mature work.

James H. Grady
Architecture of Neel Reid in Georgia, 1973

THE ART of the suburban country house in America reached its peak in the first three decades of the twentieth century. The classic statement of this in Georgia is the LaGrange estate of Mr. and Mrs. Fuller E. Callaway, Jr. It is classic in its architectural style, in its perfection, and in the precedent it set. Few before it and few afterwards have matched its excellence.

Neel Reid (1885-1926) never received a larger residential commission, and it established the importance of his firm. (Reid's original partner was Hal Hentz; they were joined by Rudolph Adler in 1915, and Philip Shutze in 1919 although he left for awhile, returning in 1923, and becoming a partner in 1927 after Reid's death.) Philip Shutze has said: "The only 'grand' house that the young artist got to plan was the Fuller Callaway man-

sion in LaGrange." Had Reid not died at age 41, no doubt he would have helped create other houses of this magnitude, but never would he have had a more ideal opportunity.

The site was perfect – a hillside overlooking a garden that was established in 1841. The garden was made up a series of dwarf boxwood parterres and descending terraces, created by Mrs. Sarah Coleman Ferrell, and laid out according to formal Italian Renaissance and Baroque patterns. But perhaps even more important, Reid had ideal clients. The Fuller Callaways were both Georgia natives who appreciated the Ferrell Gardens and wanted a classical house to complement them. Reid placed their house on the site of Mrs. Ferrell's frame cottage at the edge of the five landscaped acres that she had developed for more than sixty years. Mrs. Ferrell specifically asked Fuller Callaway, a public-spirited textile millionaire, to purchase these acres and continue to look after them after her death; Mr. Callaway accepted this trust and the results are apparent. He and his wife, Ida Cason, and his son, Fuller, and his son's wife, Alice Hand, have added features to the gardens which only complement them. The house seems to have been there as long as the gardens, and together they seem to have been there even longer.

The gardens now consist of the original five acres and one-half acre more; the entire estate is approximately 1500 acres, much of it within the city limits of LaGrange. The extraordinary executive ability which transformed the textile business in LaGrange, and created this home, also transformed the community. Hills and Dales is only one aspect of the beauty which the Callaway family has brought to LaGrange, a west Georgia town which has become one of the textile manufacturing centers of the southeastern United States.

Neel Reid described this house to Mrs. Fuller Callaway, Sr., as "Georgian Italian," meaning an English country house of the Georgian period in the Palladian style. Setting aside such considerations, a visitor writing in the guest book in 1919 simply said: "A house whose beauty is surpassed only by its gracious hospitality." The nine bedrooms and nine bathrooms at one time served several generations of the Callaways who lived under its spacious red tile roof. A "country house" was supposed to be gracious, spacious, and beautiful. The Callaways and their architect succeeded admirably.

Dr. Catherine Howett described Hills and Dales as Reid's "masterwork" (1982) and she, as did James Grady,

OPPOSITE: The gardens were begun in the 1840's. "God is Love" in the foreground was one of the mottoes spelled out in boxwood by Mrs. Sarah Coleman Ferrell. Mrs. Ferrell called her garden The Terraces; it consisted of five acres. In 1912 Fuller E. Callaway, Sr. purchased the property to preserve The Terraces, enhance it, and build this house which was completed in 1916 on the site of the original house. Beginning on Vernon Road the estate consists of 1500 acres.

compared the house to the suburban villas of Charles A. Platt, especially Timberline mansion in Bryn Mawr, Pennsylvania. Platt and Reid designed houses and gardens which were unified and harmonious compositions, merging indoor and outdoor spaces for living and for show. Like Platt, Reid helped with decorating interiors, selecting antique furniture, porcelain, fabrics, and appropriate paint colors. Thus a Reid house was a synthesis of design ideas from related styles and periods.

Neel Reid's formal education in design began at the Columbia University School of Architecture where he studied in 1905 and '06 and in Paris at the École des Beaux-Arts in 1906 and '07; he got practical experience in New York in the office of Murphy and Dana until 1908 or '09 when he returned to Atlanta and set up practice with Hal Hentz, who had also studied in New York and Paris. That was Reid's formal training, but he seems to have been an artist from birth, and in his youth he

LEFT: The Living Room. French doors open off of this room into the first terrace of the garden. The fireplace wall was changed in 1949 according to a design made by Philip Shutze, FAIA; previously there was a Caen stone fireplace. The interior decoration has evolved over the years since 1916; the latest "housekeeping" was done with the help of David Richmond Byers III of W.E. Browne Decorating Company, Atlanta. The panelling is Circassian walnut. ABOVE: The Double Staircase, looking into the Living Room.

absorbed influences from numerous sources, including from the already-executed works of such men as Platt, whose architecture he took as a model of good taste.

Reid placed the house so that the south elevation faces the Ferrell Gardens, centering the pediment on a fountain which is on axis with a pool on the lower terrace. The center three windows of this garden façade mark the location of the living hall, a monumental space with the principal staircase descending on the north side.

These three windows open as doors onto the first terrace with its central fountain. They are separated by four engaged (attached) Ionic columns supporting the embellished pediment. The house has three principal façades: north, south, and east, with important entrances on each; the service end of the house is on the west. The motor approach is on the east and is dominated by a semicircular portico in the Ionic order. Above the door on this façade is the date "1916."

ABOVE: The Music Room (originally the Drawing Room). Neel Reid designed this lovely room in the late-eighteenth century French style of the time of Marie Antoinette. An oil portrait of Mrs. Fuller E. Callaway Sr. (Ida Cason 1872-1936) is reflected in the overmantel mirror. Through the window is a glimpse of the garden and fountain of the first terrace. OPPOSITE: The Library: This room on the northeast corner of the house is English Renaissance in character and is panelled with Circassian walnut. The oil portrait above the mantel is of Fuller E. Callaway, Sr. (1870-1928).

When the designs for this house were made in 1914, an influential book had just been published, the *Architecture of Humanism* by Geoffrey Scott. Reid does not seem to have been a theorist but his houses and gardens exemplified the architecture of humanism. Geoffrey Scott dealt with the ancient Vitruvian principles: a good plan, for a certain purpose, and a well-built, symmetrical structure, handsomely ornamented – all in all a delightful experience as art. Reid designed buildings for the use and enjoyment of classically-educated people, who adhered to the traditions of classical civilization as passed to them from the Renaissance; this house and garden is all of that. As the architect and the client intended, it is a place designed for the delight of human beings.

As long ago as Pliny the Younger (A.D. 62-113) there were descriptions of villas like Hills and Dales right down to the boxwood gardens. Pliny wrote, "Sometimes the box are even made into letters." As they are here. Pliny described a house such as this as a "Villa Urbana," or country house near the city. "The complete villa," as he described it, could be Hills and Dales as though Neel Reid had used Pliny as one of his historical references. Pliny described the "master's part," the "caretaker's part," and the "outbuildings" – all arranged for beauty and convenience among landscaped grounds.

In 1931 Hills and Dales was included in *Southern Architecture Illustrated* in a series of handsome black and white photographs; at that time the house was fifteen years old and the Ferrell Gardens of the 1840's were almost ninety. But the house was already comfortably wedded to the site and the place already seemed at least a century old. When these color photographs were made in the summer of 1982, Hills and Dales represented 140 years of domestic life and architecture; a beautiful merger of the Old South and New on five and a half acres. When the distinguished architect described this creation as "Georgian Italian," perhaps he meant it in more ways than one. Certainly Hills and Dales has become as much Georgia Georgian as English Renaissance Georgian, and it represents several generations of privately-funded conservation which deserves much applause.

LEFT: The Breakfast Room, on the southwest corner of the garden façade. BELOW: The Dining Room. The coffered ceiling, designed by Neel Reid, was modeled of plaster by Italian artisans. The needlepoint on the armchairs was done by Mrs. Alice Hand Callaway. OPPOSITE ABOVE: The eastern end of the fifth terrace with GOD spelled in dwarf boxwood. This was planted in the 1840's by Mrs. Sarah Coleman Ferrell and has been maintained since 1912 by the Callaway family. OPPOSITE BELOW: Looking from the sunken garden on the lower terrace to the south elevation or garden façade. The garden consists of six terraces.

TWO STATELY HOMES OF DRUID HILLS
The Walter Turner Candler House/Lullwater House
1925-'26
The Charles Howard Candler House/Callanwolde
1917

Atlanta, Dekalb County

In every wealthy home here, recently built, the style of architecture and of interior decorations follows the fashion of some earlier period. The modern art became tiresome and lost its value. The result is an absolute return to the old fashions – to the colonial, to the early English...

Atlanta Journal
July 18, 1915

"EARLY ENGLISH" was the style that the Candler brothers, Walter Turner and Charles Howard, chose for their suburban manor houses. They built them about

the time that the family, led by the patriarch, Asa Griggs Candler (1851-1929), sold the Coca-Cola Company for $25,000,000 to a syndicate headed by Ernest Woodruff (father of Robert Winship Woodruff). Their homes are grouped together here because they relate in several important ways (Callanwolde, the Charles Howard Candler House, is on page 173). Literally the houses were related – they were built by brothers who shared the same source of wealth, and they were both located in Druid Hills, the northeast Atlanta neighborhood the family opened in 1908, and lastly they were "Period

OPPOSITE: 1483 Clifton Road, Lullwater House. Home of the Presidents of Emory University since 1963. Emory purchased the 185-acre estate from its original owner, Walter Turner Candler (1885–1967), in 1958. Candler was the fourth child of Asa Griggs Candler, founder of the Coca-Cola Company; a businessman and sportsman, he was an Emory College alumnus, class of 1907. The house is 6/10's of a mile from the main road; the property is adjacent to Emory, which Alistair Cooke, the English man of letters, described in 1977 as having the "most beautiful campus in America."
ABOVE: Principal Stairway. As with early English country houses, Lullwater House seems to have evolved over several periods. The English Renaissance style entrance and stairhall appears to date from the late-seventeenth century, but the exterior is Tudor. (That was the architect's intention.)

ABOVE: Rear Elevation, Lullwater House. The house sits on a hill above a twelve-acre lake formed from South Peachtree Creek; the property now consists of 154 acres. The fieldstone to build the house in 1925 was quarried on the grounds. The house has some 7500 square feet of living space. BELOW: The Living Room of Lullwater House is reminiscent of a "long gallery" in a Tudor period house. This room is Elizabethan, the Age of Oak; the parget ceiling and the early Renaissance mantelpiece are authentically Elizabethan in style and complement the exterior.

Houses" similar in style: an academic eclectic interpretation of the domestic architecture of Tudor England (with pre-Tudor and post-Tudor features). But perhaps more important is their relation to Emory University, the institution of higher learning (situated in Druid Hills) that the Candlers promoted, endowed, attended, and directed for many years. Both houses have belonged to Emory and the Walter Candler place, Lullwater House, is now the Emory University President's Home.

This is a family story but the story of a truly exceptional family with the highest standards of stewardship, and these houses bring it all into focus. There were other Candler houses in Druid Hills but these are the best preserved. Of the two, the one adjacent to Emory's main campus which has housed Emory University's presidents since 1963, more nearly approximates the way it was when it was new and the main house of Walter Candler's Lullwater Farms. Charles Howard Candler's Callanwolde is now a cultural center belonging to Dekalb County.

The whole of Druid Hills, some 1500 acres, is a Candler landmark. Asa Griggs Candler, the founding father of The Coca-Cola Company – in the 1880's and 90's – had by 1905 begun to concentrate on additional projects, among them real estate development, including the construction of the Candler building, a skyscraper. In 1908, with several friends, he paid Joel Hurt, creator of Inman Park, $500,000 for the unfinished Druid Hills subdivision. Hurt had engaged Frederick Law Olmsted to plan it in 1892. The Candlers used Olmsted's ideas to make the rolling terrain into a large landscaped park centering on Ponce de Leon Avenue, a wide residential boulevard built east from Peachtree Street towards Dekalb County. In effect Druid Hills became the Candler estate with these two houses as mansions on different parts of the large "plantation." In 1916 Asa Candler moved into his place on Ponce de Leon, presumably the main house, but later Walter Turner and Charles Howard outdid their father. (In 1916 controlling shares in Coca-Cola were divided equally among the five Asa Candler children with Asa retaining a share.) In 1914 Asa had given his brother Bishop Warren A. Candler of the Methodist Episcopal Church South a check for $1,000,000. and a deed for 75 Druid Hills acres to encourage the founding of Emory University on the site it still occupies (now expanded in acreage by seven or eight times). Emory College, the Methodist school at Oxford, Georgia, became the namesake, the undergraduate division, and parent institution, moving to the Druid Hills campus in 1919. The campus architect was Henry Hornbostel of New York, who was also the architect of Callanwolde. Later, the Atlanta firm of Ivey and Crook did much of the architectural work at Emory, after their effective job for Walter Candler. (Ivey and Crook was formed in 1923 and Lullwater House was one of their most important

980 Briarcliff Road N.E., Callanwolde, the Charles Howard Candler estate, 1917, Henry Hornbostel, Architect. Candler was the eldest child of Asa Griggs Candler; he was Chairman of the Board of the Coca-Cola Company and of Emory University. The house was deeded to Emory upon Mrs. Candler's death, later becoming a Dekalb County cultural center. The original estate had 27 landscaped acres.

early commissions. Lewis E. Crook was the designer – he had interned with Neel Reid – and Ernest D. Ivey supervised construction.)

In a manner of speaking Emory University was at first the school of higher education on the Candler estate; and, of course, the economic base of the estate and of the university was not cotton but Coca-Cola, as it has remained to this day. Over the years, members of the Candler family have given considerable endowment funds, particularly Charles Howard, the eldest child. (But the largest contributors have also been Coca-Cola magnates: the brothers Woodruff, Robert and George. Together as a family they have made gifts in excess of one-hundred million dollars to Emory – during their lifetimes.)

That these Candler Medicis of America's favorite soft-drink formula both chose the pre-eighteenth century, early English style for their mansions is probably due in part to the sylvan setting of Druid Hills. Their half-timbered and castellated manors certainly look at home on these tree-surrounded, druidical sites. Both look for all the world like stately homes of Tudor England. And possibly, too, it could be related to the fact that the English Reformation took place during the Tudor period, and the Candlers have been devout Protestants for many generations.

In 1977 Alistair Cooke came to Emory University and in a subsequent BBC "Letter from America" broadcast (November, 1977) he told his listeners in Great Britain that he would vote for the "Campus of Emory University in Atlanta [as] the most beautiful in America." Cooke admired Emory's "plunging hills and gardens and little lakes, all set off with towering trees." He concluded: "Visiting Emory was like walking into the Garden of Eden." Cooke said: "The new President of Emory University told me that his aim was to make the university worthy of its noble setting." The president to whom Alistair Cooke referred is Dr. James T. Laney who, with his wife and family, makes this early English house his home. Cooke was the Laney's house guest. Certainly this fine house with its English park, made an important contribution to the splendid impression Emory made on the famous British lecturer and writer. His observations about American civilization are heard and read throughout the English-speaking world.

William Makepeace Thackeray, a nineteenth-century Cooke counterpart, also liked Georgia, and he too stayed in the finest houses. Perhaps the landmark homes of Georgia will always be this state's most appealing and memorable asset. Two of Georgia's stateliest beauties are these Tudor Revival manors in the lovely northeast Atlanta suburb of Druid Hills.

Oak Hill – Home of Martha Berry
1866-1942
Mount Berry, Floyd County

Portrait of Martha McChesney Berry (1866-1942) painted by Leon Gordon in 1932 for *Good Housekeeping* magazine when Martha Berry was selected as one of the twelve most outstanding women in America. This portrait was reproduced in the magazine. It hangs at Oak Hill above the drawing room piano. In the portrait is the original Berry School's log cabin and the Collegiate Gothic dining hall built by the Henry Fords in 1927.

Every morning when she is at home she still drives over the grounds, peculiarly her own domain because it has been so literally built by her. Site for a new building is selected, change in a road is directed, new paths are laid out.

Tracy Byers, *Martha Berry, The Sunday Lady of Possum Trot,* 1932

Miss Berry always had plans in her own mind first, and then they would appear on the blueprints. Eventually they would appear on the campus.

Dr. Inez Wooten Henry
Undated Manuscript, Martha
Berry Museum, Berry Schools.

MARTHA McCHESNEY BERRY was the architect of Berry Schools: "architect (from Greek *architekton,* master builder), one who designs buildings and superintends their construction; second, one who plans and achieves a difficult objective." In each of these dictionary senses of the word, Martha Berry was the architect of her schools.

Located on the southern end of the Blue Ridge Mountains, she was the kind of architect that Thomas Jefferson had been on the northern end: Oak Hill was her Monticello and the schools, her University of Virginia. She used her family home and her schools as demonstrations of her beliefs: their architecture being an integral part of her educational program; the buildings at Berry Schools were examples to the students of how learning and hard work could transform their lives and let them enter the mainstream of history. Each building at Berry, including Oak Hill – which she herself modeled into its present classic revival form – was part of a master plan. As early as 1910 she had in mind the design and layout of the entire campus that existed at her death in 1942; although it was not until the 1920's and 30's that she was able to carry out many of her dreams.

She conceived the idea of the school in her own cabin-study near the main house at Oak Hill and by 1901 had built a white-washed schoolhouse on Possum Trot Road across U.S. 27 (now the Martha Berry Highway). She built the first schoolhouse on the 83 acres her father, Captain Thomas Berry, had left her. What had started out as a Sunday School became a boarding school, initially for mountain boys, in which farming and other work was part of the education. The first dormitory was built in 1902. Miss Martha and a retired architect, Captain John Gibbs Barnwell of Charleston, South Carolina, who lived near Oak Hill, together designed Brewster Hall, the ten-room dormitory formally opened January 13, 1902. (For a time Martha lived there herself.) Until his death in 1918, Captain Barnwell and she designed everything on the place, even putting (it is said) "spires on barns and chicken houses." She would plant an alley of elms to a fine site on a knoll, let the trees grow, and then go out and find donors to construct the new building. The students learned to build what she and her retired architect planned, and to landscape, using native flowers, shrubs and trees. After Brewster Hall they built a two-story, rustic log cabin to house guests, in the center of the 83 acres. What mystified the mountain boys most was that Miss Berry forbade

Oak Hill is on US 27 in the northern suburbs of Rome at Mount Berry on The Berry Schools campus. The plantation was begun by Martha Berry's father, Captain Thomas Berry, around 1860, about the time he married Francis Rhea of Alabama. Martha was born on the plantation in 1866, but the original house was badly burned in the 1890's. In the 1920's, after The Berry School was established, Martha gave the house its present appearance on the outside – note the School's coat of arms in the pediment. The inside appearance dates from 1932 when the interior was extensively remodeled, resulting in the present room arrangement. The grounds immediately around the house are beautifully landscaped with formal gardens, and the grounds beyond are treated like an English park.

hunting and decreed that every acre was a bird and game sanctuary.

The 83 acres in time grew to 30,000, with 50 miles of winding roads and drives. Today it is one of the largest and most beautiful campuses in the United States. The collection of schools and college buildings – amidst native landscaping in the Olmsted tradition – truly must be

seen to be believed when one considers that it all started – in this century – in a one-room log cabin at Oak Hill.

In 1911 the school and surrounding area was declared the Mount Berry Post Office. This was one of the results of her friendship with Theodore Roosevelt who came to the school in 1910. By that time her donors included Andrew Carnegie, who pledged $25,000 as his first

Library: Martha Berry's father, Captain Thomas Berry, is the subject of the overmantel portrait. This is the way the room has been decorated and arranged since the 1930's; it is as it was February 27, 1942 when Miss Berry died. The house is open to the public for regular tours.

gift, if she could match it. She did, after traveling all over the eastern seaboard to tell people of the Georgia dream that she was building stone by stone. Teddy Roosevelt suggested that she begin to educate girls, as well as boys, and that became a new impetus. In 1924 Miss Berry convinced the Henry Fords to stop at Mount Berry as they made their way to the Ford plantation at Richmond Hill, south of Savannah. That first visit began a long association between the famous Detroit industrialist and the increasingly famous Georgian educator. The Fords gave an entire collegiate Gothic quadrangle for the girl's school, a magically beautiful place with a reflecting pond;

Miss Martha and a fine Boston architectural firm, Coolidge and Carlson, designed it as another magnificent segment of her developing scholastic suburb, just north of Rome in the foothills of the Blue Ridge Mountains.

In 1932 the School's first college degrees were granted, and that same year she was appointed the first female member of Georgia's Board of Regents, as well as being voted one of the twelve most outstanding women in America. Although she had the private education of a gentlewoman, she had not attended college, but she revitalized the old concept of vocational education without a single course in how to do it. She received eight

Miss Berry's sleeping porch is as it was arranged when she was living. The simplicity of this room in comparison to the elegance of the rest of the house is said to reflect the principles on which she founded the Berry Schools. On the School's coat of arms is a "Cabin for simplicity," a ":Bible for Christianity," a "Lamp of Learning for opportunity," and a "Plow for work." At the top of the shield is the School's Biblical motto, "Not to be ministered unto but to minister."

honorary degrees, as well as an award from President Franklin Roosevelt for her contributions to the underpriviledged children of the Georgia mountains for which she had originated Berry Schools in 1901 and '02. When she died February 27, 1942, she was one of the most respected and renowned women in America.

The Berry Schools, now consisting of Berry Academy and Berry College, have continued to grow and build on the foundations laid down during her lifetime. The original threefold program of study, work, and worship has continued, though somewhat modified from the days when all students worked in the school's farms and shops, many of them to pay all of their tuition and expenses. The "Gate of Opportunity" that Martha Berry designed to go at the entrance in the early days, still remains open.

She was the Thomas Jefferson of north Georgia; the heroine and architect of a landmark of twentieth-century education. And this was her Monticello, her home, the model she created for her heirs – the young people of her school – to emulate.

SWAN HOUSE AND TWO VILLAS BY PHILIP TRAMMELL SHUTZE, FAIA

Philip Trammell Shutze has been advanced to Fellowship for achievement in design. His mastery of the fundamental principles of design and the use of the classical architectural forms as well as his taste in ornamentation and detail are evident not only in his numerous residences but also in important hospitals, banks, churches, and business buildings throughout the southeast.

Citation, The American Institute
of Architects, 1951

Entrance façade (East Elevation) 3099 Andrew Drive N.W., Atlanta. Swan House, The Edward Hamilton Inman House, 1926–1928, Philip Trammell Shutze, FAIA, Architect. Since 1966 it has been part of the Walter McElreath Memorial of the Atlanta Historical Society. There are over 20 landscaped acres in the estate in the Buckhead neighborhood of northwest Atlanta. This house is a culmination of the Palladian tradition in Southern architecture going back into the eighteenth century. This portico in the Doric Order is a direct descendant of the first major portico in the South at St. Michael's Church, Charleston, South Carolina, c. 1760. (Also note comparison with the Ionic portico of the old Executive Mansion at Milledgeville, page 74.)

The Edward Hamilton Inman House, 1926-'28, *Atlanta*
Villa Albicini/The Horgan-Curtis House, c. 1926, *Macon*
Villa Apartments, 1920, *Atlanta*

WHEN EDWARD HAMILTON INMAN and Emily Caroline MacDougald Inman commissioned Philip Shutze to plan the house and grounds of their 25-acre estate in suburban northwest Atlanta, they were in their mid-40's. Philip Shutze was 36 and about to become a partner in the leading Atlanta architectural firm of Hentz, Reid, and Adler. Neel Reid, a founding member of the firm, was dead and Shutze had succeeded to the position of chief designer, a function he had performed for some time because of Reid's failing health – and because of his own considerable talent.

The Inmans and their architect were natives of Georgia. Emily MacDougald's family were among the earliest settlers of Columbus, moving to Atlanta after the Civil War. Edward Inman was an Atlantan, a graduate of Princeton, the son of Hugh Theodore Inman and nephew of Samuel Martin Inman, brothers who made a fortune in the cotton business. S.M. Inman and Company of Atlanta was one of the top cotton brokerages in the world. Edward Inman inherited his father's fortune and, with Philip Shutze's help, he and his wife created a masterpiece of domestic architecture.

Three years after they occupied the house, Edward Inman died of a heart attack, but Mrs. Inman continued to live at Swan House – the name she gave her home. She lavished attention on its fundamental beauty with an English country house kind of interior decoration (most of which survives) and gardening, which also may still be seen – much of it as it was during her lifetime. In 1966, the year after Mrs. Inman's death, her hope that the estate, with the house, grounds and furnishings, would become the property of the Atlanta Historical Society was realized. And soon after the Historical Society purchased the property, it opened the principal rooms, gardens and grounds for tours, using bedrooms and service areas as offices.

After a few years the Historical Society built a functional headquarters on the property so that the entire house could be shown as though Mrs. Inman were still at home. (She had said that three of her legacies were spent making the place as she wanted it.) One by one, previously closed rooms have been put back as they had been originally. These splendid color photographs show much of what may be seen during one of the very popular and well-conducted tours.

But why has a house of less than 75 years been opened as a museum? And why is it considered a mas-

terpiece? The simplest answer, of course, is that it is beautiful; many of the talented people who made it possible no longer live, and with them their talents, expert training and experience have passed into history. The

world that existed prior to the Great Depression is as gone as any that has been destroyed by war or revolution. Perhaps the answer is not so simple after all and requires elaboration.

The place, inside and out, is a culmination of the domestic architecture of Georgia – which may never be equalled. It is a quintessential example of Georgia's love of beautiful houses and gardens in the classic revival tradition and as expressions of social and cultural status. It is the villa ideal, long courted in Georgia, ideally realized. It is what Georgians have been expressing architecturally, with varying degrees of success, since the houses of William Jay in Savannah one hundred years before. And expressed here with consummate knowledge and taste. Moreover, in 1965 and '66 when the place became available, it was a museum-quality arche-

ABOVE: Swan House, Garden façade facing Andrews Drive. The architect Philip Shutze has said: "It is supposed to be an English Kent house, but the cascade in front is pure Italian. I sketched this in an Italian garden about the time of World War I." (This façade is reminiscent of the Villa Corsina, Florence, which is baroque in style.) OPPOSITE: Circular Entrance Hall looking into the Stair Hall. These areas, separated by a screen of Ionic columns, flow into one another towards the garden side of the house facing Andrews Drive; they combine to create a "great space" which seems like a courtyard. The principal rooms open into this light-filled "atrium," which is filled with beautifully-executed architectural elements, ultimately derived from Andrea Palladio (1508-1580). The free-standing, spiral staircase, needless to say, is an elegant *tour de force*.

type of Atlanta's golden age of suburban architecture. And it was by one of those architects who had hclpcd to create the era, of which this was one of the true landmarks.

The beauty of the design consists less in the details, though they are perfect, but rather in the fine adaptation of the various parts to the whole, creating a unity of effect, a sense of proportion and scale and a complete assimilation of the structure with the physical site out of which it seems to emerge, as though it were an expression of the hillside.

When Mr. Shutze was advanced to Fellowship in the AIA, reference to that quality of his work was made in this way: "Shutze's knowledge and appreciation of scale, color and texture, both for interior and exterior use, has made it possible for him to create structures which are pleasing, useful and appropriate in their environment." Environmental appropriateness has been one of the concerns of architects in the twentieth century and much has been written about it – but less built. The Italian Renaissance villa wherein those ideals of appropriateness were first realized in western civilization,

Philip Shutze designed this golden-brown English Renaissance style room (the Christopher Wren period) to complement the style and color of the carved wood swag above the mantle-shelf. This ornate antique carving of fruit and flowers was done in the early eighteenth century in the manner of Grinling Gibbons (late-seventeenth century). It was in the Inman's Ansley Park house. The Shutze designs – drawn full scale – were carried out by the carver H.J. Millard of Bath, England, and Atlanta. Mr. Millard did the superb carving throughout Swan House. The door to the left opens into an arcaded porch (page 188) which leads to a boxwood garden. This room is arranged and decorated as it was during Mrs. Inman's lifetime.

then restated in Georgian England (by the Anglo-Palladian of Lord Burlington's circle) was the classical prototype. Mr. Shutze studied and mastered it to find a design vocabulary for his own century.

When he became "FAIA" in 1951, Philip Trammell Shutze was 61 and had begun to retire from the full-time practice of architecture, although he kept his folio-lined office in Atlanta's Candler Building. He was 92 in 1982 when he received the Arthur Ross Award of the Classical America Society. The citation read: "For a Lifetime Devoted to Upholding the Classical in its Finest Tradition." The award was presented at the National Academy of Design in New York City with Mrs. Vincent Astor and the President of the Classical America Society, Henry Hope Reed, officiating. There was a

kind of perfect symmetry in receiving that award at 92 – appropriate to Mr. Shutze's classicism. That award nicely balanced the Rome Prize which he received when he was 25 for three years of post-graduate study at the American Academy in Rome. That top prize, received in 1915, followed a B.S. degree from the newly opened School of Architecture at Georgia Tech (class of 1912) and an M.A. from Columbia University (1913). Undoubtedly Mr. Shutze was an academically trained architect, and proud of it. But he also had several years of internship with Hentz, Reid, and Adler, the Atlanta firm that he joined permanently in 1923, becoming a partner in 1927. He operated the partnership until his retirement – when the firm ceased to exist – except in the beautiful structures it had created throughout Geor-

gia and the southeast.

We have already shown Neel Reid's Hills and Dales at LaGrange. Here are three of Mr. Shutze's villas: Swan House in Atlanta has star billing; the Villa Albicini in Macon; and the Villa Apartments in Atlanta are in supporting roles. None of them has yet attained even 65 years but the classical perfection of each is already valued as though it were of the sixteenth century and by Andrea Palladio, or of the eighteenth century and by the English Palladian William Kent. Perhaps they are – in spirit. As Mr. Shutze said in 1978, "You don't copy the past; you adopt the beauty of the past to your present needs and, in the process, you make each design uniquely your own."

LEFT: Mrs. Inman refered to this sitting room as her "Morning Room." It was decorated in 1928 by Mrs. Inman, Mr. Shutze, and Ruby Ross Goodnow Wood of New York, a native of Monticello, Georgia. Mrs. Wood was one of the first professional decorators in America. She was the author of *The Honest House* (1914), and she was Elsie de Wolfe's ghost writer for the better known *The House in Good Taste* (1913). Elsie de Wolfe and Ruby Ross Wood practically created interior decorating and this room exemplified their approach, both recommended chintz-covered sofas for that "English-country house look." Billy Baldwin, Mrs. Wood's protege, has said that her credo was "to arrange beautiful things comfortably." (Note carved swans on the Shutze-designed Corinthian columns of the chimneypiece.)

ABOVE: Mrs. Inman's Bedroom, second floor. Swan House, with its eclectic mix of periods – antiques and reproductions – reflects the taste of the era and the good taste of the owner, Emily Caroline MacDougald Inman. Furnishing the house was one of her chief interests for forty years. An Atlanta belle, she was devoted to the beautification of her 25 acres in the heart of Buckhead. And this has continued with the leadership of Edward H. Inman's niece, Mrs. Ivan Allen, Jr. (Louise Richardson), an Atlanta Historical Society Trustee.

ABOVE: Detail of Dining Room (with views towards Andrews Drive). Mrs. Inman purchased a pair of swan console tables in Bath, England in 1924. They are attributed to Thomas Johnson (1714–1775), a noted London designer and carver of the Chippendale period. The Chinese wallpaper was imported from England for the house. Mr. Shutze designed the carved wooden cornices for the curtains, and they were executed in Italy. A Shutze sketch of this wall is on file at the Historical Society showing the cornices and the curtains as part of the compostion; in that way the entire house, inside and out, was meticulously planned. RIGHT: The Dining Room (with a glimpse of the Great Hall). Philip Shutze designed this room in the manner of the English Palladian school of William Kent, and H.J. Millard carved the details. Shutze has said: "A close collaboration of architect, owner, and decorator accounts for the resulting unified composition." (William Kent, 1685–1748, was the great designer of eighteenth-century English country houses, using a broad approach to the prototypes he had studied in Italy; he combined architecture, landscape architecture, and interior decoration to create a "unified composition" of the sort Shutze achieved with Swan House.)

Porch on South Elevation, overlooking formal garden. The pool and fountain are similar to one at the Villa Cicogna, Lombardy. (This stuccoed and arcaded space is one of Georgia's most monumental "screened porches.") Note that the entrance to this garden is exactly on axis with the carved eagle at the edge of the garden.

LEFT: Villa Apartments, 200 Montgomery Ferry Drive, N.E., Atlanta, Ansley Park, 1920. Philip Shutze worked for Hentz, Reid, and Adler for some months in 1920 when he designed this apartment building (now condominiums). ABOVE: The Villa Albicini, Horgan–Curtis House, Rivoli suburb, Macon (adjacent to and on axis with the Wesleyan College campus), c.1926. This pavilion-sized villa was based partly on a chapel at the Villa Cuzzano, near Verona, with elements from the Villa Corsini, Florence. Henry Hope Reed of the Classical America Society described this house as "opulence on a modest scale . . . a truly exotic wonder in the Baroque spirit, seldom seen outside of Italy."

Albert Howell House

1931-1932   Albert Howell, *Architect*

Atlanta, Fulton County

This was Pop's dream house; Albert fell for Italy.

Caro du Bignon Henry Howell McDowell
June 6, 1982

THIS WAS A YOUNG ARCHITECT'S dream house in 1932. He and his bride Caro du Bignon Henry were married in 1930. They took a five-month wedding trip to romantic, out-of-the-way places, returned to Atlanta, and lived in an apartment while this house was being built. It stands on an elevation above Peachtree Creek, on lands originally acquired in the 1830's by Albert Howell's family as part of the operation of the old Howell Mill. Albert's share consisted of seven acres.

This scion of Atlanta's Howell clan was one of the first native Atlantans, if not the first, to study architecture; he followed a usual route at that time, the schools of architecture at the Georgia Institute of Technology and Columbia University, and then several years at the École des Beaux-Arts in Paris. That is where he met his bride-to-be; she was residing in Paris with her mother. It was natural that they should be introduced, as they both were from old, well-known Georgia families, although Caro du Bignon Henry did not grow up in the home state of her ancestors. (The du Bignons were originally French, coming to Georgia in the eighteenth-century and purchasing Jekyll Island as their plantation.)

Albert practiced architecture, beginning in 1929, with McKendree A. Tucker (Mac). A small Italian villa they did for Mrs. Hunter Cooper, on Andrews Drive in Atlanta, in the beginning of their practice, is similar to Albert's own home, but because it may be seen from the street it is better known than his dream house. Mrs. Hunter Cooper's house was included in *Southern Architecture Illustrated* in 1931; it shows how well the Italian idiom can be adapted to suit a suburban Atlanta landscape, especially when the color of the stucco matches the sienna tones of Atlanta's soil. Tucker and Howell were also included in the famous book on modernistic architecture by the Museum of Modern Art, Philip

Terrace and Balustrade of Muses, the Albert Howell House garden.

Entrance façade. Albert Howell based this on the front of a small villa by Andrea Palladio. The panels with reclining figures are by the Atlanta sculptor, Julian Hoke Harris.

Johnson's and Henry Russell Hitchcock's, *The International Style, 1922-1932*. Their entry was decidely not an Italian villa but a small, functionalist science museum in the mountains of Highlands, North Carolina.

That was a transitional time, from the academic eclectic, Beaux-Arts aesthetic, to the new Germanic, Bauhaus approach. (See Harold Bush-Brown's *Beaux-Arts to Bauhaus and Beyond,* 1976; Bush-Brown was head of the department of architecture at Georgia Tech during the time that Albert Howell studied there.) Even though to survive in those days as architects, Tucker and Howell sometimes designed in the International Style, Albert's heart was in the traditionalism and classicism of his villa on Peachtree Battle Avenue.

In 1982 his conception was 50 years old. It would not be unlike what a young architect of today might hope to build if he were of the new school of classicists and eclectics, which has been given the name Post-Modern. Albert Howell might or might not approve of this trend, but as an illustration of what he thought about the modernists, your scribe and chronicler can give a personal testimony. In 1956 when this writer asked Mr. Howell about Frank Lloyd Wright, America's native modernist, Albert answered – characteristically with a pun – "Wrong! Frank Lloyd Wrong." And in a manner of speaking, that was the beginning of this text.

ABOVE: Terrace and garden façade. These hidden terraces are used for growing flowers and vegetables. Villa, in Italian, signifies not the house alone but the house and grounds, and the garden – whether for show or gardening – is an essential part. LEFT: Garden façade. This was based on a villa in Guy Lowell's *More Small Italian Villas and Farmhouses,* 1920. The house has the scale and proportions of a pavilion, as the French call it.

ABOVE: Principal Entrance, an octagonal room with four panels –
Italian countryside views – by Athos Menaboni. They were painted
on site for the house when Menaboni first came to Atlanta; he is a
native of Livorno, Italy, and has become world famous for his pictures
of native birds and other wildlife done in both oils and watercolor.
LEFT: Stairhall looking into Dining Room and side Entrance. The
arabesques and birds of paradise were painted by Paul Chelko and
Harvey Smith; Smith helped the Howells with interior decoration for
many years. The design of the dining room mantlepiece was inspired
by a fireplace in the Villa dei Collazzi, built in the early sixteenth
century in Tuscany. (Not a copy but an imaginative rendering of precedent.)

LEFT: Drawing Room with glimpse of octagonal Entrance Hall. The room has been so arranged and decorated for many years.
TOP: Library with glimpse of garden through doors. The portrait of George Washington, attributed to Gilbert Stuart, was acquired in Washington, D.C., by an ancestor of Mrs. Howell's.
ABOVE: Screened Porch with view of the Howell hydrangeas and some of the wooded acreage around "Pop's dream house."

MID-TWENTIETH CENTURY, 1933–1966

IN 1933 GEORGIA celebrated 200 years. And the chaste neoclassical façade on the right became a world-famous image associated with the state. Personal politics aside, this little white frame cottage at Warm Springs was – for a dozen years – the most famous house in Georgia. Franklin Delano Roosevelt's years of special association with the old Meriwether County spa, that he bought in 1927, are documented in *The Squire of Warm Springs* by Theo Lippman, Jr., 1977. Roosevelt first came to the springs as a young lawyer in 1924 seeking relief from the crippling effects of infantile paralysis. Warm Springs seemed to help, so in 1927, with a family friend – the architect Henry Toombs (1896-1967) – he began to transform the Victorian watering place into a colonnaded village of neoclassical buildings on the hill above the springs. (Toombs was originally of Cuthbert, Georgia, and a relative of the fiery Rebel, Robert Toombs; he was a graduate of the University of Pennsylvania's School of Architecture and once worked for the celebrated firm of McKim, Mead, and White.) The design of Roosevelt's first cottage was based on a one-story version of a local Greek Revival house with a dog-trot central hall, but without columns. After Roosevelt made Warm Springs a regular part of his life, he decided to build the now-famous place shown here. Begun in the fall of 1931, construction was completed in the spring of 1932; there was also a guest house and a combined servant's quarters and garage. Total cost was $8,738.14, including architect's fees.

Sited on the north slope of Pine Mountain overlooking a wooded ravine, the house was supposed to look like it belonged there, so that the style chosen was antebellum classical with the simplest of columns in the Tuscan Doric order. The interior was paneled throughout with yellow Georgia pine and furnished with "early-American" reproductions made in Dutchess, New York. Franklin and Eleanor first stayed in the house on April 30, 1932, while he was seeking the presidency and still Governor of New York. On May 5, he wrote Henry Toombs: "I can't find words to tell you how delighted I am with it." After his election and inauguration, his retreat began to be called The Little White House – a Georgia vernacular miniature of the one in Washington, D.C. It remained his favorite White House until he died there, April 12, 1945, thirteen years after that first spring when the house was brand new. (It is now a museum.)

Brand new, however, is a key idea, for almost no one wanted houses to seem new. Republicans and Democrats alike (especially Republicans) expected architecture of all kinds, but particularly domestic architecture, to be conservative and traditional. One of the best ways to communicate those qualities was by adapting early American architecture to present needs and purposes. We have seen that Martha Berry did this with her own house at the Berry Schools; in fact hers was a major example of the use of the southern classical house (sometimes called Southern Colonial) to symbolize a value system – in Miss Berry's case an ethic based on education and work. Franklin Roosevelt and his Georgia-born and beautifully-educated architect, were saying with that four-columned porch: "Franklin is here to stay awhile and wants to be welcome and welcoming. He is the Squire of Warm Springs."

This aspect of architecture, its literary and symbolic nature, is ancient. In classical times a temple front on a house was rare and had special meaning; Palladio put them on almost all of his villas to signify the power of the landlord, and the same symbolism has prevailed ever after: it has to do with hierarchy and order. This associative aspect of architecture dies slowly. (In the so-called Post-Modern era it is being revived.)

Each of these houses from the 1930's until the 1960's is an example of early-American revivalism. The first of them came at the same time as the formal opening of Colonial Williamsburg, Inc. in the mid-1930's. Each was designed by an architect and is a special phase of what developed from advancing architectural scholarship in America. The domestic architecture of our Colonial and Post-Colonial eras provided design precedents. In several instances – at Pebble Hill and The Little White House – the early architecture of Georgia itself was one of the starting points for the design. In one case the inspiration was Jeffersonian – the Hightower House, and in another, it was colonial Virginia – the Martin House. The early-American reminiscenses of one house were so subtle and the synthesis of diverse sources so ingenious, that it transcended them to become a modern vernacular house that, to put it simply, is American: the Patterson-Carr House. Each of these houses is a handsome synthesis of early American sources and that is part of the reason that they are landmark homes.

These are Southern houses, consciously regional, but the overiding architectural purpose was an American cultural identity as opposed to European. We have seen a selection of houses largely European or Italian in style and planning. And from them the architects of these early-American houses have applied planning principles to create a similar harmony between the indoors and outdoors – which is especially appropriate in Geor-

Franklin Delano Roosevelt Cottage, The Little White House,
1931-1933, Warm Springs, Henry Toombs, FAIA, Architect.

gia where the climate encourages outdoor activities
almost the year around. One of these places is especially
related to Georgia's appealing winter climate and spec-
tacularly beautiful early spring: the Augusta National
Golf Club. With it are two famous cottages on the Club
grounds: Mamie Eisenhower's and Bobby Jones's.

Because Mamie's Cabin looks very much like The
Little White House, we can say that early-American
revival architecture in Georgia transcended personal
politics: FDR could hardly be confused with a Repub-
lican, and Ike and Mamie Eisenhower could not be
accused of being Democrats, anymore than the builders
of Pebble Hill, Ohio Republicans, who were related to

Senator Mark Hanna. (Of course, Southern Democrats
have been politically close to Republicans when it was
expedient.)

These early-American revival houses do seem to
express a conservative national consensus which is related
to domestic values rather than to party politics; to an
Americanism and patriotism in the sense of homeland
and country (rather than of government and tax collector). Alfred Frazer, author of *Key Monuments of the History of Architecture* (1965) wrote: "More than any symbol
of security, Americans revere the owner-occupied,
detached house – almost always called a home." For
many people during the years of the Great Depression
and after World War II, some version of early American
has meant home; here are some of Georgia's most outstanding examples of a trend that in fact has not yet
ended.

THE AUGUSTA NATIONAL GOLF CLUB

The Dennis Redmond Plantation
1850's
The Bobby Jones Cabin
1946
The Mamie Eisenhower Cabin
1953

Augusta, Richmond County

ABOVE: The Club House of the Augusta National Golf Club was built in 1854, of concrete, as the main house of Dennis Redmond's indigo plantation. In 1857 the house and acreage became the property of P.J.A. Berchman's family which created the Fruitlands Nursery. That is when the magnolia lane leading up to the front of the house was planted. The nursery ceased operation in 1910, and in 1930 the place – about 365 acres – was purchased as the site of the Augusta National Golf Club. A group led by Georgia's famous golf champion, Robert Tyre Jones, Jr. (Bobby), converted the former plantation house and nursery into the present private club and golf course. The formal opening was January 1, 1933. The Masters Golf Tournament is held here every spring. TOP: Panoramic view within the grounds of the Augusta National Golf Club at the tenth tee. On the right is the Bobby Jones Cabin, 1946, and in the right middleground is the Eisenhower's Cabin, 1953, built by the Club when Dwight David Eisenhower was President of the United States. Both cabins remain the property of the Augusta National but they retain their original brass nameplates and many of their original furnishings.

It was the nearest thing to a home they could call their own in their entire married life.

Clifford Roberts
*The Story of the Augusta
National Golf Club*, 1976

CLIFFORD ROBERTS referred to the Eisenhower Cabin built by the Augusta National Golf Club for Mamie and Ike when Dwight David Eisenhower was President of the United States. (Clifford Roberts and Robert Tyre Jones, Jr., were co-founders of the Club in 1930.) The Eisenhowers made 29 trips to their cabin while he was President, and Mrs. Eisenhower often stayed here after the General's death.

During one week every spring, this is the most famous golf course in America. Television cameras scan the beautiful golf links during the Masters Tournament and, after the tournament is won, the club reverts to being a very private place – for members only. Many know that Atlanta golfing hero, Bobby Jones, created this golf club paradise and tournament, but few know the history of the property and of the main club house, and how part of the beauty of the setting is due to a nationally famous nursery located here from 1858 until 1910.

The clubhouse was constructed as the main house of Dennis Redmond's indigo plantation in 1854. It is believed to be the first concrete dwelling erected in the South. The cement was made of lime from a nearby source, with gravel and sand from the property. Redmond said that his house was built of "artificial stone." The walls are 18 inches thick, and there are three floors crowned by an 11 × 11 foot cupola which was used originally for observing the fields. Galleried porches 9½ feet wide encircle the first and second floors. The architecture is unique in Georgia because it resembles Louisiana plantation houses; there is not an exactly comparable classical revival house in the state. The unique architecture set the pattern for the early-American design of later buildings at the club.

The golf course was built on the 365-acre Fruitlands Nursery which replaced Redmond's plantation in 1857. Fruitlands was begun by Dr. Louis Berckmans with his son, Prosper Julius Alphonso Berckmans, in 1858. P.J.A. Berckmans was a trained horticulturist and the Berckmans' nursery was almost as well known in its day as the golf club and tournament are today. When the golf course was under construction in 1931, P.J.A. Berckmans, Jr., returned to help with horticulture – some 4000 trees and shrubs were saved and relocated; he suggested that each of the eighteen holes in the course be associated with a flowering plant or tree (hole number 11, for example, is White Dogwood).

The long, double row of magnolia trees that the Berckmans' set out before the Civil War is intact as the impressive driveway into this exclusive sanctum which the world glimpses every spring.

This is one of the unique landmarks of a state which has long been host to presidents, whether they be Democrats, Republicans or corporate chief executives. George Washington was the first U.S. President to come to Georgia; he visited Augusta in the spring of 1791 when it was the state capital. Governor and Mrs. Telfair entertained with a sumptious ball. Perhaps that ball could be said to have been the beginning of a tradition in Augusta which continues to this day in the festivities "during the Masters," which is the city's Mardi Gras, St. Patrick's Day, and Rites of Spring. These photographs, however, show the Augusta National as Bobby Jones and Ike Eisenhower and the other members have known it – a beautiful and serene Shangrila, devoted entirely to golf.

Pebble Hill is a pastoral architectural setting which harkens back to a pre-twentieth century agricultural world. The plantation buildings could be called Early American Revival for there are echoes of several American Georgian styles, among them the Jeffersonian. Also, in the main house of 1936 — which replaced the antebellum house — may be seen the influence of Thomas County classicism and John Wind, who designed the original house that burned in January 1934. But the reminiscences are not confined to early America; the picturesque silhouette of the dairy-barn silos is Norman French.

William R. Mitchell, Jr.
Landmarks, The Architecture of Thomasville and Thomas County, Georgia, 1980

Pebble Hill Plantation

1936 – and earlier   Abraham Garfield, *Architect*

Thomas County

THE HISTORY of Pebble Hill Plantation parallels the history of Thomasville and Thomas County. The plantation was begun when the county was founded in the 1820's and has persisted through every phase, flourishing to the present. It is being carefully prepared to show as a museum under the auspices of the Pebble Hill Foundation which was created by the late owner, Mrs. Parker Poe. Elisabeth Ireland Poe (1897-1978, known as Pansy and "Miss Pansy") inherited the estate from her mother in 1936. She has bequeathed Pebble Hill so that it can be shown to the public in prime condition (as it was during the height of the winter season when it was ready for company). The late Mrs. Poe's husband, Parker Barrington Poe, of Texas and New York, has directed the renovation to prepare the plantation for visitors.

Elisabeth Ireland Poe's family acquired Pebble Hill as a potential winter home and shooting preserve in 1896 (the year before Pansy's birth). Her grandfather, Howard Melville Hanna (Mark Hanna's brother) purchased the first part of the property – that containing the old plantation house – when he was still a comparatively young man. He and Mark Hanna, their families and cousins, practically adopted the county as their second home, beginning a family tradition which has continued for many generations. Some years before Pansy Ireland Poe's death, Pebble Hill had become her principal residence; she had transferred her state citizenship to Georgia. And she chose to be buried at Pebble Hill in the old walled cemetery.

Kate Benedict Hanna (1871-1936), Pansy's mother (Howard Melville Hanna's fourth child), married Robert Livingston Ireland of New York in 1894. There were two children: Pansy in 1897 and her brother Robert Livingston Ireland, Jr., in 1895. After Kate's marriage, her father gave her the "frame dwelling house known as Pebble Hill" with considerable acreage. During her lifetime she added to the old house and to the land around it, turning the grounds and gardens into a showplace. "Over the years," wrote Dr. William Warren Rogers, "Kate moulded Pebble Hill into one of America's most handsome estates." *(Pebble Hill, The Story of a Plantation,* 1979.)

Kate Hanna Ireland and R. L. Ireland were divorced in 1919 and in 1923 she married Perry Williams Harvey. Kate Harvey called upon her friend, the architect Abraham Garfield of Cleveland, Ohio (son of the former President), to help her enlarge the main house – a frame classical revival cottage of the 1850's – and build a village of red brick dairy barns for an outstanding herd of Jersey cattle. By 1928 this was accomplished; the barns were designed to resemble Thomas Jefferson's University of Virginia (there is even a Jeffersonian serpentine brick wall). And, for their picturesque silhouette, Norman French towers were built at various points in the composition (they serve as silos). At that time the Georgian Revival wall and gatehouse on U.S. 319 was built.

Then tragedy struck in January 1934, during the high point of the winter season, when Pebble Hill had house guests. Luncheon was underway when the attic caught fire from defective bricks in one of the old Pebble Hill chimneys. Fed by the longleaf pine of the old landmark, the flames spread quickly, but many furnishings were saved. Kate Harvey's east wing with its lovely arcaded loggia (page 204) and Georgian Room (page 205) was not harmed.

Almost immediately construction was begun on a replacement for the antebellum house, with Garfield as architect. Completed in the winter of 1935-1936 it is a two-story brick version, painted white, of the original house that had been designed by Thomas County classicist John Wind (1819-1863, designer of Greenwood Plantation, page 22). It is a larger-scaled interpretation of the John Wind original, built for John W. H. Mitchell, Esq., that had been an H-shaped frame house with square slender columns, a wide hall, and eight rooms. The new house is also H-shaped (on the front) with similar columns rising two stories from brick piers – set out from the porch floor, as was the Thomas County custom. The interior of the new part of the house has a particularly fine space (shown on page 206): a staircase curving up into a rotunda, which is lighted by a Palladian window overlooking the rear gardens.

Of the Thomas County plantations with long and varied histories, the history of Pebble Hill has most nearly paralleled that of the county itself. Begun by Thomas Jefferson Johnson, an original settler who led in establishing the county and county seat, Pebble Hill took on new luster during the winter resort era when the Hannas first came to the county. And due to Elisabeth Ireland Poe, who inherited the estate from her mother in 1936, this "pastoral architectural setting" will continue to be preserved. The public will be able to experience the special Thomas County world that Pansy Poe loved and Pebble Hill evokes.

TOP: East Wing Loggia, 1920's. ABOVE: View of rear of East Wing showing exterior walls of the Loggia and Georgian Rooms, 1920's. RIGHT: Georgian Room, East Wing, 1920's. This room has recently been reopened after being closed for many years. The Thomas County wildlife wall murals are by Palm Beach artist, J. Clinton Shepherd. When the Pebble Hill house burned in 1934 only the east wing (consisting of the loggia and this room) was saved. It was incorporated into the present Pebble Hill, which Abraham Garfield designed for Kate Harvey in 1935-'36. Many of the trophies in this room were prizes won by Elisabeth Ireland Poe, a champion horsewoman (and sportswoman in general, whose love of nature and animals is well represented here).

Principal Stairs, looking north. This stairway and rotunda is in the part of the house
designed and built in the mid-1930's after the fire.

TOP: Exterior of the stable, originally the dairy barn, built in 1928 and revamped in the 1940's by Mrs. Parker Poe (Elisabeth Ireland) as a stable for her fine horses. Originally it housed champion Jersey cattle and was a self-contained dairy operation. ABOVE: Stable courtyard with low Jeffersonian serpentine wall in foreground.

The Patterson-Carr House
1939   Philip Trammell Shutze, FAIA

Atlanta, Fulton County

*After 1930, Philip Shutze confined himself largely to the vernacular, at least
with his residences. His clients no doubt had some influences in this.*

Henry Hope Reed,
Classical America IV, 1977

AN EXAMPLE of the early-American vernacular
in which Philip Shutze worked after Swan House,
and after other European and English classical idioms,
is shown here in the perfection of its pastoral spring
beauty. Shutze's Julian Hightower House (following on
page 212) is as American but by comparison more formal and neoclassical yet no less perfectly beautiful. (Mr.
Shutze's American is as good as his Italian and English.)

   The Patterson-Carr House is designed to seem to
be an eighteenth-century farmhouse which has grown
by a process of addition and become more sophisticated
with the years of growth. The whole seems to be made
up of parts, all in domestic scale, which have been beautifully assembled and composed. It is like a lovely lady

who has grown poised with the years, developing a
personality that is itself a work of art: harmonious, well-
balanced and informal in its personal sense of worth.
The place has that patina and sensuality that derives
from beauty which has aged gracefully – with a hap-
piness of spirit that comes from acceptance of maturity
as a blessing. In other words, this is a house with an
attractive personality: natural, unpretentious and self-
assured. It is early American, but decidely not "hay-
seed." It is the kind of house that Emily Post wrote
about in 1930 in her book, *The Personality of a House.*
The phrase "suitability and taste" also comes to mind,
used since Edith Wharton and Ogden Codman, Jr.,
wrote *The Decoration of Houses* (1897) and Elsie de Wolfe

Entrance from brick-paved court. The design acknowledges that people will be arriving by motor car. The house was designed as though it were in a rural setting, far from main roads, and to seem as if it evolved and was added to over the eighteenth and early-nineteenth centuries: an early farmhouse somewhere east of the Mississippi.

wrote *The House in Good Taste* (1913). It has personality inside and outside and, though informal, it is not decorated as if it were a "farmhouse."

This house is of the very essence of the revival of early-American architecture to fulfill the needs of the twentieth century that Stanford White and others originated around 1900 and that David Adler of Chicago perfected, but no less so than Atlanta's Neel Reid. This is a 1930's consummation of what they were doing in the 1910's and 1920's.

The classical Vitruvian principles have been realized within an American-Georgian format: useful space, well-built structure, and delightful effects to please the user and the observer. One of these effects is the way the house is designed as part of the total landscape, an element in the whole composition – rather than dominating it. It is an indoors/outdoors kind of house with a garden vista or garden access for each principal room. And then to create the effect of a bower *in* the house, there is an Athos Menaboni dogwood mural in the L-shaped entrance hall. To punctuate this effect, the hall opens into an enclosed garden (page 211).

To produce such a farmhouse in Georgia had taken more than 200 years; the house looks delightfully like it might have actually developed during two centuries, growing with successive generations and owners. With the Patterson-Carr House, Shutze practically defined the Anglo-American concept of a house that is one's *home:* "A dwelling-place, abode; the fixed residence of a family or household; the seat of domestic life and interests" (Oxford University Press, 1901). The Patterson-Carr House just may be the ideal home and hearth that 200 million Americans dream about. And it may be that domestic-scaled architecture for American living that the imaginative Frank Lloyd Wright tried to produce in the middlewest; but with few exceptions failed because his designs looked so strange.

This *looks* as the American (and the Georgia) house, and the American (and the Georgia) home, and the American Georgian-style house ought to look; especially when the dogwood and cherry trees planted down the lane are showing spring colors; when the white-rail fence and pickets and the white-and-yellow clapboards are warming in the sun; and when the deep green of the

ABOVE: Entrance to enclosed side garden off of main hallway. The hand-painted mural of native dogwood was done for the house in 1939 by Atlanta's favorite artist of flora and fauna, Athos Menaboni, originally of Livonia, Italy. OPPOSITE TOP: Paneled sitting room. Edith Hills Interiors, Inc. has been Mrs. Carr's standby for help with decorating. Edith Hills works in the traditions of the great lady decorators, begun by Elsie de Wolfe and Ruby Ross Wood in the 1910's and 20's. (More than anything, however, the house reflects Anne Carr's own taste and beauty.) OPPOSITE BOTTOM: Dining Room, with combination window/door leading onto a screened porch overlooking gardens.

mounded boxwood is pungent by the arched and shuttered entrance door. This is suburban Atlanta at its best. As Stafford H. Bryant of the Classical American Society wrote in 1977: "Atlanta did not have the first, or even the largest of the great leafy suburbs, with each dwelling in its own large park, but in northwest Atlanta may well be the culmination of the entire movement."

The Patterson-Carr House is a distinct part of that culmination: an American suburban house that has the ambience of the rural countryside and of a house that is not brand new – but antique; but at the same time has

all of the latest conveniences, is only 15 minutes from a major shopping mall and 30 minutes from the financial district. (The garage is always an important part of a suburban house.) With every modern domestic amenity, this house fulfills every requirement of a dwelling in the twentieth century and has the good manners and refinement of several generations of good architectural breeding.

The house has been the home of Mr. and Mrs. Julian Carr since the 1960's; it was built by the Fred Pattersons in the late 1930's.

Julian Hightower House

1947-1949   Philip Shutze, FAIA

Thomaston, Upson County

Grace and Julian Hightower's place at Thomaston is one of my favorites.

Philip Shutze, September 10, 1981

THE HIGHTOWER HOUSE is the last great country house built in Georgia in the tradition that reached fine flower in eighteenth-century England in the hands of William Kent. And it is the last great house that Philip Shutze did in Georgia before his retirement (a suburban house in Greenville, South Carolina, was his very last). It is most probably the last great country house built in America in the classical tradition as revived during the American Renaissance of the last part of the nineteenth century; which then extended into the twentieth, becoming even more refined in the hands of Shutze and his colleagues (such men as David Adler of Chicago).

Moreover, the Hightower House is a culmination of the American country house as a type – ultimately going back to the great houses of Virginia, American versions of the English prototypes. This house makes specific references to the kind of architecture and estate which Thomas Jefferson's genius gave a new impetus and new form, in the example he set with his villa, Monticello, and with those of his friends whom he helped: James Madison, for example. Madison's Montpelier (c.1810) was one source of the American classical vernacular which Shutze used in planning this splendid house for his friends, Grace and Julian Hightower of Upson County, Georgia. But more than any of the other Georgia country houses that are comparable in quality, this house is truly a *country* house, for it is several miles outside of town – out in the county – on a large developed tract (3800 acres) with an 80-acre lake which was planned as part of the total composition.

The house is approached through a well-tended, park-like woods, on a winding drive that follows the natural contours of the rolling terrain. The drive opens onto a great lawn — a closely-cropped meadow – which sweeps without interruption to a gleaming white Jeffersonian portico. In the Tuscan Doric order, it is set against rose-red bricks and enframed by the deep green of towering hardwood trees. It is on axis with the viewer, down a straight, earth-colored drive. This drive becomes a line of sight cutting through the lawn, aimed for the front entrance, directing the eye – if one could see that far – through the wide central hall of the house to the

OPPOSITE: Entrance façade. ABOVE: Garden façade.

garden door and then out onto a deep terrace, partly enclosed by boxwoods. Then the line of sight continues down a low flight of stairs onto a sloping lawn which descends to the edge of a placid lake, a wide expanse of water bordered by tall Georgia pines on the far shore. Symmetrical, orderly and perfectly composed, with a greater degree of formality in the architecture than in the landscape (and greater elaboration inside than outside), it is all in the eighteenth-century Anglo-Palladian country house manner. The house is only an element in the total landscape and the landscape is like a great open meadow.

The English Palladian, William Kent, was the first to do that. As Horace Walpole (1717-1797) has said: "Kent was the first to leap the fence and see that all nature is a garden." This revolutionized both the relation of house to landscape and the landscape itself: baroque and geometrical elaborations – parterre gardens and cascades of water (as Shutze used at the Swan House) were no longer

ABOVE: Dining Room. This room has been arranged and decorated in this way since 1949. OPPOSITE: Dining Room detail. H. J. Millard carved this chimneypiece, as well as all other such features throughout the house, based on Philip Shutze's designs.

used. The Julian Hightower House is a mid-twentieth century example of that school of design.

In the late 1940's when the Hightowers had Shutze do this house, its supreme quality of neoclassicism may well have been unique at that time in the United States. It certainly was the only one in Georgia. It was, in a manner of speaking, an anachronism, for the country house era was supposedly over, and classicism and academic eclecticism was theoretically dead (even despised in some circles). Client and architect achieved an ideal architectural form of the kind that Geoffrey Scott championed in *The Architecture of Humanism* (1914).

Mrs. Hightower has said that the site was selected about 1940 and plans laid to build, but the war intervened. The Tuscan portico nestles in its background of trees as though it were a classical garden pavilion in the distance on a great mid-eighteenth-century estate such as Stowe. It is a serene and neat setting of the kind that Kent (and later Capability Brown and Humphrey Repton) devised with great artifice, moving heaven and earth to make the landscape seem picture-perfect. Walpole said:

"An open country is but a canvas on which a landscape might be designed. Any tract of land whose characteristic expressions have been strengthened by art and which the spontaneous arrangements of nature have improved by the hand of taste, ought to be considered a garden." That is the kind of total garden one finds under the Georgia sun at the Hightower House.

Inside, formality and Kentian classicism prevail, which is in keeping with the Georgian revival exterior. (On the terrace façade, for example, Shutze used a Palladian, or Venetian, window, in the manner of Kent, above a one-story classical porch.) Shutze once explained how interior and exterior details were handled. He said: "We made models and castings of all detailing; then we found the artisans to execute our designs." The wood-

TOP: View from Stairlanding through Palladian window. ABOVE: Music Room. This was originally an open porch. Philip Shutze and his assistant, James Means, enclosed it for the Hightowers in 1962. ABOVE RIGHT: Drawing Room. Mrs. Hightower called on the late Charles Townsend of W. E. Browne Decorating Company, Inc. to help her, and since his death, David Richmond Byers III.

carver, Herbert J. Millard, a native of Bath, England (who was brought to Atlanta from Cincinnati, Ohio, to do the woodcarving at the Swan House) worked on almost every structure Shutze designed, including the Hightower House. Here Mr. Millard did the doorway entablatures and chimneypieces. The chimneypiece in the dining room is especially outstanding; a marble one at Houghton Hall, Norfolk, England, by William Kent, was the precedent for Shutze's design.

It was Kent who first provided the kind of professional service Mr. Shutze performed for the Hightowers, designing the inside and outside as a harmonious unit. Also, as with Kent's Houghton Hall, the Hightower House has large formal rooms that are always

ready for company; their chief function is the formal display of works of art and fine furniture, especially chosen to compliment the architecture.

As Mark Girouard has written in his *Life in the English Country House* (1979): "The architects and builders of country houses were . . . producing buildings designed to fit the particular way of life of the landed gentry." Members of the Hightower family have long been the textile magnates of Thomaston. They have played the role in Upson County of the English gentry and this reflects that role. Moreover, as Girouard has written, "A classical portico could be more than a symbol of its owner's culture and education. It could also symbolize his place in the social order."

That is what the great classical country houses of the South had always done; they had stood for the established order, the timeless, ancestral and civilized values dating back to Greece and Rome, to the Mother Country of England and the Mother Colony and State of Virginia. This house, built only a few years after World War II – in the first years of the Atomic Age – is in that tradition. It shows that, despite monumental changes, Georgians had not lost their sense of the old order, of hierarchy and civilization; and that Georgians in 1948 still believed in the eternal verities as expressed in the classic French saying: "Plus ça change, plus c'est la même chose." (The more things change, the more they remain the same.)

Home of Mr. & Mrs. Thomas E. Martin, Jr.

1965   James Means (1904–1979), *Architect*

Atlanta, Fulton County

James Means was possibly the last living architect trained in the 18th century manner, before the schooling of architects became institutionalized and codified. He learned as Christopher Wren's generation did – from apprenticeship to master designers and from the original books. All designs by James Means were purely Means, but have fooled experts who guessed them to be genuine 18th-century buildings.

The Houses of James Means
Mrs. John Ray Efird, Editor, 1979

PEGGY SHEFFIELD (MARTIN) rode horseback over these fields and meadows when she was growing up in northwest Atlanta, before suburbia extended endlessly. She often crossed this Nancy Creek bridge near the northern end of "Broadlands," the Hugh Richardson's great Buckhead estate (which covered numerous acres from West Paces Ferry Road along Northside Drive to Broadlands Road). After her marriage to Thomas E. Martin, Jr., she and her husband created – on her former riding turf – one of the most serenely handsome and beautifully sited of all of the houses by James Means: an evocation, inside and out, of the James River plantations of Tidewater Virginia. (Both had graduated from Virginia colleges and Thomas Martin served as a national president of the University of Virginia Alumni Association.)

To say that the Martins' place is one of the finest that Means helped to create is truly saying something, as a glance through the book about his works would show. There were about 50 houses, each of them a handcrafted masterpiece that was not only eighteenth century in style and detail but eighteenth century in spirit as well. The domestic scale and classical proportions that Means learned during his apprenticeship – first with Neel Reid and then with Philip Shutze – was matched by the scholarly knowledge of period ornamentation and down-to-earth craft skills he also learned. He was one of the first to work for the firm of Hentz, Reid, and Adler; and then one of the last – helping Philip Shutze until the firm went out of business in 1950.

Jimmy Means' career is unique for his day. He went to work for Neel Reid as an office boy in 1917 when he was only fourteen. At first he worked part-time, and then he went to the office more and more to learn, in time becoming the firm's best draftsman and assistant. Upon graduation from high school, he enrolled in architecture at Georgia Tech but soon was back full-time (by choice) at Neel Reid's side, learning from a master of the old school. During those years Means began to work with Philip Shutze who was also interning with the firm but, unlike Means, was following an academic course. When Shutze settled into the firm to stay, Means and Shutze worked together daily until Shutze retired and closed the business. It had been a large office, with many talented men. The well-known Atlanta modernist, John Portman, worked there for a time, as did many others who later made names for themselves. Jimmy Means was not the least of these. He was never a registered architect, but he produced the best homes built in Georgia in his day.

The Thomas E. Martin House was one of his largest private commissions. (His largest was for the Georgia Stone Mountain Authority: finding, moving and reassembling 17 buildings from around the state to create a facsimile plantation complex as part of the Stone Mountain Park.) Means was well known for his love of

OPPOSITE: Entrance façade. The house faces east towards Northside Drive and is a considerable distance from Fairfield Road, with acres of pasture between the front door and Northside Drive. It is a country house in a suburban setting. ABOVE: Nancy Creek looking at south elevation. This bridge was built in the 1930's on the northern edge of the Broadland's estate, which starts at West Paces Ferry Road and runs north to Broadlands and Fairfield roads.

TOP: Drawing Room. Mrs. Martin and David Richmond Byers III of W.E. Browne Decorating Company, Inc. have collaborated in decorating the house to complement the American-Georgian architectural style. The pair of Hong paintings, next to the Irish Georgian secretary desk, is especially fine. The rug is Oushak. Above the fireplace is an oil portrait of an eighteenth-century Martin family not unlike the Thomas E. Martin family of this century and this house. ABOVE: Master Bedroom. James Means designed interior shutters throughout the house. Appropriate accessories match the subtlety of Means's scholarly architectural taste.

The Stairhall is designed in the spacious James River plantation tradition. Mrs. Martin has said that this was James Mean's favorite room in the house.

old houses and authentic, old building materials. He used salvaged materials in his own work (but only if the old house or building from which the materials came was past saving, or past using in toto as part of one of his own compositions.) He knew the craftsmen and contractors who could do what he wanted, but there were few of them left.

When Jimmy Means died, it was the end of an era. He had worked alone since 1954 (he and Edward Vason Jones, another Georgia classicist, had worked together for four years). No one working in Georgia had his unique lifetime knowledge of the classic architectural tradition that he had learned directly from Reid and Shutze and had kept alive in his own work. As his daughter, Mary Catherine Means (a noted preservationist with the

National Trust) has written: "James Means continued to produce uniquely elegant classical homes until quite recently, yet he was relatively unknown beyond his circle of clients and staunch admirers. As more scholarly attention is paid to the undercurrent of classicism in twentieth-century architecture, James Means may yet achieve national recognition."

One of his staunchest admirers and most faithful clients was Peggy Sheffield Martin who, from horseback, first saw this site where she and Thomas Martin had Means build their Tidewater Virginia house. "Purely Means," but one almost has to rub his eyes. Is that Carter's Grove or Westover across that meadow? No, it is the subtle melding of the two in the architectural alchemy of James Means.

RIGHT: Dining Room looking into the central hallway; the tall, lacquered clock stands near the front door. The Martins found this eighteenth-century southern dining table of mahogany near Aiken, South Carolina. The William and Mary chairs are exceptional as is the Queen Anne English mirror. The chinoiserie wallpaper was painted for this room. Through the uncurtained, shuttered windows is a glimpse of the meadowland setting of this early-American revival house (to rival anything actually built in the period from which it was derived.) TOP: Sitting Room, looking through central hallway to the Library. The child's chair next to the hearth was made on Mr. Martin's great-great grandfather's plantation near Eatonton, Georgia. (It is made of Persimmon wood.) Mr. Martin once said about his home: "A joy to research, design, build, and live in . . . " ABOVE: Boxwood Garden, enclosed with a Jeffersonian serpentine wall. Souvenir bricks from Virginia plantation houses are inserted in the end wall of the wing facing the garden. Some of the Virginia bricks were collected for that purpose during Mr. Martin's tenure as National President of the University of Virginia Alumni Association.)

Twentieth Century
1967–1983

IN THE LAST 16 of the 250 years covered by this book, the first home to appear is not a "house" but an apartment in a 26-story Atlanta tower built in the late 1960's. The tower is now made up of condominiums but the owner of this home-in-the-sky was the first she occupied it.

Home for many people throughout Georgia (but especially in the capital city of Atlanta) is an apartment or a condominium, and the single-family suburban house is no longer the absolute ideal for people of any age group

resident when it was built as the first "luxury highrise" on Atlanta's Peachtree Road. In 1967 she was the first to sign a lease on one of the units in the building as it was being constructed. Then she and her long-time interior decorator made her apartment – from the concrete walls out – into exactly what she wanted. It was an empty shell when they began and, today, a dozen years later, her home is almost exactly as it was the day

or economic bracket. Of course, not everyone lives near the top of a 26-story luxury highrise – with a doorman – but such "machines for living in," as the French called them after World War I, are a part of an era that cannot be overlooked. Because of its obvious beauty and its spectacular view of the modern Atlanta skyline, this was chosen as a representative apartment/condominium. The collection of European paintings alone is exceptional, but the entire design – now more than a decade old – is still quite fresh and exemplifies a style of decor that has characterized the ambience in which fashionable people have lived in major cities in much of the twentieth century. A glass-topped cocktail/coffee table is the symbol of it all.

Following this chic condominium is Georgia's large new Governor's Mansion (called the State Executive Center) on Atlanta's millionaires' row of West Paces Ferry Road. No book on the landmark homes of Georgia could exclude the current home of the state's governmental executive and his wife. (Georgia has not yet had a lady governor.) Next, somewhat out of chronological sequence, we have included a glimpse of the Plains, Georgia, home of a governor who, needless to say, became a U.S. President. His home is the kind of dwelling that many people in the twentieth century have built and which is usually called "ranch style." It is a good example of that characteristically American one-story brick house. Following Jimmy and Rosalynn Carter's house at Plains is the St. Simons Island home of a well-known collector of early Georgia-made furniture of the late eighteenth and early nineteenth centuries – the furniture of the first settlers of the Georgia Piedmont. Then, in contrast, there is a highly formal house in southwest Georgia, the main façade of which started life as part of the front of the million-dollar Howard Theater in Atlanta. The theater was designed in 1920 by Philip Shutze and, in the late 1960's, the center five segments of the top story were adapted to make a pavilion-like home on a suburban street in Moultrie. The architect who made that successful and decidely unusual adaptation was Frank McCall of Moultrie. McCall's weekend home at Sea Island follows the converted Shutze façade. It is a two-story house covered with stucco and reminiscent of early nineteenth-century townhouses in New Orleans. After Frank McCall's two works comes the next to the last house in this section of the book. Completed in 1980 on a beautiful Chattahoochee River site in the northern suburbs of Columbus, Georgia, it is the handsomely appointed new home of a public-spirited couple. Their home embodies characteristics of traditional Georgia houses but with a contemporary flair (especially in the great room overlooking the river). The last house in this section was completed on Sea Island in the summer of 1982 as the eventual permanent home of an Atlanta couple whose family has grown and married. Their house seems to prefigure new architectural and decorating directions and is a clearcut example of Post-Modern-

ism. It was designed by Ed Cheshire, AIA, of St. Simons Island, a Harvard-educated Georgian who is keeping up with the Joneses in American architecture, if not going them one better.

And on that positive note this section of 250 years of landmark homes will end. In this series from 1967 to 1983, the houses are of our own era, there will be less text than was needed for older houses. The photographs, therefore, will do more of the "talking" so that one can focus on the visual qualities of these landmarks from 1967 to 1983.

Dr. Kenneth Coleman ended his *Georgia History in Outline* (1978 edition) with this statement: "Georgia's material environment has changed more than her people. There is an innate conservatism often balanced by liberal change." And he goes on to say that people disagree as to what is "progress" and what is "change." From what we have seen up to 1967 we would agree that the people of Georgia have been conservative, and it has been reflected and expressed in the character of their homes. This continues in these last 15 years. The state's domestic architecture has almost always expressed changes in the material environment with a conservative aesthetic. This has continued. Georgia's architectural conservatism has been a conscious conservatism with a bias for classical architectural values, symbolized by symmetrically placed entrances and porticos – even on assymetrical and picturesque Victorian houses: the Hay House in Macon for example, and the Lapham-Patterson House in Thomasville. This bias for symmetry will be seen in the Norman White House by Ed Cheshire which ends the houses in this section.

This conservatism has been expressed in recent years with the conservation of historical architecture throughout the state. The concluding section of the book (beginning on page 262), therefore, will be on the accomplishments in the preservation of individual Georgia houses (public and private) of whole neighborhoods, many of which have been declared historic districts. To encourage the continued preservation of the houses we have shown and discussed throughout this section (some of which are restorations or renovations) has been one of the main reasons for this 250th anniversary book. Fifty years from now in 2033 (the 300th anniversary) perhaps a book such as this will need to be twice as long to cover the old landmarks, newly restored and preserved, and the new landmarks of the last years of the twentieth century and the first years of the twenty-first.

Plaza Towers Apartment
of Mrs. Robert R. Snodgrass

c. 1967

David Richmond Byers III, *Interior Architect*

Atlanta, Fulton County

It could be argued that the very stylelessness of many modern apartment buildings is an asset, as a blank canvas is an asset to a painter. It is to the obvious credit of the decorators that they have created such elegance or casual pleasantness in spite of the spaces they have had to work with.

Russell Lynes
"Enter the Decorator"
The Finest Rooms, 1964

AS THIS SKYSCRAPER apartment building was being constructed, Mrs. Robert Snodgrass and David Byers of Atlanta's W.E. Browne Decorating Company were planning her apartment. It was not the first time they had conferred on such matters. David Byers had helped Mrs. Snodgrass with other apartments, but it was to be the first in a modern highrise building. The twin towers of these 26-story luxury apartments were the first to be built so high in residential Buckhead. Mrs. Snodgrass had been a longtime apartment dweller; she liked the idea of being near the top of a building; and this is her "cliff" overlooking downtown Atlanta.

She had been an art collector for most of her life and needed the assistance of David Byers in designing a setting that suited her and her things. Her "pictures" (as they would be called in England) are a treasure that needed suitable surroundings. Because each unit of the tower was essentially just alike – a blank canvas – client and decorator felt fortunate to get an apartment before construction was completed so that her one-bedroom unit could be finished according to their specifications.

One writer has said that the architecture of such buildings reflects the standardization of the mid-twentieth century. But Mrs. Snodgrass's taste is anything but standardized. So, with the help of a contractor friend and one skilled carpenter, Mrs. Snodgrass and David Byers went to work to set a Louis XV scene for her eighteenth-century French furniture and nineteenth-century French paintings. They made a comfortable and stylish home-in-the-sky scaled to Mrs. Snodgrass's petite person and exquisite taste; a suitable environment for her possessions, complementing and enhancing their museum quality. As Russell Lynes, author of *The Taste-makers* and of a series of eagerly read essays in *Architectural Digest,* has written: "A home is meant to reflect the personality of its inhabitants. The room is most successful as an example of the decorator's art that seems least contrived by its contriver, that most amiably and handsomely reflects the image of its owner and that at the same time seems to have happened spontaneously." Lynes goes on to say, "It is the function of the decorator to vanish."

Thus far in *Landmark Homes of Georgia* the interior decorator, as such, may not have vanished altogether, but he has not been featured as have architects. However, those who know David Richmond Byers III, originally of Baltimore, Maryland, know that he may design woodwork but doesn't just disappear into it – at least not in the personal sense. The interior decorating field has traditionally been dominated by lively personalities and David Byers is possessed of one himself. The decorating business, as we know it today, was conceived in this century by a noted "personality" and titled taste-maker named Elsie de Wolfe – Lady Mendl. David Byers has done well in this highly competitive business, how-

Terrace overlooking Atlanta and Peachtree Road. Mrs. Snodgrass has been a "cliff-dweller" for many years.

ABOVE: Sitting Room looking into mirrored Dining Room. Over fruitwood chest (Louis XV, Rouen type) is Mrs. Snodgrass's Chagal. The Louis XV moldings and doors were designed by David Richmond Byers III, who helped the owner convert the empty shell of the apartment. RIGHT: Dining Room. The mirrored left wall magically increases the size of the room and doubles the decorative impact of the carefully chosen and arranged items.

ever, not because he does or does not vanish, but because he has the distinct advantage of knowing his "Torus from his Scotia," an expression he uses to mean that designers like himself ought to know and be able to use the classical language of architecture (a universal language which interior decorating continued to speak even when contemporary architecture did not). He had a talented mentor when he started in the field: the respected Charles Bennett Townsend of the W.E. Browne Decorating Company. David went to work there in 1946, thirty-six years ago; he went for a summer, after graduating from the University of Virginia's School of Architecture, and remained, as he has said, "to pay taxes in Atlanta." He is now decorating for a third generation of clients and "goes where he is invited" in Georgia and elsewhere.

David Byers has worked in several houses already shown in *Landmark Homes* but no identifiable personal style has been noted. (In that sense, the proper vanishing act was achieved.) Mr. Byers has been invited to help decorate some nice places in this state; therefore it is inevitable that some of them would appear here – just as several of Philip Shutze's designs have been included. The Georgia Governor's Mansion, which is the next house in this series, is one of those places; David Byers was the consultant decorator for the Fine Arts Committee in charge of that work. (He has also worked with similar committees in Washington, D.C., at the White House and the U.S. Diplomatic Reception Rooms.)

ABOVE: Music Room/Library. Two Utrillo paintings over a banquette covered in tobacco-leaf chintz. The chest is Austrian in the Louis XVI/Directoire style with Haitian paintings by the artist Botello above. (The color of this room is "headache yellow" – according to the owner and decorator.) RIGHT: Sitting Room. The collection of original oil paintings throughout the apartment is of museum quality. Over the sofa is a Vuillard, 1892. Edouard Vuillard (1868-1940) was a French painter of the "Nabis" school, a group of artists devoted to home life, including the making of paintings of intimate interiors filled with domestic detail and exquisite patterns. The way this room was decorated complements the painting and is, in spirit, similar to the ideals of the "Nabis."

Mrs. Snodgrass's apartment was done at about the same time as the new Governor's Mansion. Russell Lynes's criterion that the personal stamp of a decorator should not be apparent – except in high standards of quality – is demonstrated when the two places are compared. In comparison to Mrs. Snodgrass's apartment, the Governor's Mansion (pages 232-235) was a decidely different problem to help solve: less personal, more public, more formal, and, for a lack of a better word, more "historic." It was also more in the category of what people ordinarily think of as a landmark. But Mrs. Snodgrass's home-in-the-sky has at least four landmark aspects itself: first, such a "home," as opposed to a house, would have been nearly impossible until the development of elevators and steel-cage construction; second, it was the very first unit in those still highly desirable skyscraper apartments (themselves a first in the well-to-do Buckhead neighborhood); third, it is a characteristic kind of habitation in an era of mobility, and it can stand for all such apartment/condominium homes created for the more urban way of life of twentieth-century Georgia; and fourth, it has a quality and distinction that few places of its kind achieve. Its stylishness has lasted so well that the apartment (now officially a condominium) is as it was when she moved into it.

Governor's Mansion
1966-1968

Atlanta, Fulton County

"It's a question of quality and taste, not money!"

Mrs. Albert Thornton,
Chairman of Furniture and Furnishings,
Georgia Fine Arts Committee; quoted in
"New Governor's Mansion" by Andrew Sparks
Atlanta Journal-Constitution Magazine, March 3, 1968

W E HAVE SEEN the old Governor's Mansion of
1838 at Milledgeville (pages 74-77), a classical
revival house of exceptional quality; one writer judged
it to be an "acknowledged masterpiece." It served the
purpose for which it was built until 1868, and was the
home of eight governors. (Now restored and open to
the public, it is again the property of the state.) Neo-
Palladian in architectural character, it was part of the

ABOVE: 391 West Paces Ferry Road N.W. The Mansion faces
south. The first floor has state rooms designed for formal recep-
tions and other official gatherings; the second floor is the Governor's residence and the ground floor has a large reception hall and
dining room, a kitchen, a laundry and other service areas. The
Mansion is open to the public during the week; large groups
require reservations. The estate consists of 18 acres. RIGHT: State
Reception Hall with Circular Stairhall seen through flanking
Ionic columns; the State Dining Room is to the right. In the
stairhall a rare French porcelain vase, c. 1810, with a medallion
portrait of Benjamin Franklin sits on a marble top pier table
attributed to Charles-Honoré Lannuier. These are characteristic of
the valuable and interesting objects gathered to furnish the Mansion. Placed on a marbleized pedestals in niches at either side of
the entrance into the State Dining Room are bronze busts
stamped "Houdon 1778" identifying them as the work of the
noted French sculptor, Jean Antoine Houdon.

ABOVE: State Drawing Room (with Family Drawing Room in background). This room measures 40' × 25'. The furnishings are American-made pieces of the Federal period, 1790-1825, among them two mahogany sofas attributed to the workshop of Duncan Phyfe, the New York cabinetmaker. On the wall are two American-made "Bulls Eye" gilt mirrors, topped with Federal eagles. The Aubusson tapestry-weave carpet was made in France in the early nineteenth century. David Richmond Byers III of W. E. Browne Decorating Company, was the consultant for interior decoration. OPPOSITE: Sunken Garden, west side of Mansion, with Italian marble figures of the Four Seasons. This and the terraces are part of the old Robert Foster Maddox estate, Woodhaven. This terraced garden was "the first formal garden of any pretentions in Atlanta," according to the *Garden History of Georgia* (1933). Much of the old planting on the site remains and many of the trees are quite ancient because the Robert F. Maddoxes retained them when they developed the property before World War I. Edward L. Daugherty, ASLA, of Atlanta, was the consultant for landscape architecture.

Jeffersonian classical revival. Jefferson believed that the early American republic should express its aspirations with architecture reminiscent of the buildings of the ancient civilizations of Greece and Rome. Classical architecture was the official style of the early American republic, and the old Georgia Governor's Mansion was a monument of that revival when it was still more Roman than Greek; still Jeffersonian and Neo-Palladian.

With that precedent in mind, no one was surprised in 1966 when the State of Georgia decided to build a new classical revival house for governors. But many people were delighted that the executive mansion at 205 The Prado in Ansley Park would be replaced. Built in 1910, a large granite bungalow vaguely Prairie School in style, it was considered ugly, but it had been the home of eleven governors before it was retired and demolished. (House Resolution 235-694, authorizing the new Governor's Mansion, described the one in Ansley Park in these somber words: "cold, gray, austere and medieval.")

The site of the new mansion on West Paces Ferry Road was a 75-acre estate belonging to Robert Foster Maddox. (Eighteen acres would be purchased.) The site was suggested by a special Governor's Mansion Committee of the Georgia General Assembly. This committee also suggested that the style of the new mansion should be "in keeping with Georgia's Southern heritage." An Atlanta architectural firm, A. Thomas Bradbury & Associates, was chosen to design the building, and P.D. Christian Company was the contractor. Construction was begun in 1966 and the house was dedicated in January 1968.

Thirty fluted columns in the Doric order surround the rectangular body of the house supporting an unornamented wooden cornice. These columns, made of California redwood, rest on a porch floor paved with St. Joe brick laid in a herringbone pattern; there is no balustrade. The columns measure 24 feet in height. The

front entrance is based on an Asher Benjamin design of the 1830's. In overall form, the house is more like the vernacular classical revival of the Delta country of the Gulf Coast than it is the classical revival of Georgia; the unusually large scale contributes to that quality. It is one of the largest houses ever built in the South in the columned mode; of course, a large mansion was what was intended.

Decisions about gardens, grounds, and furnishings were made by a Fine Arts Committee of Georgia citizens. General Chairman was Henry D. Green assisted by Mrs. Carl Sanders (wife of Governor Carl E. Sanders, Governor of Georgia from 1963 to 1967). Governor Sanders appointed the committee in July 1966. The first governor to occupy the new mansion was Lester G. Maddox, Governor from 1967 to 1971. (He was not related to Robert Foster Maddox whose estate occupied the site from 1911 until 1967).

The Fine Arts Committee assembled an outstanding and nationally recognized collection of early nineteenth-century antiques and art objects. For the most part, these antiques were American-made and in the Federal style (circa 1825 seems to have been the cut-off date for what was chosen). It was felt that this furniture style was compatible with the architecture of the building. In fact, much of the collection is somewhat earlier than the kind of furnishings that were typical of Greek

Revival houses in Georgia, especially those outside of Savannah, but the style of the house is not exactly in keeping with the vernacular precedents of Georgia anyway. The results are more than creditable and the building's formal beauty and dignity is a source of pride for Georgians. Many people think of this mansion as the actual home of Georgia's governors since the antebellum period; the whole ensemble effectively speaks the symbolic language of classical architecture – to which people seem to respond instinctively.

The architects, the Fine Arts Committee, and everyone concerned with the project achieved their goal, which was to build a fine new Governor's Mansion which would be "in keeping with Georgia's Southern heritage." Two-million dollars was the cost of 24,000 square feet on an 18-acre estate. From the vantage point of 1982/83, that seems economical for a place of this scale, which must function as a family residence and as a mansion for state occasions.

(As this is written, Governor and Mrs. George Dekle Busbee and their family occupy the mansion. When George Busbee came into office, the term was four years. He was inaugurated in 1975 but a constitutional amendment adopted in 1976 allowed him to succeed himself, and he was easily reelected to a second term in 1978. Governor Busbee's term will expire in 1983 during the 250th anniversary year.)

Home of President and Mrs. Jimmy Carter
1961
Plains, Sumter County

The first words of Governor Jimmy Carter's inaugural address on January 12, 1971, were: "It is a long way from Plains to Atlanta." But in five years he would travel a much greater distance – from Plains to the White House.

James F. Cook
Governors of Georgia, 1979

ON NOVEMBER 15, 1976, Jimmy Carter became the first man from the Deep South to be elected President of the United States since 1849. *Time* magazine described the reaction in the Carters' hometown: "For Plains, Georgia, a normally placid farming community of 683 citizens, there would never be another day like this one: Election Day, 1976 – family reunion and carnival and the world's front page all rolled into one."

The Plains of Dura, a biblical reference, was the first name of the settlement. In 1885 the town moved to the site of the newly built railroad and the name was shortened to Plains. Jimmy Carter's family came to the area in 1904.

This was the hometown residence of Jimmy and Rosalynn Carter during both his terms as Governor and as President and is still the Carter's permanent address. The comfortable, one-story home is similar in style to a great many American houses built since the 1950's. As the Plains White House and the home to which one of the world's most famous couples has returned, it is one of Georgia's important landmarks.

LIVING WITH EARLY GEORGIA FURNITURE AND OTHER EARLY AMERICANA
The Home of Mr. and Mrs. Henry D. Green
1970

St. Simons Island, Glynn County

My first interest in antique furniture began in 1936 when I moved to Athens and was privileged to live in the home of a collector of Georgia-made pieces. There began my first experience of "Living with Antiques."

Henry D. Green, *Furniture of the Georgia Piedmond Before 1830,* Exhibition Catalogue, High Museum of Art, 1976.

ABOVE: Mr. Green was his own architect; he designed the house around his and his wife's roles as grandparents and collectors of early Americana. BELOW: Sitting Room. The chimneypiece was made in Athens, Georgia about 1800. the woodwork was designed by Mr. Green to complement the old chimneypiece. The old tiles are Dutch delft. The mantleshelf garniture is oriental export, c. 1775. The pair of candlesticks on the mantleshelf is Bow, c. 1760. The brass fireplace equipment is American from about the same time as the chimneyplace. The two small tables are New England, c. 1810. And the overmantel painting is by William Trost Richards, signed and dated 1870.

THE HENRY GREENS are Georgia natives. Mrs. Green (Frances Yates) was born in Atlanta; Mr. Green was born in Camilla, Mitchell County, and moved to Atlanta when he was eleven. He graduated from Georgia Tech in Civil Engineering, married, went into the road-building business, reared a family, and retired to St. Simons Island on the coast of Georgia near Brunswick. He was his own architect for the home they built to suit their roles as grandparents and as leading collectors of antiques, especially those of the Georgia Piedmont plateau before 1820 or '30.

The name Henry Green is synonymous with the concept of collecting and studying antique furniture made during the early years of the settlement of the Georgia upcountry. Mr. Green is the very first to acknowledge that he learned much from several people when he started out collecting; among them Mrs. Charles Brightwell, Henry Eugene Thomas, and Jake Bernstein — all of Athens, Georgia. Mrs. Brightwell had Georgia-made pieces and Mr. Green lived in her house for awhile when he worked in Athens in the late 1930's. Henry Eugene Thomas was a superb furniture craftsman who loved antiques and especially those that he could find locally; he sold some of them in his shop, which was an early source of Mr. Green's collection. Jake Bernstein had a large furniture store in Athens but his first love was fine old furniture, which he stored in a warehouse. He opened his warehouse only to serious collectors and sometimes sold them something if he liked their attitude. Bernstein and Henry Thomas sometimes sold to outstanding dealers from New York City, among them Joe Kindig and Israel Sack.

Georgia-made sideboards often ended up in the North with their origins overlooked. The dealers knew that they had to sell them as being from someplace that

ABOVE: Sitting Room. The portrait of the lady in blue is English, attributed to Sir Peter Lely, c. 1670. The sofa is by Duncan Phyfe. The tea table is Philadelphia, c. 1725; the secretary desk is New England, c. 1820. The pair of chairs are two of Mr. Green's prize early-Georgia pieces; c. 1780-1800; the wood is Black Cherry although at one time before wood analysis was common, "applewood" was the generic name everyone used for any native wood they couldn't identify. Note carved tassels in the splats of this pair of chairs which demonstrate the simple beauty of Georgia piedmont furniture. OPPOSITE: Master Bedroom. The four-post bed is from Athens, Georgia, c. 1825, mahogany. The desk-and-bookcase is from Wilkes County, 1780-1800, walnut, with southern yellow pine secondary wood. Mr. Green has owned this exceptional Georgia-made piece for over 30 years. Over the Charleston-made, Thomas Elfe, mahogany chest of drawers (c. 1765) is an American mirror, c. 1815. The "Martha Washington" chair is American and the tilt-top candlestand is Wilkes county, Georgia, both c. 1810.

people thought antiques came from. The Georgia antiques had regional characteristics, but there were few, if any, students of that specialty then – and none for Georgia, except some of the Georgians mentioned here. So it was natural and easy for northern dealers to attribute a piece of Wilkes County furniture to someplace in Virginia, or possibly to the Eastern Shore of Maryland, where southern antiques were supposed to have originated. Mr. Green says that Mr. Maxim Karolik once asked him increduously, "You have antiques in Georgia?" As a matter of fact, Henry Green knew that we didn't, in a manner of speaking, because many of the best things had been shipped to the North. He knew, too, that Georgia-made objects which remained in the state were rarely identified as having originated here.

Furthermore, very little was known about the general subject of Southern furniture. The first Williamsburg Antiques Forums of the late 1940's and early 50's began to try to sort things out. The first exhibition ever made of Southern-made furniture was at the Virginia Museum of Fine Arts in 1952. Colonial Williamsburg, Inc., *The Magazine Antiques,* and the Virginia Museum sponsored the exhibit. Henry Green was responsible for the selection of Georgia pieces. Miss Alice Winchester,

who was the editor of *Antiques* in those years, encouraged Mr. Green and came to Georgia to see what he had found. She has written: "It was Henry Green who introduced me to the early furniture of the Georgia Piedmont. Serving as consultant for the 1952 exhibition, he gave me an eye-opening tour of the Piedmont, visiting old towns and old houses. He taught me to see the features . . . that distinguish the furniture, and to appreciate the history and character of the region that produced it." That is the very real contribution that Henry Green has made: a scholarly understanding of the aesthetics and craftsmanship of Georgia-made furniture and of the history and culture of the early settlers who owned it. The Gilbert-Alexander House (pages 46-49) in Wilkes County is a landmark example of one of the rare houses in the Georgia upcountry that has retained some of its original furniture.

After many years of study and collecting, Henry Green organized an exhibition at the High Museum of Art in Atlanta during the American Bicentennial. The title of the exhibit, as mentioned in the quotation at the front of this account, was "The Furniture of the Georgia Piedmont Before 1830." (Two Atlantans helped him a great deal: Mrs. Katherine Gross Farnham and Mrs.

Callie Huger Efird.) The published catalogue of that exhibition is itself a collector's item, containing a lifetime of information on a beautiful and interesting part of early Georgia culture. Without Henry Green, it might possibly have gone unresearched and unheralded.

These photographs, therefore, show some of the favorite things of a uniquely well-informed Georgia collector of early Americana, who has learned as much as

he possibly could about the antique furnishings he and his wife have lived with and used, especially those of his native state of Georgia. Henry Green's home is a landmark because of the collection it houses and because the collector has shared with the world a unique and expert knowledge of the furniture of the Georgia Piedmont before 1830; the very phrase is Henry Green's.

ATLANTA THEATER FAÇADE ADAPTED
Home of Robert B. Wright, Jr.

1962   W. Frank McCall, Jr.; Adaptation, *Architect*

1920   Philip Trammell Shutze; Theater, *Architect*

Moultrie, Colquitt County

The Howard Theater may be the only American instance of a building clearly based on Palladio's Palazzo Chiericati at Vicenza. It has been dismantled in its original setting, but a portion used in the most ingenious and sympathetic way possible. Robert B. Wright, Jr., and his architect, W. Frank McCall, made the center five bays of the top story of the theater into the façade of his house in Moultrie, Georgia. What was in its original state a full palazzo is now a very tidy pavilion; our Italian Palladian theater now has the quality of an eighteenth-century English adaptation.

H. Stafford Bryant, Jr.
Classical America, 1972
Volume 1, Number 2.

ROBERT B. WRIGHT, JR. is often known as Brother Wright. He is a large-scaled gentleman and this house is in proportion with his full height. It had long been his intention to build a "classical house." He had collected furniture and other decorative items for many years, towards the eventual building of a home; some of the French furniture in the house today was purchased before 1960. That year he saw a newspaper article about the impending demolition of Atlanta's Paramount Theater, a cinema on Peachtree Street (where the new 55 story Georgia-Pacific tower is presently being constructed.) The Paramount was originally called the Howard. It was built for Troup Howard at a cost of one million dollars and was opened December 13, 1920. It had become a much-admired Atlanta landmark, especially in the days when Atlanta was much like a small town and people went "downtown to the movies." It was always considered quite exceptional, and Brother Wright had an idea about how to use the classical façade to an advantage.

The Atlanta firm of Hentz, Reid, and Adler was the original architect; the designer was Philip Shutze during the months that he worked in that office while he was still involved with his Italian studies (and before he was permanently attached to the firm). Shutze based his design on the Palazzo Chiericati by Andrea Palladio, a city palace of 1550 which fills one side of a plaza in Vicenza, Italy. Because it is a city palace it made a good prototype for a theater in an important Atlanta setting, at a kind of plaza formed by converging streets. Shutze's Italian essay at the site was to be torn down for a plain and uneventful high-rise insurance office.

But that is enough about the theater, it is Brother Wright's idea and how he carried it out that counts. Actually he went immediately to Atlanta on Monday after seeing the weekend newspaper story and bought the top story of the limestone front while he stood in the street talking to the demolition contractor. (The contractor said that he didn't want to have to tear it down.) They made a deal and Wright called his architect and life-long neighbor, Frank McCall, back in Moultrie to tell him what he had done, and Frank said carefully: "Fine, I think we can build with it what you want."

In the fall of 1960 all of the four-foot thick limestone was delivered to Moultrie on a caravan of a dozen flat-bed trucks: the entire facade of the theater, not just the needed portion. And, not only that, but the myriad pieces were unnumbered. That, however, was where Philip Shutze came back into the story; he still had a copy of the original blueprints and agreed to send Brother Wright a copy. Then Wright and Frank McCall went to work to adapt the center five segments of the top story as the façade of the "classical house" he had long meant to build. (Photographs taken before demolition also helped in sorting out the enormous puzzle.)

All of the pieces that they intended to use were fitted back together, with only an occasional difficult moment. It took over two years to do, from purchase of the limestone façade to completion. Paul Summerford and Son of Moultrie was the contractor; the project seemingly involved everyone in town and was the "town topic." Twenty Tallokas Road – an Indian name – had definitely become the major landmark of Moultrie, somewhat in the category of the great pyramid.

Everything architectural back of the entrance façade, of course, was conceived by Brother Wright and Frank McCall. Nothing from inside of the theater was used except the bronze door frames in the entrance hall. Otherwise all other ornamentation, the cabinetwork and the plasterwork, was especially designed for the new structure which they built to go with the five segments of the top story of the theater. (Brother Wright still has the rest of the large limestone pieces in a field somewhere in Colquitt County.)

Frank McCall was an ideal architect to help, for

OPPOSITE: The owner bought the mahogany front doors in Havana, Cuba, in 1958, planning even then to build a "classical house" to go with them; he was also collecting European decorative arts of various periods. When an Atlanta theater, built in 1920, was about to be demolished in 1960, he decided to buy part of its façade to use in composing this house. He continues to perfect the grounds; the fountain dates from the late 1970's.
ABOVE: Entrance Hall. The bronze door frames are from the Howard Theater. Frank McCall designed the ornaments on the doors and they were hand carved in Florence, Italy; he also designed plasterwork throughout the house and it was executed by Italian artisans. The Louis XV wall clock keeps perfect time. Mr. Wright's taste is eclectic and his collection is aimed at delighting the eye.

Drawing Room. The chimneypiece is Louis XVI, of aubergine marble, with bronze doré mounts.
The splendid rug is a Savonnaire ordered for the room in Madrid, Spain from the Royal Tapestry
Works. The chandelier is of the French Empire period. The picture over the sofa is an oil painting of
the school of Murillo (1617-1682), the Spanish painter of biblical subjects; this is The Birth of Christ.
Mr. Wright's Renoir is one of the most contemporary art objects in the room; it is a charcoal sketch of
Renoir's friend Monet. One of the theater door frames in bronze surrounds the door
into the dining room.

not only is he from Moultrie but he is one of the last of the eclectics of the kind that worked in the era when Philip Shutze designed the Howard Theater. McCall is well-known as a designer of fine houses who attends to all aspects of the work, including furnishings. ("The Hedges" his own holiday residence at Sea Island will follow next in this series of landmarks of our own era.)

The Brother Wright house was completed in 1962 but it has been paired with Frank McCall's Sea Island house of 1976. A long-time project, it was not until 1979, for example, that the fountain in the entrance court was placed where it had been destined; a young architect

in Frank McCall's office, John Hand, was the designer. They based it on a fountain of Philip Shutze's design at the Swan House (1926), which itself was based on one that Shutze sketched in Italy during his Rome Prize Days.

But that is eclecticism and classicism. Architects adapt classic, time-tested precedents, refining them and putting them to new uses. McCall's adaptation of Shutze's theater façade as a pavilion-sized town house is an excellent demonstration of this. The result is the "classical house," furnished with his growing collection of European decorative arts, that Brother Wright had set out to build.

Dining Room. This table setting with vermeil, and lace, and crystal, and with the Directoire candlesticks lighted, expresses the spirit of the decor throughout Brother Wright's classical house. The Directoire chandelier was bought in France for the house. This room was designed around the Louis XVI marquetry cabinet, a piece that he purchased before the house was designed.

THE HEDGES
Sea Island Residence of
W. Frank McCall, Jr., Architect
1976

Sea Island, Glynn County

McCall, an architect, actually has more than a dozen Sea island homes: twelve completed, three under construction, and five on the drawing board. And his architectural attention to proportion and detail makes these homes distinct. "Designing residences is still my first love," he confesses.

Georgia Journal, 1981
Volume 1, Number 4

THE REIGNING MASTER of domestic architecture in Georgia is W. Frank McCall, Jr. of Moultrie. This is the house he designed for himself at Sea Island to use on weekends and holidays. At the threshold is a "corner stone," a small block of Georgia marble engraved with the date July 4, 1976. This is the house a specialist in house architecture designed for himself in the American Bicentennial year; it is one of over a dozen houses that he has designed and supervised at Sea Island – Georgia's finest coastal resort, a family and residential retreat developed in the 1920's and 30's by Alfred William Jones. But throughout Georgia, Frank McCall's name is synonymous with well-designed houses to which he has given his personal supervision as construction proceeded.

Frank McCall does a great deal for other people, professionally and personally, and has received many awards for his public-spiritedness. Without a doubt he has helped to transform his home town, as a ride through Moultrie would demonstrate; it is a ship-shape town and McCall has been the captain of architecture. His annual Wonderful Welcome to Spring, an American Cancer Society benefit, has brought outstanding people in his field to Moultrie to speak, and has helped to raise the level of public awareness of architecture, the decorative arts, and aesthetics generally. Frank's influence in this handsome southwest Georgia town is apparent up and down every street. His own designs of course have led the way and Frank McCall, without too much hyperbole can be compared with those architects in Renaissance Italy whose influence brought the Renaissance to their own neighborhood. That is what he has done for Moultrie and much of the part of georgia which is on his regular "beat" – from the Moultrie area to Sea Island. (He has done beautiful work at Thomasville; one of his restoration commissions was the Hardy Bryan House, the headquarters of Thomasville Landmarks, Inc.)

McCall learned from other architects after he graduated from Auburn. He has done the same favor for younger architects himself. Because his office has continued to use the traditional-eclectic-historical approach to architecture, it has been a rare educational experience for architects who have come out of school not knowing the Doric from the Ionic order. Or, at least, not knowing how to design using the classical orders as the fundamental organizing principle of their architecture. A few years with Frank McCall has remedied that and many have gone off on their own, prepared to do houses in the McCall tradition; although, sometimes, the younger men have given their work a Post-Modern twist, as we shall see with the Norman White House at Sea

---

ABOVE LEFT: The Hedges derives its name from the thick hedges of oleander and myrtle protecting it from the street. Located in the center of the Island, near the northern end, it is designed more like a town house than a beach house because it is not on the ocean; but the sea is only a block or two away. Based on a London Regency house that was built on a mews, it was given a coastal Georgia flavor by the stucco, the coloring, and the vented cupola.

Entrance Hall and Staircase. The staircase is placed to the side to conserve space in the Charleston townhouse manner. The Chinese Chippendale design of the stairs is based on a staircase at Bohemia (1745) in Cecil County, Maryland. Frank McCall's eclecticism actually makes his designs "modern;" traditional precedents are combined in a modern house for comfortable present-day living. It is not an attempt to recreate any particular early house. Elements from many places are combined but related carefully in scale and proportion. The furnishings are also an eclectic assortment that the architect's informed taste has allowed him to combine in a fresh and contemporary manner. The stairs lead to the Drawing Room and the bedrooms on the second floor.

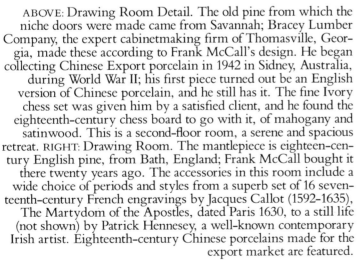

ABOVE: Drawing Room Detail. The old pine from which the niche doors were made came from Savannah; Bracey Lumber Company, the expert cabinetmaking firm of Thomasville, Georgia, made these according to Frank McCall's design. He began collecting Chinese Export porcelain in 1942 in Sidney, Australia, during World War II; his first piece turned out be an English version of Chinese porcelain, and he still has it. The fine Ivory chess set was given him by a satisfied client, and he found the eighteenth-century chess board to go with it, of mahogany and satinwood. This is a second-floor room, a serene and spacious retreat. RIGHT: Drawing Room. The mantlepiece is eighteen-century English pine, from Bath, England; Frank McCall bought it there twenty years ago. The accessories in this room include a wide choice of periods and styles from a superb set of 16 seventeenth-century French engravings by Jacques Callot (1592-1635), The Martydom of the Apostles, dated Paris 1630, to a still life (not shown) by Patrick Hennesey, a well-known contemporary Irish artist. Eighteenth-century Chinese porcelains made for the export market are featured.

Dining Room. The chintz fabric on the walls has a pagoda motif which has been repeated in the rest of the decoration of this centrally-located dining room. The shape of the cornice for the curtains was designed by the architect to echo the pagoda of the wall-covering. The rug is Chinese; the leather of the chairs reflects the blue in the chintz, in the rug, and in the porcelain. (Architecture and interior decorating are conceived and coordinated in this house to delight the eye and refresh the spirit during a holiday or weekend at the beach.)

Island (pages 258-261) designed by Ed Cheshire, originally of Moultrie and now of St. Simons. Cheshire worked with Frank for several summers while he was an architectural student at Georgia Tech and before he went off to Harvard for a post-graduate architectural degree.

We have just seen one of the notable houses Frank McCall helped to create – the Robert B. Wright, Jr. house at Moultrie; now we have the pleasure of being Frank's company at The Hedges, his own "cottage" at Sea Island; it is a key to his domestic architecture, and as we peer into his own place we can see why he is a master of traditional design.

In the tradition of Neel Reid, McCall usually designs the entire residence, from helping to select the site to choosing the fabrics for the chairs – which he has also helped select.

Select is the key word; the concept of selection, of taste and suitability; of choosing what is suitable from a wide selection of periods and precedents; of having "taste and information," as one of Georgia's leading interior decorators has phrased it. Frank McCall has

Garden Room. This is the "living room" of the house; it is a blending of many elements, many styles and periods for comfort and visual delight. It runs most of the length of the rear of the house and is perfectly designed for the main purpose of the house: holidays and weekends. (The formal living room is the Drawing Room on the second floor.)

brought traditionalism and academic eclecticism right into the last quarter of this century. He is well-grounded in the fundamentals of architecture: matters of proportion and scale, as well as in the ornamental styles to grace the structures he builds. And then he chooses what is suitable for the given situation; this is academic eclecticism and, ironically, it is modern – even though it is traditional.

His architectural degree comes from Auburn University in Alabama; and then he began a series of internships with excellent southern architectural firms, first working with Miller, Martin, and Lewis of Birmingham after graduation. Frank McCall had grown up in Moultrie where he decided to be an architect,

although he says, "I'd not met one." Residential architecture was always his first priority. In January 1946, after serving in the U.S. Army Corps of Engineers – designing airfields, hangers, and barracks – he came back to Georgia and joined the firm of W. Elliot Dunwody, Jr. in Macon. Dunwody (now retired) was one of the best of the Georgia traditionalists. McCall was with Dunwody for eleven years. In 1957 he returned to Moultrie to open his own office, an office that looks like an old shoe but turns out work that looks as though it came from the house pictured here – which in a very real sense it does.

Home of Dr. and Mrs. Clarence C. Butler

1980

Columbus, Muscogee County

Far from the hills of Habersham
Far from the valleys of Hall
....
...the lordly main from beyond the plain
Calls o'er the hills of Habersham
Calls through the valleys of Hall.

Sidney Lanier,
"Song of the Chattahoochee,"
1877

AS THE CHATTAHOOCHEE RIVER (the western boundary of Georgia since 1802) flows south from its origins in the north Georgia counties of Habersham and Hall – as it flows towards "the lordly main" of the Gulf of Mexico – it passes through a beautifully hilly

suburb, north of Columbus, called Green Island Hills.

On a fine elevated site above the river bank, the Clarence Butlers have built an exceptionally fine country house, just to suit the present needs of the two of them – their children are no longer at home. Spacious and

Entrance Hall looking into the River Room. This arch in the Temple-of-the Winds Corinthian order was designed by Neel Reid about 1920; it comes from an Atlanta house that had to be dismantled.

gracious, it is designed to fit the site as well as it fits the various facets of their lives. There are formal and informal spaces; indoor and outdoor living areas: a deck and a plunge; there is a large River Room overlooking the Chattahoochee River through tall sliding-glass doors with arched transoms: a great space comfortably furnished with antiques and modern sofas and chairs; and there is a jacuzzi in the master bathroom that takes so much

water to fill that Mrs. Butler could easily wish the Chattahoochee flowed right through the house á la Frank Lloyd Wright.

Mrs. Butler, however, knew exactly what she wanted to build; the Frank Lloyd Wright mode was not it. She sketched it out after they found the land, and it was going to be according to no one else but Sarah Turner (Weezy) Butler (whose life-long nickname must be used once in this account, so that people will know who it is).

Mrs. Butler had three experts help her with various problems: for architecture, Edward Warner Neal, AIA, Columbus; for landscape architecture, Julia Orme Martin, ASLA, Atlanta; and for interior decoration, David Richmond Byers III, Atlanta. With this fine team led by a client-captain who knew her goal, the splendid results were inevitable. Mrs. Butler could not have agreed with what the Dutchess of Marlborough said in 1732 about the designers helping her with Blenheim Palace: "I know of none that are not mad or ridiculous, and I really believe that anybody that has sense with the best workmen of all sorts could make a better house without an architect, than any has been built these many years. I know two gentlemen of this country who have great estates and who have built their houses without an architect, by able workmen that would do as they directed which no architect will, though you pay for it."

Almost all of the furniture and accessories in the house already belonged to the Butlers when they decided to build. They planned the house to suit their things and to fit their pattern of using them in everyday living. Part of the decor that they obtained especially for the new house – not furnishings exactly but in the category of antiques – was some important architectural woodwork. It was designed by Neel Reid for an Atlanta house that had to be dismantled; the pediments used in the River Room (page 253) are from that house. A similar decorative item that they acquired especially to go in the house was an old Georgia mantlepiece in the Federal style. Used in the drawing room, it came from the John Walker Plantation at Mulberry Grove, Harris County, Georgia. Also in that category was an eighteenth-century, folk-art wood carving of an American eagle. It was purchased in New York City, from a famous dealer in early Americana, to go where it was placed. It is in the

BELOW: River Room Detail/Informal Dining Area. The contrast of modern glass doors and antique wood is characteristic of this room where nature – especially the river – is an evolving and abiding decoration. OPPOSITE: The River Room. Clients, architect, and interior decorator created this great space; its dramatic scale but liveable proportions results from their collaboration. Its soaring volume is a surprise as the rear element of a house so traditional at the entrance. It takes advantage of the sloping site and the view towards the undeveloped Alabama bank of the Chattahoochee River.

LEFT: Drawing Room. This room was designed around the Federal style mantlepiece from Harris County, and the Butler's collection of antique furniture, a mixture of American and English. The English architect's desk holds a copy of Richard Pratt's influential book on architecture and decorative arts, *The Golden Treasury of Early American Architecture;* it was an influential publication on early Americana and was an inspiration for this book on Georgia. TOP: Master Bedroom. ABOVE: Master Bath.

ABOVE AND OPPOSITE PAGE: Plunge, Deck, and rear façade. Julia Orme Martin, ASLA, of Atlanta, helped with landscape architecture. Edward Warner Neal, AIA, of Columbus was the consultant for architecture.

River Room on a pedestal above the main entrance into the room. A feature of the house also in the category of antique wood was the flooring – Georgia heart pine from the old Eagle and Phenix Mills in Columbus. (One of Mrs. Butler's grandfathers was President of that mill during its heyday. Columbus was founded in 1828 as a trading town on the Chattahoochee; it became and remains an important textile center.)

Many houses in this modern/traditional manner have been built throughout Georgia since the Second World War, and especially in the last twenty years. The taste for eclecticism in architecture and interior decoration seems to have intensified as interest in modernism has waned. It is as though the two concepts have met in the middle, so that the River Room has a Chinese Chippendale balustrade on one wall and sliding glass doors on the other. This taste for mixing diverse features, old and new, seems to be growing. The Clarence Butler's house is a significant example of that taste, built as Georgia neared its two hundred and fiftieth birthday.

The Butlers are natives of Columbus; they have greatly contributed to the life of their Chattahoochee River home town. Today it is the second largest city in Georgia. As it grew, however, the Butlers and about a dozen other leading citizens became zealous advocates of historic preservation, giving the town's past a priority along with its present and future. Their home reflects this special respect for tradition which also allows possibilities for adapting the old for new and lively uses.

POST-MODERN PAVILION-BY-THE-SEA
The Norman E. White House
1981-1982

Robert Edward Cheshire III, *Architect*

Sea Island, Glynn County

*I like elements which are hybrid rather than 'pure' . . . I am
for richness of meaning . . .*

Robert Venturi, *Complexity and
Contradiction in Architecture,* 1966

THIS POST-MODERN pavilion is the final of the series of houses built between 1967 and 1983, and it is the last house in this section of the book. The architect, Ed Cheshire, is a native of Moultrie who practices from a St. Simons office. A graduate of the Georgia Tech School of Architecture, he has a post-graduate architectural degree from Harvard. Some of his practical experience came from summer work in Frank McCall's architectural office in Moultrie. He and his clients, the Norman E. Whites of Atlanta would all be the first to agree that they have built an uncommon house which in one sense, at least, is a landmark: the neighbors have dubbed it "The Battleship." The Whites were unsure that the Sea Island Company would let them build it. But here it stands. Ed Cheshire has made a startling composite by designing the wings in the Shingle Style (of the 1880's and 90's) and the central trunk in the International Style (of the 1920's and 30's). It is a "hybrid" of the sort that Robert Venturi's Post-Modern manifesto advocated. The Shingle Style was a highly textured, imaginative interpretation of early-American vernacular architecture, and the International Style was a smooth-surfaced interpretation of the aesthetics of modern machinery, and of such things as ocean liners. (Thus, "The Battleship.") The hybrid works, however, and is a wonderful composite of rough and smooth, a complex and contradictory composition in the Post-Modern manner.

Philip Johnson, a leading modernist who has become a post-modernist, has said, "We cannot *not* know history." In the 1930's, he discarded eclecticism and now seems to want to return to it. A younger eastern architect, Kevin Roch, stated: "We desire to restore a broader range of architectural forms and meanings through use of ornament, cultural symbols, and historical references, all of which the Modernist had discarded." Another post-modernist (or "revivalist," as he was called in the *New York Times*) is Richard Meier, the New York

Cheshire says that the Norman White House is a "programmatic" design solution. He designed the house first, to fit the site, that is to take full advantage of a small lot with a diagonal view of the Atlantic Ocean; second, to fulfill the client's list of specific requirements, and last, to work within the budget. The result is, he agreed with this writer, a "planned collision" of the revived Shingle Style and the revived International Style.

Mrs. White, who has a degree in interior design

OPPOSITE: Entrance façade. Post-Modern architecture consciously makes hybrids. Here the Shingle Style of the 1880's and 90's is combined with the International Style of the 1920's and 30's. It is an example of what Post-Modern architect and theorist Robert Venturi called "complexity and contradiction" in a book with that title. ABOVE: Beach façade. This elevation is similar to the International Style houses that Europeans began building in the early 1920's; the Frenchman Le Corbusier, for example. In America sometimes it was called "Art Moderne" because it was considered French and modern. Ed Cheshire has, in the true spirit of post-modernism, combined that approach with reminiscences of the Shingle Style. Landscape architecture was by T. M. Baumgardener and Associates of Sea Island, the firm which has long done the landscaping for the Sea Island Company.

City architect of the new High Museum of Art in Atlanta (to be completed in 1983). The High Museum will be in Meier's well-known International Style revivalist manner.

Perhaps the best description of the movement is Leland Roth's: "Post-Modern architecture is rooted in its context, makes allusions to the past, and employs applied ornament." In other words, the younger architects, such as Ed Cheshire, are designing buildings that are not concerned with structural or engineering aesthetics, as the modernists were: they are using ornament and historical precedents, and they are site-oriented; the context – in the widest possible sense – in which a building is constructed influences its design.

and practices in Atlanta as Mary White, ASID, was an ideal client for a house of this slightly more radical appearance than those of her neighbors. She started the entire design process when she asked for an open, informal plan emerging from a curved kitchen that would be truly part of the rest of the house. Combinations of textures especially appeal to her, and that is why she liked the exterior contrast of shingles and smooth concrete.

This Post-Modern house represents the avant-garde architecture of our era, but in fact, is a very conservative avant-garde house; it is totally symmetrical and almost classical in the orderliness of its appearance; the form of the house exactly expresses the plan – which is a Beaux-

Arts principle. The Whites report that their neighbors like the house, now that it is completed, and feel that it fits in far better than expected. Some have noted its resemblance to the original International Style house on the beach several blocks south (page 28). The shingle-covered wings and roof help to blend the house with the

site and soften the effect of the exposed concrete.

Two hundred and fifty years of domestic architecture, therefore, concludes on a conservative note. A respect for the old, and the creation of the new, meet in a conservative middleground in the Norman White House. The fresh new eclecticism it represents should

LEFT: Sitting Room view of the Atlantic Ocean. Sea Island, one of the barrier Golden Isles of Georgia, was first developed as a resort in the 1920's and 30's by Alfred W. Jones and Howard E. Coffin. TOP: Sitting Room with view into kitchen wing. Mrs. White wanted a curved kitchen which was open to the main part of the house. This was one of the requirements which began the open plan and the exterior form of the house. ABOVE: Entrance and Principal Stairs. In foreground, a Hans Godo Fräbel glass Calla Lily; in background on wall of stairway "Cherokee Syllabary" by Betty Foy Sanders.

be welcome in a state where the old eclecticism never ceased to be admired (especially if the precedents revived were popular to begin with). Perhaps this house does sum up the landmark homes of Georgia, for in 1982 it leaves us with the concluding idea that the fundamental character of the domestic architecture of Georgia has been conservative, with a great respect for the customs and manners of architecture as it has been inherited from the past.

The preservation and conservation of Georgia's domestic architecture follows in Section III.

SECTION III
HISTORIC PRESERVATION IN GEORGIA: LANDMARK HOMES AND NEIGHBORHOODS

Savannah Historic District, Monterey Square, with Pulaski Monument and Forsyth Park fountain in far distance. This square was laid out in 1847 as the town expanded south from the original four Oglethorpe wards and squares; Monterey is one of 24 within the district, the largest historic district in the central city of any major urban area in the United States (2.2 square miles). On the right are the paired Charles Rogers houses, 1858, and next to them the red-brick Hugh Mercer House, c.1860.

SECTION III
Historic Preservation in Georgia:
Landmark Homes and Neighborhoods

The significance of a work of architecture, however exhilarating it may be as an isolated object, rests within a well-defined social and visual environment.

Professor Henry A. Millon
Key Monuments of the History of Architecture, 1965

WE HAVE SEEN key monuments of domestic architecture in Georgia from the founding of the colony until the eve of the two hundred fiftieth birthday year – arranged in order of their construction. That arrangement related the houses to each other as architecture which was developing through numerous styles and periods. It also related the houses to major social, cultural, and historical patterns. It formed a panorama of architecture, interiors, and gardens.

The eighteenth-century houses were in the eastern part of the state, near the Savannah River, because that was the first area to be settled; only in eastern Georgia can one find Colonial houses. Because the houses are chronologically arranged, that is made clear. The very first dwelling shown was an eighteenth-century frame house at Augusta; the second was the house of a Cherokee Indian in North Georgia, completed in 1805 when that part of the state was still Indian territory. Even though those two houses, and the others, were photographed as "isolated objects," they were related to larger issues in discussion, as the chronological sequence proceeded. Each was chosen *because it stood out* (from its neighbors in the community) and represented an important aspect of the environment in which it was built.

In this concluding section the ABC's of house preservation in Georgia are discussed, and some of the fundamental landmarks of preservation are shown. Also we broaden the photographic coverage somewhat to include a series of views of neighborhoods which have been renewed by historic preservation. Many of these neighborhoods have been given special status, either locally or nationally, as "historic districts." The street-scape photographs demonstrate visually that the preservation and conservation of environments – as opposed to individual landmarks – have become major concerns in Georgia. This will help to balance the impression this book would give that only great houses and stately homes are of consequence. Within the main body of the text numerous landmarks in historic preservation, as such, have been shown – for example, the Beath-Griggs House

in Atlanta's Inman Park (pages 144-149). Those will not be repeated but, when they are mentioned, page references will be noted. Major preservation landmarks that were not explored earlier in the book will be included in this last section – for example, the Davenport House in Savannah – but coverage will be limited to one exterior photograph.

The appendix has information about houses and districts in Georgia that, as of August 1982, were in the National Register of Historic Places and that had been declared National Historic Landmarks: two related programs of the United States Department of the Interior. The number of Georgia places, of all kinds, in the National Register – some 900 as of 1982 – gives an indication of the intensity of interest in preservation in Georgia. The greatest percentage of National Landmarks and entries in the Register are houses and residential districts.

This concluding section emphasizes accomplishments – and ignores problems – in the preservation, restoration, and rehabilitation of houses and neighborhoods throughout Georgia. It, as with the rest of the book, is arranged chronologically to show how historic preservation has developed in the state from the turn of the century. Georgia's preservation accomplishments have paralleled, and sometimes exceeded, those of the rest of the nation.

As the reader knows, this book is dedicated to the Georgia Historical Commission, the state historical agency that was constituted in 1951 and disbanded in 1973. It was a national leader; but in 1973, its functions were dispersed among other departments within state government. Van Jones Martin and this writer began their careers when the historical commission and the Department of Archives and History were both under the aegis of Ben W. Fortson, Jr. (1904-1979). The historical commission's accomplishments were great and set a high standard during the 22 years of its operation. The first and second houses in Section Two were restorations done by the historical commission. They will not be repeated here, but they were important milestones in historic preservation in Georgia (see pages 38-45).

The very first historic preservation milestone in Georgia was Meadow Garden. The Daughters of the American Revolution raised the money to save it in a national campaign. It was the home of George Walton during the last years of his life; he had been one of the Georgia signers of the Declaration of Independence. Dedicated in 1902, the property was purchased by the DAR over a period of several years; it is now the responsibility of the Georgia and Augusta DAR's. Meadow Garden was one of the first successful attempts in the United States to save an entire structure as a memorial – as opposed to erecting a monument or marker. Meadow Garden was identified with the concept of the Founding Fathers, and the campaign was modeled on the successful effort to save Mt. Vernon. That was where historic preservation began in America – in commemoration and patriotism, and in the realm of historic house museums. As this chronicle proceeds we will see that preservation moves away from that towards more diverse goals, but always the past is revered as being an important and useful part of contemporary life.

The next successful attempt to save an old house began in 1909 with the death of the renowned Georgia writer, Joel Chandler Harris of Atlanta. His home, The Wren's Nest, was secured by a lady's memorial association in 1913. It has been open to the public ever since, and in recent years has been the prime landmark in the revitalization of West End, the Victorian period neighborhood around it in southwest Atlanta. The Wren's Nest is in Section Two, pages 134 and 135.

Next in this series of early-twentieth century preservation successes is the Andrew Low House in Savannah (pages 96-99); in 1928 it became the headquarters of the Georgia Society of Colonial Dames in America.

Liberty Hall in Crawfordville (pages 132-133), the home of Alexander H. Stephens, Vice-President of the Confederacy, became his official memorial in 1932 when it was deeded to the State by the United Daughters of the Confederacy.

When Fort Frederica National Monument (page 18) was established at St. Simons Island in 1945 the preservation of the tabby and brick ruins of some of Georgia's earliest houses was assured. In 1947 the state's purchase of Jekyll Island meant the preservation of the cottages within the Millionaire's Village (page 26). That was one of the first neighborhood or district preservation efforts in Georgia, although recreation was the prime reason for the purchase of the historic island. The village of cottages is in fairly good condition today and is a tourist attraction; no one resides in the houses, but the Crane Cottage (pages 158-159) has been adapted as an administrative building and is a sample of what has

been accomplished on Jekyll Island since 1947. At about the same time that the State took possession of Jekyll Island, The Little White House at Warm Springs was opened to the public as a museum (July 25, 1947) furnished just as it had been on April 12, 1945 when President Roosevelt died there (pages 198-199).

In 1951, the Georgia Historical Commission was created within the Department of the Secretary of State Ben W. Fortson, Jr. "Mr. Ben," as he was known, was

Meadow Garden, 1230 Nelson Street, Augusta. This was the last home of George Walton, a Georgia signer of the Declaration of Independence; when he lived here during the last years of his life it consisted of only the left half of the cottage – note remaining low front door on the left. In 1901 it became the property of the Daughters of the American Revolution and as such is one of the first historic-house museums in America and the first in Georgia. Still DAR property, it is a National Historic Landmark and is open to the public.

one of the real leaders in promoting and preserving Georgia's Heritage, as has already been mentioned. The first house museum the Commission undertook was the Chief Vann House at Springplace (pages 42-45). Soon after the Historical Commission was underway, Fortson appointed Mr. Joseph B. Cumming of Augusta as the Chairman; he served in the position until Governor Jimmy Carter dispersed the activity during his governmental reorganization. The Executive-Secretary for many years was Mary Gregory Jewett (1908-1975). Mrs. Jewett was one of those who formed the Georgia Trust for Historic Preservation in 1973.

The Owens-Thomas House Restoration (pages 50-57) in Savannah, was undertaken in the early 1950's by the Telfair Academy of Arts and Sciences. It was an initial effort to do something about Savannah's deteriorating landmarks and is still one of the inspirations for Savannahians and visitors to Georgia's first settlement.

ABOVE: Isaiah Davenport House, 324 East State Street, Columbia Square, Savannah. Columbia Square dates from 1799, this house from 1820-21. In 1955, when it was about to be demolished, several public-spirited ladies formed Historic Savannah Foundation to start preventing such destruction. Restored and furnished, it was the Foundation's headquarters until the William Scarbrough House became a similar Foundation project in the 1970's. Still owned by Historic Savannah, it is a house museum open to the public.

BELOW: Midway Museum, US 17 Liberty County. This building was built as a museum of early Midway history. The design was based on local, eighteenth-century prototypes; it does not reproduce any particular "raised cottage" but is similar to one that stood at nearby Riceboro. The architect, Thomas Goree Little, designed this for the Georgia Historical Commission in the mid-1950's. It was originally called the Midway Colonial Museum; it was the dream of numerous Midway descendants who wanted to commemorate the early history of "Georgia's cradle of liberty" and the almost vanished civilization documented in Robert M. Myer's *Children of Pride* (1972). Open to the public.

About the same time, the Juliette Gordon Low Birthplace was purchased by the Girl Scouts of America; the Andrew Low House (pages 96-99) where Daisy Low lived when she formed the first girl scout troop, is the Low memorial we have included in *Landmark Homes of Georgia*.

Then in 1955, the preservation of a major landmark of the modern historic preservation movement in Georgia (and in America) was achieved in Savannah: the Isaiah Davenport House. From that effort, came the formation of the Historic Savannah Foundation, Inc. A change in the direction of historic preservation was signaled in the saving of this superb early-nineteenth-century brick house. Isaiah Davenport was only incidental to the effort – although it must be noted that he designed and built the house. But it was not to memorialize an individual, nor just to preserve an important example of Savannah's architecture – although that was one of the reasons – but it was to stop urban decay right there, and it was to become part of an overall plan to save the entire historic context which surrounded the house – a district of some two square miles (see pages 262-263). The founders of Historic Savannah Foundation saw their certifiably historic downtown district rapidly disappearing, and there had even been talk of cutting streets through the middle of squares... one square had already become a parking lot. It was not the historical associations with the landmark but the landmark itself – its physical presence – that moved people to act. Without its graceful curved front steps and American Georgian dignity, Savannah, they knew, would be less like itself, less "historic" in appearance. The visual environment of the square on which it had stood since 1820, would have been irrevocably altered. Thus it became a key monument in the historic preservation movement in Savannah, the anchor and rallying point – and it is still one of the most popular sites in town.

In 1956, '57, and '58, the Georgia Historical Commission had several projects. The old White House at Augusta, sometimes called the Mackay House, and now officially called the Ezekiel Harris House, became State property and in time was opened as a house museum; it is on pages 38 through 41. An important attempt to remember an entire historic community was commenced at that time by the *building* of a house museum. This was done at Midway, Liberty County, Georgia. The Historical Commission did not reconstruct a particular Midway dwelling but designed a museum structure based on the kind of Colonial period cottages, raised on a high basement, that were the vernacular houses of the area; a particular house that had been at Riceboro was one of the prototypes; another was Wild Heron (page 18) which still stands between Savannah and the historic Midway community.

Also in the late 1950's there was a preservation

project in Atlanta, sponsored by the High Museum of Art. The Redman Thornton House, a story-and-a-half, eighteenth-century dwelling from Greensboro, Georgia, was moved to the grounds of the High Museum, carefully restored to its original appearance, and decorated with appropriate late-eighteenth-century furnishings. The kinds of scholarly restoration procedures that have been developed by Colonial Williamsburg, Inc. were used. The project was seen as an adjunct to the museum's initial decorative arts program, rather than historic preservation, but the restoration techniques used were an inspiration to many people who wanted someday to restore a house of their own. In the 1960's when the Atlanta Art Association and other cultural organizations needed the land on which the Thornton House had been placed, it was moved again, to Stone Mountain Park to be part of the complex of antebellum Georgia plantation buildings there, a restoration village very similar to places such as Sturbridge Village in New England. The Thornton House remains a fine restoration, although the chimneys are now about a foot shorter than they were originally. (Stone Mountain Park is owned by the State of Georgia and operated by the Stone Mountain Memorial Association; it is just east of Atlanta off of U.S. Highway 78.)

Between 1962 and 1964 at Thomasville, Georgia, a splendid and exacting true reconstruction took place. It is unlike anything that has been accomplished elsewhere in the state. In 1962 the main house of Fair Oaks Plantation burned to the ground but the owners, the Brigham Brittons, decided to reconstruct their winter home exactly as they and generations had known it. It was designed and built in the 1850's by John Wind, the Thomas County builder-architect, for Richard Raines Mitchell. The Brittons and a local architect in Thomasville put the house back exactly as it had been. This private reconstruction, in the most technical sense of that word, set a standard for such activities that would be hard to meet and impossible to excell. Historic preservation activities in Thomasville and Thomas County are among the most successful in the state. The private standards set by Fair Oaks and by another Thomas County landmark, Greenwood Plantation, have been inspirations for Thomasville Landmarks, Inc., founded the same year as the Fair Oaks reconstruction. (Greenwood Plantation is one of the oldest ongoing private preservations of an outstanding Georgia landmark. It has been the winter home and hunting lodge of the New York Whitney family since the turn of the century. Their care of this masterpiece of classical revival architecture, built in the early 1840's, has been exemplary from the time the property was acquired in 1899.) To save an in-town historic house, Thomasville Landmarks was incorporated in 1965. The Hardy Bryan House, c. 1840, the first two-story dwelling built in the town, became

ABOVE: The Thornton House, Stone Mountain Park, Stone Mountain. This story-and-a-half, late-eighteenth-century settler's cottage was originally restored in the 1950's by the High Museum of Art, Atlanta. In the 1960's the house was moved to this location as a part of an antebellum plantation complex. Open to the public.
BELOW: Fair Oaks Plantation, Thomas County. This is the finest reconstruction done in Georgia. The 1850's plantation house designed by John Wind burned to the ground in 1962. This exact reproduction (1964) was made by the owner with the help of a Thomasville architect, Roderick Brantley. (The carved acorn and oak-leaf medallion in the pediment was not on the original house. It replaces a lozenge-shaped window as the owner's homage to other fine Thomas County decorated pediments by the builder-architect, John Wind.)

the organizations's long-term goal. Not until 1980 and '81 was the house finally put into the condition shown here. But it was the organization's vigilance, until it could acquire the property and begin the total reconstruction, that saved the house; it in now the organization's headquarters.

A similar long-range preservation/restoration pro-

ABOVE LEFT: Greenwood Plantation, Thomasville. Built for Thomas Jones in the early 1840's, it was designed by John Wind, an English immigrant, builder-architect. A masterpiece of the American classical revival, it has been carefully conserved by the Whitney family since 1899. Two of the characteristics of Thomas County's classicism were pediment medallions and columns set out from the porch on brick piers. When Stanford White looked at it for the Whitneys about 1900, he said that it was perfect as it was, and the Whitneys, with only minimal changes, have so maintained it ever since. ABOVE RIGHT: Hardy Bryan House, 312 North Broad Street, Thomasville, c. 1840. Headquarters of Thomasville Landmarks, Inc. Saving and restoring this house – accomplished in 1980 – was one of the long term projects of Thomasville Landmarks. Open to the public. (Note that this is a simplified version of Greenwood Plantation: a pediment medallion, a second-floor balcony, and columns on brick piers set out from the porch.)

ject was begun in 1964 in McDuffie County near Thomson. The Old Rock House (page 20) was the place, an eighteenth-century structure built of field stones. There is nothing exactly comparable in the entire state. Not until 1981 was the house put into mint condition, but without a local organization, and several vigilant ladies, it would not have survived. Also in McDuffie County is the privately-restored Thomas E. Watson Birthplace, completed in the mid-1970's at the late U.S.

Birthplace of United States Senator Thomas E. Watson (1856-1922) at Hickory Hill, Thomson, McDuffie County. Watson's family restored this clapboard-covered log cabin as his memorial in the mid-1970's.

Senator's estate, Hickory Hill.

In 1965 and '66, the Old Governor's Mansion at Milledgeville was restored (pages 74-79); it too set high standards for the community in which it has stood since 1838. Preservation in Milledgeville has been outstanding in the neighborhood and historic district manner that has become the generally accepted approach. After Savannah, Milledgeville was one of the first towns to do a city-wide survey of its treasures as part of an overall preservation plan. Milledgeville had been laid out as the capital of Georgia in the first decade of the nineteenth century and the town layout itself became one of the historical resources the preservationists wanted to protect. An historic district with local controls, and national registration – as provided by the Historic Preservation Act of 1966 – was created on the pattern of the Historic District of Savannah (and, before that, of what had been done in Charleston, South Carolina). In 1966, the United States Department of the Interior began participating with the states in historic preservation activities through the National Register of Historic Places. Most of old Milledgeville is listed in the National Register.

Columbus was the *first* town in Georgia outside of Savannah, however, to make the important step of inventorying and planning for the preservation of great numbers of potentially useful old houses – and other older structures within the cityscape – all mostly in rundown condition. Historic Columbus Foundation was organized in 1966, and in 1967, began the work which has resulted in the preservation of the Columbus His-

ABOVE: Milledgeville Historic District, South Liberty Street. In the foreground is the Orme-Sallie House, c.1821. Professor Janice A. Hardy, the expert on Milledgeville preservation and architecture, has written: "South Liberty Street is a microcosm of Milledgeville's architectural heritage, the whole evolution of taste and fashion are visible here." The Milledgeville Historic District includes essentially the same area that was planned as the capital of Georgia in 1804. The 3,240 acres – four public, and eighty-four residential squares – are all on the National Register of Historic Places. BELOW: Historic District, Columbus, Muscogee County. In the foreground is the Historic Columbus Foundation Headquarters and, in the far background, the Muscogee County Courthouse. The Columbus District is largely residential, nineteenth century, along a plateau above the Chattahoochee River. This neighborhood was going to be bulldozed as part of an urban renewal program in the mid-1960's when Historic Columbus was organized, did an inventory, and in 1969 got the area declared a district, locally and nationally. It was the first Georgia district to be put on the National Register of Historic Places (outside of the National Landmark Savannah District). Along this street is the Foundation's first headquarters, the Walker-Peters-Langdon-Kyle House, 716 Broadway; this, and several other nearby Foundation-owned houses, may be toured.

ABOVE: Westville, Stewart County. According to a leaflet distributed by Westville Historic Handicrafts, Inc., this is a "functioning living history village of relocated, authentically restored (original) buildings, depicting the pre-industrial life and culture of Georgia's pioneer days up to 1850." Here is the Edward McDonald House, c.1850, and its lattice-work gazebo. Westville is one-half mile south of the town of Lumpkin and is open daily. LEFT: Lower Greene Street Historic District, Augusta. This part of Augusta has been called "Old Town;" it is on a plain formed by the Savannah River. The neighborhood has an odd nickname, "Pinched Gut." This photograph was taken in the 400 block of Greene Street, within walking distance of the Richmond County Courthouse. The area was added to the National Register of Historic Places in 1980. BELOW: Macon, Bibb County. This is part of a concentration of houses on College Hill that was pinpointed in Macon's architectural survey in 1970. It has not been declared a historic district but has the qualities we associate with that kind of neighborhood. In the background is the Walter T. Johnson House, 1238 Jefferson Terrace, designed in 1911 by Neel Reid. In the foreground is the Randolph-Whittle House, 1231 Jefferson Terrace, 1840. Two schools of architectural thought face each other across a street within the same neighborhood. OPPOSITE TOP: Ansley Park Historic District, Atlanta, during the Spring dogwood season. This district was entered on the National Register of Historic Places April 20, 1979. The register nomination said that Ansley Park was Atlanta's "first automobile suburb." Now it is considered almost downtown. This 15th Street townscape shows the mixture of architecture that characterizes the neighborhood; in the background is a Colony Square Tower. The house in the middle of this photograph is also illustrated on page 30.

ABOVE LEFT: Baltimore Block, Atlanta, Fulton County. The Headquarters of the Georgia Trust for Historic Preservation is 11 Baltimore Place. This row was built in the 1880's in the manner of Baltimore row houses. In the 1930's and 40's it became an artist's colony in the spirit of Greenwich Village. The Georgia Trust's location here helps to continue the block's preservation and identify the Trust's broad preservation concerns. ABOVE CENTER: The Yancey-Shaw House, "Claremont," 906 East Second Avenue, Rome, Floyd County. This is possibly the finest Second Empire style house in Georgia. Built before 1880, it is being restored by the Charles Shaws. Their work was recognized in 1981 by an Outstanding Restoration award from the Georgia Trust for Historic Preservation. Rome is a north Georgia community founded in the 1830's that cares about its rich heritage; throughout *Landmark Homes* examples of its concern may be found. ABOVE RIGHT: The Gould House Condominiums, Augusta, Richmond County. Converting this mansion into three condominium units was a long-time project of Historic Augusta, Inc. The surrounding neighborhood is called Summerville and sometimes the Sand Hills. Located at Milledge Road and Walton Way, the crossing is called Gould's Corner.

toric District, a large neighborhood near the Chatta-hoochee River. Local recognition was given the area and it was added to the National Register of Historic Places in 1969 – the second such district in Georgia. (Savannah's district was named a National Historic Landmark, even before the creation of the National Register, under an earlier federal program based on the Historic Sites Act of 1935; it is the largest historic district in the central city of any major urban area in the United States.)

This view of the Columbus Historic District shows the headquarters of the Historic Columbus Foundation with several of the Foundation's nearby preservation projects. In 1980 additional old downtown Columbus

residential areas were added to the National Register. The residences and other buildings within those areas are awaiting private investors to renovate them, probably in some adaptive way for commercial purposes. (There are income tax incentives under the Economic Recovery Act of 1981 that encourage the rehabilitation of income-producing "certified historic structures" of the kind that are included in historic districts. Columbus has been one of the towns to take advantage of these new incentives.)

Near Columbus – 35 miles south in Stewart County – out from the little courthouse town of Lumpkin, is an assemblage of southwest Georgia buildings called Westville. It was begun in the mid-1960's as a way of

ABOVE LEFT: Americus Historic District, Sumter County; designated in 1976. ABOVE RIGHT: Brunswick Old Town Historic District, Glynn County; designated in 1979. BELOW: Covington Historic District/Floyd Street, Newton County; designated in 1974.

saving isolated antebellum buildings, moving them into a village especially created for the purpose. Opened in 1970 it has set standards for such work that have helped elevate the quality of restorations throughout the state. Many Columbus people have helped in this notable project which was begun by Dr. Joseph B. Mahan of Columbus, with the help of the Sam Singer family of Lumpkin.

During the mid-1960's a number of historic preservation organizations were formed throughout the state, modeled on the Historic Savannah Foundation, Inc. (The National Trust for Historic Preservation helped in all of these activities sending representatives from its Washington, D. C. headquarters before it had a Southern Regional Office at Charleston, South Carolina.) Historic Augusta was incorporated in 1966. One of its major projects was the Broad Oaks or Gould's Corner Condominium preservation; a unique adaptive-use approach to a large house in the historic Summerville neighborhood, of which the old Gould house was probably the most outstanding single landmark. Not until 1977 was the house put into top condition and occupied. Another area in Augusta that had concerned the organization was a deteriorated downtown neighborhood near the Richmond County Courthouse, along Greene and Telfair Streets. Progress has been made there largely through investments by private citizens. This lower Greene Street Historic District was added to the National Register in December, 1980. That was an encouragement for further investment and neighborhood rehabilitation.

Macon's historic preservation movement was also begun in the mid-1960's. The Middle Georgia Historical society was the initiator and leader, and the most determined of all their members was the late John J. McKay, Jr. who never gave up on its goals. One of these was to purchase the Sidney Lanier Cottage as the society's headquarters that was achieved in 1973 (page 134). John McKay's long-time work also resulted in an unusually large number of nominations to the National Register from Macon. For many years of dedication, John McKay in 1980 received the Distinguished Service Award of the Georgia Trust for Historic Preservation.

The Georgia Trust was an outgrowth of the work of the Georgia Historical Commission. A series of historic preservation conferences organized and sponsored by the historical commission was begun in the spring of 1969 at Athens. At the Macon conference in April 1973, the Georgia Trust was formally organized as the membership organization to continue the annual conferences, serve as an auxilliary to the historical commission, and promote historic preservation throughout Georgia. Twenty-five trustees were named, this writer among them. Mrs. Mary Gregory Jewett of the historical commission was the first president. The offices of the Georgia Trust were soon located in Baltimore Block,

the only group of Victorian rowhouses in Atlanta. This helped to insure their preservation. Built in the 1880's, this row was the first downtown Atlanta (mini-) neighborhood preservation accomplishment, dating back to the late 1930's; but Atlanta had grown up – and been torn down – around it. A major project of the Georgia Trust developed in 1977. The Board of Trustees accepted the continued preservation and restoration of Macon's Johnston-Felton-Hay House as its responsibility, and that remains one of its most demanding and significant projects. (See pages 120-129.) One of the Georgia Trust's most popular programs is the recognition of private restoration and preservation achievements. The Yancey-Shaw House, "Claremont," a Second-Empire Victorian landmark at Rome, was recognized as an Outstanding Restoration in 1981. The owners, Mr. and Mrs. Charles C. Shaw, received their award at the annual spring preservation conference that year. These Georgia Trust awards have helped to maintain high standards and are highly regarded recognition for much hard work.

The annual state historic preservation conference was held in Atlanta in the spring of 1976. By that time even modern Atlanta had preservation projects to see. The Atlanta Historical Society's Swan House (pages 178-188) was a showplace house-museum in Buckhead. But there were whole neighborhoods to show, among them Inman Park and Ansley Park. Inman Park was already a great success by 1976 (see pages 144-149). But Ansley Park had also consciously entered the business of preservation. Ansley Park was developed in the first decade of this century and had seen some relatively bad days in the late 1940's. In the 1950's, however, a few young couples began to renovate houses as residences. By the 1970's it was considered a very desirable in-town neighborhood again, and had never suffered the really bad times of Inman Park, but Atlanta had definitely grown up around it, and Colony Square, a high-rise mid-town office and residential park, was on Peachtree Street right at its door. (The Ansley Park Historic District was added to the National Register of Historic Places, April 20, 1979.)

Neighborhood preservation success stories have been repeated throughout the state, for example, in Americus, Brunswick, and Covington. Because this has had to be only the ABC's of historic preservation in Georgia up to 1983, they are the towns with which we conclude. Historic preservation began with houses as isolated objects and has broadened to include the social and visual environment in which they are found. Literally, therefore, we end with these ABC's of Georgia preservation: Americus, Brunswick, and Covington. There are many more letters in the Georgia preservation alphabet, but these will have to stand for similar communities and neighborhoods; they represent the future of the past in Georgia.

Appendix A
National Historic Landmarks: Houses and Residential Districts

Twenty-six of the 41 National Historic Landmarks in Georgia are either houses or districts; these 26 are listed below by county, with their locations. The National Historic Landmark program was authorized by Congress in 1935 within the U.S. Department of the Interior, National Park Service. A district, site, building, structure, or object that the National Park Service adjudges to be *nationally* significant receives a bronze tablet. Among the National Landmarks that have been featured in *Landmark Homes of Georgia* are the Johnston-Hay House; the Owens-Thomas House; the Savannah Historic District, the Lapham-Patterson House, and Meadow Garden (which the Park Service designated a Landmark in 1982). Several that could not be included in the main body of the text are illustrated here in black-and-white.

Baldwin County

Former Governor's Mansion
120 S. Clark Street, Milledgeville

Bibb County

Johnston-Hay House
934 Georgia Avenue, Macon

Raines-Carmichael House,
118 Georgia Avenue, Macon

Chatham County

Green-Meldrim House
Macon and Bull Streets, Savannah

Juliette Gordon Low Birthplace
10 E. Oglethorpe Street, Savannah

Owens-Thomas House
124 Abercorn Street, Savannah

Savannah Historic District
Bounded by E. Broad, Gwinnett, and W. Broad Streets, and the Savannah River

William Scarbrough House
41 W. Broad Street, Savannah

Telfair Academy
121 Barnard Street, Savannah

Clarke County

Henry W. Grady House
634 Prince Avenue, Athens

Floyd County

Chieftains
80 Chatillon Road, Rome

Fulton County

Joel Chandler Harris House
(Wren's Nest)
1050 Gordon Street, Atlanta

Martin Luther King, Jr.
Historic District
Bounded roughly by Irwin, Randolph, Edgewood, Jackson, and Auburn Avenues, Atlanta

Gordon County

New Echota
near Calhoun

Liberty County

St. Catherine's Island

McDuffie County

Thomas E. Watson House
310 Lumpkin Street, Thomson

Muscogee County

Octagon House (May's Folly)
527 1st Avenue, Columbus

Richmond County

Stephen Vincent Benet House
(President's Home, Augusta College)
2500 Walton Way, Augusta

Bellevue, NHL
LaGrange

Robert Toombs House, NHL
Washington

Chieftains, NHL
Rome

Meadow Garden
1230 Nelson Street, Augusta

College Hill (Walton-Harper House)
2216 Wrightsboro Road, Augusta

Stephens County

Traveler's Rest (Jarret Manor)
near Toccoa

Thomas County

Lapham-Patterson House
626 N. Dawson Street,
   Thomasville

Troup County

Bellevue (Benjamin Harvey
   Hill House)
204 Ben Hill Street, LaGrange

Walker County

John Ross House
Lake Avenue and Spring Street,
   Rossville

Wilkes County

Robert Toombs House
216 E. Robert Toombs Avenue,
   Washington

Tupper-Barnett House
101 W. Robert Toombs Avenue,
   Washington

Raines-Carmichael House, NHL
Macon

Taylor-Grady House, NHL
Athens

Appendix B.

The National Register of Historic Places

Congress Authorized the Department of the Interior, National Park Service, to begin compiling the National Register in 1966. As of August 1982, Georgia had 899 entries. Kept in Washington, D.C., the Register is a growing expansion of the National Landmarks list to include places of state and local significance. Buildings, structures, sites, objects, and districts are nominated. The State of Georgia has been helping the National Park Service to compile the Georgia list, county-by-county, since 1969. For further information contact:

Historic Preservation Section
Georgia Department of Natural Resources
270 Washington Street, S.W.
Atlanta, Georgia 30334

Many of the places in *Landmark Homes of Georgia* are in the National Register. Some that were not in the main body of the text are shown here and on page 276.

Swanton House
Decatur

Photo by Jim Lockhart
Herndon House
Atlanta

Montrose
Augusta

Appendix C

Marshall Row
Savannah

Orange Hall
St. Marys

This is an outline map of Georgia for general reference. It gives only the places where houses and historic neighborhoods are featured.

Reid-Lawrence House
Eatonton

Richard Russell House
Winder

Lighthouse Keeper's House
St. Simons Island

Martin Luther King
Birthplace,
Atlanta (in NHL District)

276

Note on Sources

A man will turn over half a library to make one book.

. . .

Knowledge is of two kinds. We know a subject ourselves, or we know where we can find information upon it.

Samuel Johnson, April 1775
Boswell's *Life of Johnson*, Vol. I

Landmark Homes of Georgia is based on three major sources: first, materials in written or graphic form in the author's collection, in libraries, archives, and other repositories; second, the houses and their settings as artifacts, many of which the author knew as long ago as the 1950's, and some to which he was introduced as recently as 1982 (each house was experienced or re-experienced as the photography took place, so that the text and the illustrations could be a unified); third, interviews with owners and others who knew about the places, or about Georgia architecture, gardens, and interiors in general.

Landmark Homes was not designed as a footnote book, but important sources are cited within the text, especially with the frontispiece quotations in Section II. The selected bibliography which follows is for the serious reader who might like to pursue some aspect himself; all materials of whatever nature are arranged together and listed alphabetically.

Coleman, Kenneth. *Georgia History in Outline.* Athens, 1978.

Coleman, Kenneth, et al. *A History of Georgia.* Athens, 1977.

Coles, William A., ed. *Classical America IV.* New York, 1977.

Coulter, E. Merton. *Georgia: A Short History.* Chapel Hill, 1960.

Davidson, William H. *Pine Log and Greek Revival.* 1964.

Downing, Andrew Jackson. *The Architecture of Country Houses.* New York, 1850.

Efird, Mrs. John Ray, ed. *The Houses of James Means.* Atlanta, 1979.

Garden History of Georgia. Atlanta, 1933 and 1976.

Gowans, Alan. *Images of American Living.* Philadelphia, 1964.

Grady, James H. *The Architecture of Neel Reid in Georgia.* Athens, 1973.

Green, Henry D. *Furniture of the Georgia Piedmont Before 1830.* Atlanta, 1976.

Hamlin, Talbot. *Greek Revival Architecture in America.* Oxford, 1944.

Hartridge, Walter Charlton. *Savannah.* Columbia, S.C., 1947.

Horton, Mrs. Corinne Ruth Stocker. "Savannah and Parts of the Far South," *The Georgian Period,* Part XII, 1902.

Jencks, Charles. *The Language of Post-Modern Architecture.* London, 1978.

Kelso, William M. *Captain Jones's Wormsloe.* Athens, 1979.

Lanier, Mary D., ed. *Poems of Sidney Lanier.* New York, 1913.

Lane, Mills. *Savannah Revisited.* Savannah, 1977.

Linley, John. *The Architecture of Middle Georgia.* Athens, 1972.

Marsh, Kermit B., ed. *The American Institute of Architects Guide to Atlanta.* Atlanta, 1975.

Mitchell, William R., Jr. *Handbook for Historic Preservation.* Atlanta, 1971.

————————————. "Historic Preservation and American Architecture, Emphasizing Georgia," *The Georgia Historical Quarterly,* LXIII (Spring, 1979) 39-52.

————————————. *Landmarks, The Architecture of Thomasville and Thomas County, Georgia, 1820-1980.* Thomasville, 1980.

————————————. "Seven State-Owned Historic House Museums in Georgia," High Museum of Art Atlanta, Antiques Show Catalogue. 1971.

Morrison, Mary. ed. *Historic Savannah.* Savannah, 1979.

Morrison, Mary. *John S. Norris.* Savannah, 1980.

Mumford, Lewis. *The South in Architecture.* New York, 1941.

National Register of Historic Places Inventory – Nomination Forms. Atlanta, 1969-1982.

Nichols, Frederick Doveton. *The Architecture of Georgia.* Savannah, 1976.

————————————, *The Early Architecture of Georgia.* Chapel Hill, 1957.

————————————. "Wooden Temples on Georgia Hillsides," The Walpole Society Notebook. 1976.

Owens, Hubert B. *Georgia's Planting Prelate.* Athens, 1945.

Perkerson, Medora Field. *White Columns in Georgia.* New York, 1952.

Pratt, Richard. *David Adler, The Architect and His Work.* New York, 1970.

Roth, Leland. *A Concise History of American Architecture.* New York, 1980.

Saye, Albert B. *New Viewpoints in Georgia History.* Athens, 1943.

Scott, Geoffrey. *The Architecture of Humanism.* New York, 1914.

Scully, Vincent. *The Shingle Style Today.* New York, 1974.

Severens, Kenneth. *Southern Architecture.* New York, 1981.

Smith, G. E. Kidder. *The Architecture of the United States,* Vol. II. New York, 1981.

Spalding, Phinizy. *Oglethorpe in America.* Chicago, 1977.

Temple, Sarah B. G., and Kenneth Coleman. *Georgia Journeys.* Athens, 1961.

Wharton, Edith, and Codman, Ogden, Jr. *The Decoration of Houses.* New York, 1902.

Index

Note: This is an index to places illustrated: houses, neighborhoods, and districts. The principal name of a house as used in the text is the name that appears here. Over time, houses have usually acquired more than one name, and sometimes they have a special name such as Bellevue, Boxwood, Chieftains, or Fair Oaks, without an owner's name. If this traditional name is used in the text, then it appears here, even if some may know the property by the name of an owner. Also, where applicable, and known, the name of an architect or designer is included in parenthesis after the name of a house; followed by the name of the town or vicinity, with the page number (or numbers) preceding. The first entry in the index is typical: 29 Alberson, Angus (Means); Albany. This indicates that the Angus Alberson House, designed by James Means, located in Albany, may be found on page 29.

ABC

Page	
29	Alberson, Angus (Means); Albany
272	Americus Historic District
271	Ansley Park Historic District; Atlanta
200-201	Augusta National Golf Club
27	Bach-Duncan (Reid); Macon
140-143	Baldwin-Neely (Preston); Savannah
271	Baltimore Place; Atlanta
28	Barnes-Cheatham (Reid); Griffin
80-83	Barrington Hall (Ball); Roswell
144-149	Beath-Griggs; Atlanta
274	Bellevue; LaGrange
102-103	Boxwood; Madison
272	Brunswick Historic District
268	Bryan, Hardy; Thomasville
80-82	Bulloch Hall, (Ball); Roswell
250-257	Butler, Dr. Clarence (Neal); Columbus
28, 173	Callanwolde (Hornbostel); Atlanta
170-172	Candler, Walter (Ivey and Crook); Atlanta
208-211	Carr, Julian (Shutze); Atlanta
20	Carr, Thomas, Thomson vicinity
236	Carter, President Jimmy; Plains
102-111	Cedar Lane Farm; Madison
274	Chieftains; Rome
269	Columbus Historic District
272	Covington Historic District
156-161	Crane Cottage (Adler); Jekyll Island
23	Crawford-Talmadge; Lovejoy
26	Crescent, The; Valdosta

DEF

Page	
22, 266	Davenport, Isaiah; Savannah
29	Demere, Raymond (Shutze); Savannah
24	Dinglewood; Columbus
24	Edge Hill; Rome
200-201	Eisenhower Cabin; Augusta
27	English-Chambers (Shutze); Atlanta
23	Ethridge, Olney; Sparta
267	Fair Oaks (Wind); Thomas County
112, 113, 115	Founders' Memorial Garden (Owens), Athens
18	Frederica; St. Simons Island

GHI

Page	
46-49	Gilbert-Alexander; Washington-Wilkes
31	Girard Place; Savannah
29	Goddard-Jones (Abreu and Robeson); Atlanta
62-73	Gordon-Banks (Pratt; Riley); Newnan
14, 16	Gordon, Peter; 1734 View of Savannah
271	Gould House Condominiums; Augusta
232-235	Governor's Mansion (Bradbury); Atlanta
112-114	Grant, John; Atlanta
237-239	Green, Henry; St. Simons Island
97, 100, 101	Green-Meldrim (Norris); Savannah
22, 268	Greenwood Plantation (Wind); Thomasville
151-153	Greyfield (MacClure and Spahr); Cumberland Island
38-41	Harris-"Mackay"; Augusta
275	Hatcher-Schwartz; Macon
244-249	Hedges, The (McCall); Sea Island
276	Herndon; Atlanta
212-217	Hightower, Julian (Shutze), Thomaston vicinity
162-169	Hills and Dales (Reid); LaGrange
18	Horton-du Bignon; Jekyll Island
190-197	Howell, Albert (Howell); Atlanta
145	Inman Park Historic District; Atlanta

JKL

Page	
120-129	Johnston-Hay (Thomas); Macon
200-201	Jones, Bobby; Augusta
28	King, Judy; Sea Island
275	King, Martin Luther, Jr., Birthplace; Atlanta
132-134	Lanier, Sidney, Birthplace; Macon
136-139	Lapham-Patterson (Rommerdall); Thomasville
132-133	Liberty Hall; Crawfordville
275	Lighthouse Keeper's House (Cluskey); St. Simons Island
41	Lillibridge, Hampton; Savannah
198	Little White House (Toombs); Warm Springs
96-99	Low, Andrew (Norris); Savannah
27	Lucas (Marye); Atlanta

MNO

Page	
270	McDonald; Westville
26	McGarvey (Wood); Brunswick
276	Marshall Row; Savannah
218-223	Martin, Thomas E., Jr. (Means); Atlanta
24	May's Folly; Columbus
265	Meadow Garden; Augusta
266	Midway Muscum (Little); Midway
269	Milledgeville Historic District
156-159	Mill Pond Plantation (Hubbell and Benes); Thomas County
80-82	Mimosa Hall (Ball); Roswell
275	Montrose; Augusta
174-177	Oak Hill; Rome
20	Oddingsells Cottage; Savannah
14,16	Oglethorpe Cottages; see Peter Gordon View
22, 74-79	Old Governor's Mansion (Cluskey); Milledgeville
276	Orange Hall; St. Marys
113, 116-117	Owens, Hubert B. (Owens); Athens

POR

Page	
202-205	Pebble Hill Plantation (Wind; Garfield); Thomas County
25	Peters, Edward C. (Norrman); Atlanta
150-152	Plum Orchard (Peabody and Stearns); Cumberland Island
276	Raines-Carmichael; Macon
24	Rankin; Columbus
275	Reid-Lawrence; Eatonton
50-57	Richardson-Owens-Thomas (Jay); Savannah
26	Rockefeller Cottage; Jekyll Island
20	Rock House; Thomson vicinity
30	Robinson, James (Jova); Atlanta
275	Russell, Richard; Winder

STUV

Page	
262	Savannah Historic District
60-61	Scarbrough, William (Jay); Savannah
29	Shorter Edward (Toombs); Columbus
226-231	Snodgrass, Robert R. (Byers); Atlanta
178-188	Swan House (Shutze); Atlanta
276	Swanton House; Decatur
275	Taylor-Grady; Athens
58-59	Telfair, Alexander (Jay); Savannah
267	Thornton, Redman; Stone Mountain Park
274	Toombs, Robert; Washington-Wilkes
21	Traveler's Rest/Jarrett Manor; Toccoa vicinity
84-91	Tullie Smith; Atlanta
23	Tupper-Barnett; Washington-Wilkes
92-95	Valley View; Cartersville vicinity
42-45	Vann, Chief; Spring Place
189	Villa Albicini (Shutze); Macon
189	Villa Apartments (Shutze); Atlanta

WXYZ

Page	
26	Walker-Moore; Sparta
21	Ware's Folly; Augusta
19	Washington-Wilkes Cabin; Washington vicinity
268	Watson, Thomas E. Birthplace; Thomson
30	Watt, Vance (Jones); Thomasville
270	Westville, Lumpkin vicinity
258-261	White, Norman E. (Cheshire); Sea Island
18	Wild Heron; Savannah vicinity
30	Williams, Thomas Lyle, Jr.; Thomasville
19	Willink, Henry; Savannah
132, 134-135	Wren's Nest; Atlanta
240-243	Wright, Robert B. (Shutze; McCall); Moultrie